ROUTLEDGE LIBRARY EDITIONS: LIBRARY AND INFORMATION SCIENCE

Volume 43

IF WE BUILD IT

IF WE BUILD IT

Scholarly Communications and
Networking Technologies

Edited by
SUZANNE MCMAHON, MIRIAM PALM
AND PAM DUNN

LONDON AND NEW YORK

First published in 1993 by The Haworth Press, Inc.

This edition first published in 2020
by Routledge
2 Park Square, Milton Park, Abingdon, Oxon OX14 4RN

and by Routledge
52 Vanderbilt Avenue, New York, NY 10017

Routledge is an imprint of the Taylor & Francis Group, an informa business

© 1993 The Haworth Press, Inc.

All rights reserved. No part of this book may be reprinted or reproduced or utilised in any form or by any electronic, mechanical, or other means, now known or hereafter invented, including photocopying and recording, or in any information storage or retrieval system, without permission in writing from the publishers.

Trademark notice: Product or corporate names may be trademarks or registered trademarks, and are used only for identification and explanation without intent to infringe.

British Library Cataloguing in Publication Data
A catalogue record for this book is available from the British Library

ISBN: 978-0-367-34616-4 (Set)
ISBN: 978-0-429-34352-0 (Set) (ebk)
ISBN: 978-0-367-37088-6 (Volume 43) (hbk)
ISBN: 978-0-367-37091-6 (Volume 43) (pbk)
ISBN: 978-0-429-35263-8 (Volume 43) (ebk)

Publisher's Note
The publisher has gone to great lengths to ensure the quality of this reprint but points out that some imperfections in the original copies may be apparent.

Disclaimer
The publisher has made every effort to trace copyright holders and would welcome correspondence from those they have been unable to trace.

IF WE BUILD IT:
SCHOLARLY COMMUNICATIONS AND NETWORKING TECHNOLOGIES:
Proceedings of the
NORTH AMERICAN SERIALS INTEREST GROUP, Inc.

7th Annual Conference
June 18-21, 1992
The University of Illinois
at Chicago

Suzanne McMahon, MLS
Miriam Palm, MLS
Pam Dunn, MLS
Editors

The Haworth Press, Inc.
New York • London • Norwood (Australia)

If We Build It: Scholarly Communications and Networking Technologies: Proceedings of the North American Serials Interest Group, Inc. has also been published as *The Serials Librarian,* Volume 23, Numbers 3/4 1993.

© 1993 by The Haworth Press, Inc. All rights reserved. No part of this work may be reproduced or utilized in any form or by any means, electronic or mechanical, including photocopying, microfilm and recording, or by any information storage and retrieval system, without permission in writing from the publisher. Printed in the United States of America.

The Haworth Press, Inc., 10 Alice Street, Binghamton, NY 13904-1580, USA

Library of Congress Cataloging-in-Publication Data

North American Serials Interest Group. Conference (7th : 1992 : University of Illinois at Chicago)
    If we build it : scholarly communications and networking technologies : proceedings of the North American Serials Interest Group, Inc., 7th annual conference June 18-21, 1992, the University of Illinois at Chicago / Suzanne McMahon, Miriam Palm, Pam Dunn, editors.
       p. cm.
    ISBN 1-56024-450-X
       1. Libraries–United States–Special collections–Serial publications–Congresses. 2. Libraries–Canada–Special collections–Serial publications–Congresses. 3. Information networks–United States–Congresses. 4. Information networks–Canada–Congresses. I. McMahon, Suzanne. II. Palm, Miriam. III. Dunn, Pam. IV. Title.
Z692.S5N67 1992
025.3'432–dc20   93-19928
                                                                                                      CIP

In Memoriam

Margaret McKinley

1939-1992

These proceedings are dedicated to the memory of Margaret McKinley, who died on October 18, 1992. Margaret was a member of NASIG and other professional organizations, as well as a frequent and often-cited contributor to library literature. At the time of her death, Margaret headed the Serials Department of the library at the University of California, Los Angeles. Prior to that time she held other appointments in the University of California system, including the editorship of the University of California Union List of Serials. Margaret's friends and colleagues will greatly miss her wisdom, humor and thoughtful insight. NASIG dedicates these proceedings to honor Margaret McKinley and to recognize her contributions to serials librarianship.

**If We Build It:
Scholarly Communications and Networking Technologies:
Proceedings of the North American Serials
Interest Group, Inc.**

CONTENTS

Introduction	1
Announcement: NASIG Conference Grant Awards	3

PLENARY SESSION I: JUNE 19, 1992

The Transformation of Scholarly Communication and the Role of the Library in the Age of Networked Information *Clifford A. Lynch*	5
St. Augustine to NREN: The Tree of Knowledge and How It Grows *James J. O'Donnell*	21
Webs That Link Libraries, Librarians, and Information: Evolving Technical Standards for a Networking Age *Julia C. Blixrud*	43
Landlords and Tenants: Who Owns Information, Who Pays for It, and How? *Anita Lowry*	61

JOINT PLENARY SESSION, NASIG AND SSP (SOCIETY FOR SCHOLARLY PUBLISHING), JUNE 20, 1992

Higher Education in the 90s: Growth, Regression or Status Quo *Charles B. Reed*	73

A Potency of Life: Scholarship in an Electronic Age   79
    Willard McCarty

PLENARY SESSION II: JUNE 21, 1992

Professionals or Professionless, Information Engineers or ???   99
    Karen A. Schmidt

From Past Imperfects to Future Perfects   109
    Gary J. Brown

BREAKOUT SESSION A: NEW STRATEGIES FOR PUBLISHING

New Strategies for Publishing   123
    Michele Crump

BREAKOUT SESSION B: PRICE STUDIES: WHY AND HOW

A History of Journal Price Studies   127
    Barbara Meyers

Libraries and the Use of Price Studies   129
    Deana L. Astle

Index Medicus™ Price Study   137
    Lynn Fortney

BREAKOUT SESSION C: COPYRIGHT AND LICENSING IN THE ELECTRONIC ENVIRONMENT

Copyright and Licensing in the Electronic Environment   143
    Laurie Sutherland

BREAKOUT SESSION D: PRESERVATION: FUTURE STRATEGIES FOR RETAINING THE PAST

New Books from Old: A Proposal   149
    David Cohen

BREAKOUT SESSION E: REGIONAL LIBRARY NETWORKING: NEW OPPORTUNITIES FOR SERVING SCHOLARSHIP

Regional Library Networking: New Opportunities for Serving Scholarship   157
Glenda Thornton

Regional Library Networking: New Opportunities for Serving Scholarship   161
Barbara von Wahlde

BREAKOUT SESSION F: Z39.1-YOU JUST DON'T UNDERSTAND! LIBRARIANS AND A PUBLISHER DISCUSS THE STANDARD FOR PERIODICALS FORMAT AND ARRANGEMENT

Z39.1-You Just Don't Understand! Librarians and a Publisher Discuss the Standard for Periodicals Format and Arrangement   177
Daphne Hsueh

BREAKOUT SESSION G: MARKETING TO LIBRARIES: WHAT WORKS?

Marketing to Libraries: What Works? Adapting Marketing Strategy to Changes in the Library Community   183
Nan Hudes

Marketing to Libraries: What Works and What Doesn't   197
Vicky Reich

BREAKOUT SESSION H: ARTICLE DELIVERY: AN ALTERNATIVE TO OWNERSHIP?

Article Delivery: Shifting Paradigms   207
Anne McKee

Document Delivery Vendors: Benefits and Choices   217
Martha Lewis

PRE-CONFERENCE WORKSHOP

Electronic Networking and Serials Resources: Quotidian
   Applications for the Curious and the Cynical   225
      Robin B. Devin

WORKSHOP SESSION REPORTS

Cataloging Serial Computer Files   229
      Margaret Mering

Automating Binding Procedures: Using INNOVACQ
   vs. An In-House Database   233
      Paul Parisi

The Footbone's Connected to the Anklebone, or, Enumeration,
   Checking-In and Labeling Instructions   237
      Lawrence R. Keating II

Game Shows, Elevators, Full Plates, and Other Allegories:
   A Look at the Present State and Future Possibilities of LC
   Subject Headings   241
      Sandy L. Folsom

The Changing Role of the Vendor: Developing New Products
   and Services   245
      Lucy Bottomley

Check-In with the SISAC Symbol (Bar Code): Implementation
   and Uses for Libraries, Publishers and Automation Vendors   249
      Marcella Lesher

Publishing Opportunities: Getting into Print or Getting
   Involved   253
      Ellen Finnie Duranceau

Fine-Tuning the Claims Process   257
      Martha Kellogg

Basic Training for Survival *Bonnie Naifeh Hill*	261
Cataloging Computer Files That Are Also Serials *Pamela Morgan*	265
Working Together for the Future: Librarian/Publisher/ Subscription Agents *Lynne M. Hayman*	269
The Role and Responsibilities of the Professional Serials Cataloger *Jane Robillard*	273
How to Plan and Deliver a Great Workshop *Linda Meiseles*	277
Fewer Subscriptions = Increased Library Services: How ASU and ASU West Met the Challenge *Martin Gordon*	281
Managing Reference "Pseudoserials" *Sharon Scott*	285
Collection Development Assessment for Biomedical Serials Collections *Barbara A. Carlson*	289
Auditing the Automated Serials Control System *David Winchester*	293
The Cost Effectiveness of Claiming *Elizabeth Parang*	297
Seventh Annual NASIG Conference Registrants, University of Illinois at Chicago, June 1992	301
Index	317

Introduction

The North American Serials Interest Group (NASIG) held its Seventh Annual Conference at The University of Illinois at Chicago, from June 18-21, 1992. The conference included a joint day with the Society for Scholarly Publishing (SSP). The Program Committee chose "If We Build It: Scholarly Communications and Networking Technologies" as the theme of this year's conference.

The revolution in scholarly communication, spurred by the phenomenal growth of electronic technology, will not take place in a far-distant future–it is happening around us right now. Serials librarians, vendors, and publishers have each played unique roles in the print-based model of communication. What will change for us as ink and paper become the oddity and electronic transmitters and receivers become the norm? What services will be in demand and who will provide them? Which economic models will keep us all afloat? And most importantly, can the disparate groups currently active in scholarly communication work together to build the physical, social, and economic backbone of a new model?

Speakers at this year's conference addressed these questions at three plenary sessions. On June 20, NASIG and SSP conference participants attended joint plenary sessions and concurrent breakout sessions. NASIG also offered eighteen workshops dealing with the nuts-and-bolts aspects of serials work. Papers presented by the plenary speakers, papers and reports from the concurrent breakout sessions, and summaries of all the workshops are included in this volume. We wish to thank Dena Hutto for preparing the index.

The Eighth Annual NASIG Conference will be held at Brown University, Providence, Rhode Island, June 10-13, 1993.

S.M.

© 1993 by The Haworth Press, Inc. All rights reserved.

Announcement: NASIG Conference Grant Awards

The North American Serials Interest Group (NASIG) is an independent organization bringing together many segments of the serials information chain to study and explore common interests, problems, and ideas. NASIG is currently seeking candidates for grants to attend the Eighth Annual Conference to be held at Brown University, Providence, Rhode Island, June 10-13, 1993. Through the granting of these awards, NASIG desires to encourage participation in this information chain by students who are interested in some aspect of serials work upon completion of their professional degree.

GUIDELINES

SCOPE OF AWARD: Recipients are expected to attend the entire conference and submit a brief written report to NASIG. Expenses for travel, registration, meals and lodging will be paid by NASIG.

ELIGIBILITY: Students who are currently enrolled at the graduate level in any ALA accredited library school, who do not already have an ALA accredited degree, and who have expressed an interest in serials and/or technical services work, are eligible. Applicants *must* be full or part-time students at the time of application. In order to accept an award, a recipient *must not* be employed in a position requiring an ALA accredited degree, nor be on leave from such a position, at the time of acceptance of the grant. Equal consideration will be given to all qualified applicants, with preference given to those graduating the year of the conference.

APPLICATION PROCEDURE: Application forms will be available after January 15, 1993, in ALA accredited library schools and from Harriet Kersey, Chair, Library Science Student Grant Committee. Application forms should be sent to: Harriet Kersey, Asst. Head, Information Control and Management, Georgia Tech Library, Atlanta, Georgia 30332-0900. Telephone number: (404)894-4523.

APPLICATION DEADLINE: March 3, 1993. Applications received after this date will not be considered.

AWARD NOTIFICATION: Award recipients will be notified by April 15, 1993. A maximum of six grants may be awarded for 1993.

PLENARY SESSION I:
JUNE 19, 1992

The Transformation of Scholarly Communication and the Role of the Library in the Age of Networked Information

Clifford A. Lynch

INTRODUCTION

As an institution, the modern research library is both a product and an integral part of the current system of scholarly communication. Research libraries actually underwrite a major part of the cost of scholarly publication today. As with all well-established major institutions, the library now follows its own imperatives. In re-

---

Clifford A. Lynch is Director, Library Automation, University of California, Office of the President, 300 Lakeside Drive, 8th Floor, Oakland, CA 94612-3350.

This paper is loosely based on a keynote address given at the North American Serials Interest Group (NASIG) Meeting held in Chicago, Illinois in June 1992.

The author wishes to thank Cindy Hepfer for her notes on that talk, which were invaluable in preparing this paper, and to Nancy Gusack for editorial help.

© 1993 by The Haworth Press, Inc. All rights reserved.

sponse to continued budget pressures and escalation in publication prices, many research libraries are focusing their collections more narrowly through cancellation programs and an emphasis on acquisition of journals over monographs. A great deal of management attention in libraries is concentrated on service and budget issues that concern the vitality and quality of the institution's traditional missions.

Yet, while libraries follow a trajectory of organizational evolution shaped by traditional roles and missions arising out of the existing system of scholarly communication, that system itself is at the beginning of a major revolution fueled by developments in information technology.

Information technology–computers and computer communications networks–are changing many of the existing assumptions about how people discover and communicate information, teach, and learn. New methods of creating and disseminating information are appearing. There is a tendency to equate the current system of scholarly *publishing* with the system of scholarly *communication*. Actually, publishing is just a part of the communication system that grew, at a particular time, out of a series of assumptions about technology (paper and printing), infrastructure (postal mail and libraries), and economics (institutional support of authorship through employment of faculty and institutional support of publishers through library book purchases). The idea of publishing, narrowly construed, is a very limiting concept that has become separated from its origins and taken on a life of its own–an institutional imperative much like the library. The argument today about the extent to which various forms of electronic information creation, dissemination, and communication are "really" publishing misses the essential point: These processes are clearly part of the realm of scholarly communication. It doesn't matter whether they are categorized as publishing; these processes will eventually supplant publishing within the system of scholarly communication to the extent that they more effectively meet the needs previously fulfilled by traditional paper-based publishing. It is already clear that some of these network-based electronic communications processes have enough to offer scholars to insure that the new processes will survive and grow, at least as a supplement to the existing print-based system. We do not yet understand fully what the transfigured system of scholarly communication will be. It is virtually certain, however, that some elements of the existing print publishing processes (perhaps much changed) will be brought forward, but it is not essential that publishing, as we currently view it, be fully and faithfully transported into the electronic environment.

It is also likely that at least some print-based publication will continue to meet real needs for some time. And, just as the nature of electronic "publishing" practices are different from today's print practices, tomorrow's print practices may be different from today's. The transformations in the world of scholarly communication, including changes in the roles of publishers and libraries, remind us that these roles serve the needs of research, teaching, and learning. There is no guarantee that these roles are permanent and immutable, or that their changing nature in the face of changing needs will ensure the untroubled continuity of the existing institutions that have been part of that system. These institutions developed to support a system that *was* effective (given a set of assumptions about technology and economics that were true at the time). If the system evolves in response to changing possibilities of technology, the supporting institutions run the risk of (at worst) becoming obsolete and increasingly unnecessary unless they evolve to serve the altered system of scholarly communication. In reality, since the new system will probably incorporate much of the old, the institutions will persist, even if they don't respond, but with an increasingly limited role.

This paper explores the widening gulf between the traditional system of scholarly communication–and the traditional institutions, with a particular focus on libraries, that are its products *and* its foundation–and the new, transforming system of communication. The transformation, to the extent that its outlines are currently defined, is examined; and the effects of technology on both libraries and scholarly communications are explored. Some speculations about the possible roles of libraries as institutions within a new system of scholarly communication conclude the paper.

MODERNIZATION AND TRANSFORMATION

I find that the distinction between *modernization* and *transformation* clarifies the impact of technology on scholarly communication.

This perspective was first explained to me by Paul Peters of the Coalition for Networked Information and Peter Lyman of University of Southern California. *Modernization* can be defined as the use of new technology to continue to do what you have been doing, but in a more efficient and/or cost-effective way. In the library context, one example is the use of computers to automate library processes of circulation and serials check-in. There are experiments currently underway (such as the Elsevier TULIP project[1]) which address the modernization of journal publishing. Rather than shipping paper to libraries that subscribe to journals, the publisher would ship electronic images of the printed pages. The library could then store these electronically, and print them only on demand for users. This is modernization: The same service, under basically the same economic model, is provided in a way that is (hopefully!) more efficient and cost effective. Of course, there is the potential to go a bit beyond simple modernization in this project. The subscribing institutions receive what are, in effect, "site licenses" which will encourage wider and more convenient use of the material; online browsing on bitmapped terminals is a possibility; the receiving institutions can apply optical character recognition (OCR) and feed the results into current awareness services, text search systems, and the like. But, fundamentally, the idea is one of modernization, not transformation, and it is significant that potential extensions that go beyond simple modernization all rely on development efforts by the *receiving* organization–they do not alter the role or activities of the publisher.

In contrast to modernization, *transformation* addresses the use of new technology to change processes in a fundamental way. A shift from a scholarly communication system that fixes results into print publications to one that relies on quality controlled distributed hypertext databases that are updated continuously, accessed and distributed through computer communications networks, and perhaps controlled by intelligent agent programs operating on behalf of end users, describes a potential transformation. The ability to publish relatively raw experimental data and programs that model and manipulate, not merely summarize and analyze it, represents a potential transformation in scholarly communication. The possibilities of developing distributed network-based multimedia that combine images, sounds, text, computer programs, and other objects is transformational in nature. Shared virtual reality (VR) environments, operating across the network as a "place" to perform scientific collaboration, point the way towards yet another transformation in the scholarly communications process.

There are a few experimental projects focusing on the transformational possibilities of technology. Nina Matheson at Johns Hopkins University and Richard Lucier (formerly at Hopkins, and now at the University of California San Francisco) have pioneered a methodology they call "knowledge management" and developed systems such as the On Mendelian Inheritance In Man (OMIM) database. A system called "telesophy" developed by Bruce Schatz and his colleagues provides an extensive "information environment" for researchers concerned with the nematode *C. Elegans*. Multimedia "knowledge bases" are being compiled in many institutions and in support of many disciplines. One good example of this is the Perseus project on classical language and culture. There are several experiments underway in VR-based collaboration and multimedia authoring and distribution systems.

Many of these initial transformation experiments in scholarly communication do not fit comfortably within the existing system; indeed, this is one way to identify potentially transformational characteristics. One of the most common questions raised by academics in discussions of such projects is whether such work, unlike traditional print journal publications, will be of value to the authors when they are considered for tenure and promotion. The community is still unsure how to rate work on knowledge base and software development within the traditional evaluation framework. Part of the problem is the nature of the work. Another aspect that makes evaluation difficult under traditional criteria is the intensive collaboration that is usually behind such efforts, which often brings together researchers from multiple disciplines.

At this point, both libraries and publishers are focused intensively on modernization rather than transformation. In fact, when one considers transformational activities, it remains unclear what role the library as an institution will (or should) play. While individual visionaries within the library community can offer talent, energy, and resources to support progress on transformational projects, and in this way establish a role for their organizations, it is not clear how much this role reflects individual initiative and excellence rather than any inherent organizational mission (other than, perhaps, the organizational mission to survive in a changing world), particularly when traditional library missions are considered. Of course, the new missions of the library in the transformed world are yet to be defined–and perhaps the efforts of these leaders and visionaries are pointing the way.

LIBRARIES, PUBLISHERS, AND MODERNIZATION: THE ECONOMIC STRUGGLE

The traditional library, suffering ever increasing acquisitions costs, coupled with an erosion of institutional budgeting support, is looking to modernization to reduce costs. Facing the shock of this economic squeeze, some librarians have come to view the publishing community as their natural enemy. Others view publishers as fellow victims (albeit victims with more capability for self-determination) of a system of scholarly self-aggrandizement–"publish or perish"–that is out of control. Yet others blame the whole system.

Modernization will not substantially reduce publisher charges to libraries for their goods. This is only wishful thinking. In fact, due to investments in technology, modernization may actually increase the price of acquiring published material in the near term. Some publishers are showing a propensity to amortize and recover the expenditures they are making to upgrade their production systems over rather short time horizons, leading to increased prices. And, certainly, publishers will not view new electronic product offerings as a justification for reducing existing profit margins through price cuts. It seems improbable that modernization alone will reduce costs for libraries within the framework of traditional library-publisher economic models and the forces driving the system.

Libraries are also looking at new economic models. There is some evidence that many articles in journals are infrequently, if ever, read. It is technically feasible to employ the developing network infrastructure and information technology base to move to an acquisition-on-demand model under which a library acquires individual journal articles only when a patron requests them, rather than subscribing to the journal. But it seems certain that publishers will set the article prices for acquisition-on-demand to keep their existing revenue streams (at least) constant, though libraries may be able to take advantage of a brief transitional period while publishers react to the change in acquisition patterns by altering their pricing structures. If anything, libraries have not fully considered the potential complexities of a business model where most articles are acquired on demand. They assume that prices per article would be relatively constant from one article in a given journal to another, and over relatively long time periods, perhaps readjusted only every year or two, much as is now done with print royalties collected by rights brokers like the Copyright Clearance Center. But it is easy to imagine publishers applying information technology to vary prices of articles over days or weeks, based on usage levels, topic interest, citation analysis, or media coverage. (A Nobel Prize, for example, might stimulate immediate doubling of prices for recent articles authored by the recipient.) One can imagine speculative markets in article futures much like a commodities market. Are libraries ready to develop and deploy the information system necessary to perform trends analysis, hedging, and arbitrage in such a marketplace (which will be conducted in multiple national currencies, given the strong European representation among the commercial publishers, where the currencies, themselves, also form a marketplace!), and, more importantly, to adapt their budget and acquisitions policies to the realities of this new environment?

From a more transformational perspective, it seems clear to me that we will enter a period where the economics of information access will become much more complex and volatile. Imagine a world where there are many more dissemination channels for information, ranging from traditional print publications to a wide array of network information distribution options. We will have free information, information that we are paid to read (advertising, basically), information that is sold to recover costs, information sold for a profit, information the price of which decays as the timeliness of the information itself lags, and information the value of which varies inversely or directly with the scope of its distribution. The number of pricing options will be as wide as the set of motivations for making information accessible. Imagine the corporate sponsorship of scholarly information access much like current corporate sponsorship of public television programs. This will likely be a reality in the new world of networked information.

Regarding the publisher-library conflict, it seems likely that simple modernization of the traditional publishing process will offer the libraries little economic relief, and the more realistic leaders within the library community realize this. Modernization alone will not much reduce the power of the publishers to continue to raise prices for information essential to the process of scholarly communication, or at least to maintain current revenue streams. In the long run, after technology upgrades by the publishers are amortized, there might be a very modest savings split between the publishers and their customers. But it will immediately be consumed by growth in the volume of published literature.

So there are several other ideas being raised. Passing some part of the costs for information access back to the user is a natural outgrowth of existing document delivery services and acquisition-on-demand. This route is attractive to libraries, but may prove to be less desirable than it currently seems. It opens the library up to competition, particularly in a networked environment where geography is largely irrelevant and any organization can compete for customers anywhere. If you have to pay to get information from the local library, it is logical to shop the network for better and cheaper services. Few libraries are well-equipped to cope with this competitive environment. Beyond this rather crass consideration, user fees strike at the foundation of the "purchasing collective" economics that support libraries in their current form. Further, they raise troublesome policy considerations about equality of access to information. We will undoubtedly see libraries develop multiple service tiers: a basic level free to all patrons, and one or more extra-cost service levels. But it seems likely that the boundary for the basic level of service will have to be set high enough so that while the extra-cost services that libraries may offer will generate some revenue, it will probably not be enough to really resolve the library funding crisis.

Another alternative that has been proposed for dealing with the funding crisis is sometimes called the transition from collections to access, often referred to with the slogan "just-in-time rather than just-in-case acquisitions." There are two inherent problems with this attractive "solution." First, it is rooted in the existing print world rather than the world of electronic information. In the print world, the use of material owned by the library is almost always covered by copyright law and the doctrine of first sale. A library, having acquired material, can share it through the interlibrary loan system (subject to various constraints defined by the copyright law and its interpretations, such as the National Commission of New Technological Uses of Copyrighted Work (CONTU) guidelines). Thus, a library in the print world can implement acquisition-on demand through interlibrary loan, perhaps supplemented by commercial document delivery. Commercial document delivery includes a royalty component, and, as indicated above, it appears to be the intent of publishers to adjust royalties for per-article copies to ensure the continuity of the overall revenue stream, if and when article-based acquisitions substantially reduce subscription revenues. If there is a significant shift to acquisition-on-demand, the costs will increase until there is little or no savings in using commercial services, at least when these costs are averaged across the entire library community. Some individual libraries may benefit from the reallocation of costs; others will be punished by them. This leaves traditional interlibrary loan as the main vehicle with which a library can move from an emphasis on collections to an emphasis on access, while obtaining some protection from escalating per-article royalty charges.

But for information in electronic form, interlibrary loan is usually impossible. The electronic information a library acquires is typically *licensed* rather than purchased, and the library's subsequent use of that material is governed by the contract that it signed with the publisher rather than by copyright law. The contract is likely to be more restrictive than the copyright law and to forbid any exchange of the material through interlibrary loan. The transition from print to electronic formats may ultimately eliminate much of the existing interlibrary loan support infrastructure among libraries.

The second problem with just-in-time acquisition is a policy issue. This mode of operation essentially abdicates one of the primary roles of the research library: to preserve the scholarly record and the materials for future research. This library role may be somewhat out of fashion today, but it is crucial in the long run.

A final point should also be made about the shift from collections to access. If a library wants to acquire material on demand it must acquire it, presumably, in many cases, from some larger library that either has not recognized the imperative to make the transition from acquiring just-in-case to just-in-time, or that has been unable to make the transition due to pressures from its user community, or that has made a policy decision to continue to behave like a traditional research library. This points to the development of a two-tiered system of a handful of very large, collection-oriented "traditional" research libraries that function as service centers to smaller, more agile, acquisition-on-demand-oriented libraries. These larger libraries will continue to face increasing financial pressures which will force them to charge more realistic interlibrary loan costs to the more "opportunistic" smaller libraries relying on their collections. And, as these collections become increasingly electronic, they will be unable to share more recent electronic materials limited by license restrictions.

One possible future scenario is a division of the research libraries into collection-based and access-oriented libraries. Publishers might reach agreements with the collection-oriented libraries to permit those libraries to resell information to the access-oriented libraries directly, thus avoiding the need for the publisher to mount network-based article supply servers and respond to large numbers of article-level requests. One advantage of delegating the large collection-oriented libraries as brokers to smaller libraries on behalf of publishers is that it gives the access-oriented libraries a more coherent environment in which to acquire information. They could deal with a few large collection-oriented libraries rather than with many publishers directly. In this sense, the collection-oriented libraries would compete with and partially supplant the existing for-profit document delivery brokerage services.

Libraries have sometimes proposed breaking the economic grip of the publishers of scholarly information with the extreme remedy of "taking back the means of production"—by altering institutional policies in higher education to encourage or require the institutions to retain copyright to faculty publications rather than having the faculty transfer the copyrights to publishers as a condition of publication. While this would probably make a major impact on the economic bind facing libraries, it seems unlikely that such a shift could be accomplished. Faculty would besiege university administrations, and publishers (and others) would challenge such policies in the courts and the legislatures–and likely with considerable justice. If nothing else, the bureaucratic ineptitude of many large institutions would threaten to become a major barrier to the dissemination of new knowledge–a situation meriting concern. In addition, it should be noted that the intellectual property rights that are associated with many of the new scholarly communications vehicles are extremely complex and poorly defined. Assignment of these rights is made even more ambiguous by the extensive collaboration that is often represented in these new transformational vehicles. Existing intellectual property policy at most universities does not even recognize the legal problems that are associated with these new developments, much less attempt to address institutional claims on rights associated with them. Imagine a scenario in which three collaborators from three institutions develop a multimedia database. Each of the three institutions owns its faculty members' intellectual property rights under a take-back-the-rights policy. Counsel for the three institutions become involved and begin bickering. Years pass, with the institutions (unlike the authors, who are desperate to share their work with the scholarly community) having only the most abstract motivation in most cases to resolve the problem so the work can be made available. Thus, one might argue that the "take back the rights" approach remains very much focused on a set of issues that are being rapidly redefined by changing technology, and it is unclear how to update the approach to accommodate the changing technology and its results, or even whether such an approach is really desirable. In some ways, a move towards identifying and reserving rights in a Draconian fashion might simply create one more barrier to slow the rate at which transformation of the system of scholarly communication can occur; worse, it might further jeopardize the existing system.

Within the context of modernization, then, it seems that there is little relief in sight for libraries. Budget pressures will continue.

There will be some alteration (really, narrowing) of mission on the part of many research libraries. Most may, in a real sense, cease to be research libraries in today's understanding of the term to become intermediaries between their patrons and the few remaining research libraries. To be sure, as intermediaries they will add significant value for their patrons in many cases. Libraries will work sometimes in cooperation and sometimes in competition with other libraries as they attempt to shift costs from one institution to another. Local and temporary advantages will be achieved and lost. But, ultimately, these shifts in cost allocation will stabilize. Although we will see costs remain relatively constant, the number of research libraries, as we understand the term today, will likely be reduced.

SCHOLARLY COMMUNICATION, NETWORKS, AND TRANSFORMATION

While libraries struggle with their budgetary crises and the costs and dislocations of modernization, a revolution in scholarly communications is brewing. This may eventually render moot much of the effort that libraries are making to cope with the current budget crises. Indeed, the revolution threatens to undermine much of the existing role of libraries (and publishers). A full consideration of the implications of information technology and computer communications networks for transforming scholarly communications is beyond the scope of this paper. In fact, it is probably impossible to explore fully such a topic at this time, since the ultimate results of this process have yet to be defined.

Some of the potential results have been suggested, and we should recognize that not all of these potentials are likely to be attractive to those accustomed to, and comfortable with, a system of scholarly communication based upon the refereed printed journal. There is a serious, growing problem facing network users attempting to assess the quality and accuracy of the available information. Inaccurate information lies dormant on the network, and is periodically re-broadcast, re-evaluated, and rediscredited; but it stays in various archives waiting to be found again. Completely new approaches may be necessary to cope with the problems of unauthenticated, unattributed information that propagates through the network in a series of repackaged, recombinant forms.[2]

The need to offer (at least optionally) a validation of information on the network suggests that some aspects of traditional peer review may find their way into the networked information environment; but they may be different in important ways from print mechanisms, emphasizing, instead, reviewers or authenticators as direct, individually identified sources of important, accurate material. It may be that one pays people for their reading lists of "good stuff" rather than paying the authors, or that one pays both in the networked environment. It also seems likely that it will be far easier than in the print world for anyone to make material available. Editorial staffs and reviewers may be far less important as pre-publication gatekeepers on the network. The challenge for authors may be simply getting their material read, not making it available for people to read.

The network is a place for scholarly communication and collaboration. But it is also a place to conduct commerce and a part of the infrastructure that will support business and industry, in ways ranging from conducting transactions in information through supporting corporate research. There is no firm demarcation between commerce and scholarship; one fades into the other in many complex ways. The scope of the network as an environment for both scholarship and commerce will be international rather than merely national. In the new arena of global economic competition that many envision, the network will become, in some sense, a field of battle. It is worth mentioning that we have very little experience in managing deliberate, possibly malicious attempts to introduce disinformation and misinformation into the network in support of commercial advantage or even national security advantage, at least at levels more subtle than simple electronic dissemination of print-oriented propaganda (a modernization activity).

With rare but noticeable exceptions, however, it is striking how little libraries are doing to address access and management of the developing world of networked information. They are contributing little or no financial or intellectual capital to supporting the networks or networked information, or to organizing these resources. This is perhaps the most telling point, when one considers the extent to which library budgets underwrite both scholarly publishing and, increasingly, the building of abstracting and indexing databases. Despite the fact that certain disciplines now rely on network based communications and information distribution as perhaps *the* primary medium of communication and information distribution (to be fair, primarily, but not solely in fields closely related to computing and computer communications), libraries seem to be making no effort to collect and archive this information for future use. Rather than stepping up to the challenge of developing the network as an arena for scholarly discourse, many libraries are choosing to ignore it in favor of "traditional" missions related to print-based publications. Yet, as a percentage of budget, libraries could do a great deal with a very small investment.

To the limited extent that we currently understand it, networked information is qualitatively different from print publication. Much of the library model of information management assumes that information is fixed in a given (printed) form of lasting value and long-term availability. This form is then amenable to processes such as cataloging that organize it and add value, but that require a significant investment in human labor. Such processes are familiar as means by which libraries "add value" to the printed literature. In contrast, on the network today there is a jumble of information that is ephemeral in character and information that is of lasting value. There is a compelling need for information-organizing technologies that accommodate not only the long-term information but also the ephemeral. It seems appropriate that libraries and the information science research community should undertake the research necessary to develop techniques to manage this rich but chaotic collection of information. Traditional cataloging is probably not the answer, and certainly not the complete answer.

In fact, when one considers how essential information from nonprint sources such as television broadcasts has become to our society, it is also striking the extent to which libraries have continued to focus on print-based collections and ignored these new information sources. As broadcasting and mass media merge with computer communications networks in the 1990s (as predicted by the work of organizations such as the MIT Media Lab), the full range of these nontraditional sources will become ever more important as part of the cultural, and even the scholarly record. Again, would speculate that part of the reason that libraries have not emphasized this material is that it is unclear how to organize it, provide intellectual access to its contents, and to deliver it effectively to large numbers of patrons.

The traditional publishers, as well as the libraries, have largely avoided becoming involved in the early fruits of the coming transformation of scholarly communication.

The dominant intellectual property rights owners in the emerging nonprint marketplaces are quite different and distinct from the traditional publishers, and the traditional publishers have not become much involved in the development of the new knowledge bases and other electronic communications vehicles. Perhaps that is because the operating framework of these new vehicles is so completely alien to the business arrangements that commercial publishers have found comfortable. Put another way, perhaps the commercial publishers cannot see any way, yet, to make profits from these new developments or even to position themselves into the processes. Or perhaps they have not felt it worth the effort. Surveying the developing world of network-based electronic scholarly communication, one finds a few professional societies and a few difficult-to-characterize organizations such as OCLC, but very little presence from the traditional print publishers. Much like most libraries, the print publishers are watching and talking, but committing few resources to new, non-traditional activities.

CONCLUSIONS

Libraries face some extraordinarily difficult challenges in the coming years. The transition of the scholarly communications system will not be instantaneous. During the transitional period, which may be as long as a decade, libraries will face pressures from their constituencies both to invest in the new and to continue the existing base of services. Given the budgetary pressures they face, heroic efforts will be required merely to continue the existing service base that serves the current system of scholarly communications. Finding the funding and the energy to make the investments in the developing, post-transformational system will be almost impossible under the current constraints.

Yet there is real danger if the funding cannot be found, and if the management commitment and intellectual focus cannot be mustered to address the developing networked information environment. The system of scholarly communication is starting to change, and the rate of change will only accelerate as the networked information revolution takes hold. The danger lies in the possibility that libraries, while protecting their currently defined institutional roles within the "old" scholarly communications system, will overlook the transformation of this system, and will find themselves in a much-reduced role as archivists of the past, pre-transformational records and products that print publishers continue to produce, but largely shut off from the vital mainstream of transformed scholarly communication in the age of networked information.

NOTES

1. The TULIP project is a three-year experiment designed by Elsevier Scientific Publishers and a group of about fifteen US institutions of higher education with the endorsement of the Coalition for Networked Information. The idea of the project is to spend three years providing the participating institutions with bit-mapped page images from about forty-five journals in materials science published by Elsevier or its now-subsidiary Pergamon. The sites will collect usage data, experiment with various delivery options such as print-on-demand, online browsing, and full text access using OCRed versions of the text. They will also explore new economic models such as pay-per-view rather than subscription in some cases.

2. Those interested in the future of the network might find Vernor Vinge's science fiction novel of interest: *A Fire Upon the Deep* (St. Martins Press; 1991). He depicts an interstellar society that is linked through something very similar to Usenet Newsgroups. Characters in the book refer to it as "the net of a million lies."

St. Augustine to NREN: The Tree of Knowledge and How It Grows

James J. O'Donnell

SUMMARY. As a new age begins, it is important to know what age it is that ends. As we move to networked communication, it is not the age of writing that is ending, nor specially the age of the printed book. It is rather the end of the life span of the *codex* (the familiar form of rectangular pages sewn and gathered between covers), the invention that revolutionized the arrangement and processing of information in the earliest centuries of the common era. Consideration of the modes of storage and access (including early foreshadowings of hypertext) in the age of the manuscript codex will lead to reflections on what is likely to abide in the new forms of information processing and what is likely to pass away. Forms fade, structure abides.

At the turn of an age, it is good to know where we have been. It helps a little, as we strive to discern where we are going. The transformation of our ways of knowing by electronic media is well under way and will be a watershed in the history of culture. Those who have studied with some envy earlier transformative moments, like that of the introduction of printing, thinking that to be young in those days was very heaven,[1] should not forget to be grateful that we are alive in days that are, if anything, more exciting.

All agree on the importance of two earlier moments: when writing was introduced to give the voice power over distance and when printing gave wider distribution to what the hand had written.[2] My business in this paper is to draw attention to a less well-publicized

---

James J. O'Donnell is Professor, Department of Classical Studies, 720 Williams Hall, University of Pennsylvania, Philadelphia, PA 19104-6305.

and studied moment in our past, to examine its influence on our past and on ourselves, and then to make a few suggestions about the future. I mean to do no more than sketch, suggest, and provoke. It is no accident that I do this for an audience with a keen professional interest in "serials," for I believe that the scholarly journal has rich potential for becoming a powerful engine driving the transformation of scholarly and scientific ways of knowing in the years to come. I hope to give some reasons for that optimism in the course of this paper.

I. THE AGE OF THE CODEX

Writing among the Mediterranean peoples, whom we acknowledge as ancestors,[3] began on stone,[4] but only became a useful vehicle for the dissemination of information when the technology of the papyrus roll or scroll was perfected.[5] Though the Athens of Sophocles and Plato (c. 400 B.C.) was a town almost intoxicated with the power of the written word, the real achievement of ancient literacy was consolidated a century and more later in the Greek-founded Egyptian city of Alexandria.[6] There the rows on rows of neatly docketed rolls in their pigeon-holes created the first great library and the first great generations of literary critics and consumers. Most of that treasure is now lost to us, and what survives for the most part is in fragments, unearthed from the Egyptian sands in the last century.

The ancient roll was an elegant but cumbersome form of record. Size was strictly limited. We are told, perhaps only in legend but in verisimilar legend, that the length of a "book" in antiquity (such as the twenty-four "books" that make up the *Iliad* or the *Odyssey*) was de facto defined by the size of the pigeon-holes at Alexandria. A thousand or so lines of text was all that a roll could hold, and that roll itself was a bulky long sheet of papyrus, averaging twenty to thirty feet in length. To shuffle through a roll looking for a passage was time-consuming and bothersome. To manipulate twenty-four of those in order to control one of Homer's epics is to our taste a seriously user-hostile environment.

There was already a humbler form of information-processing

technology at hand for day-to-day purposes: the wax tablet. In its simplest form, this was a sheet of wood, hollowed out, with melted wax poured in the hollow. A dry stylus would incise letters which the thumb could then erase at will. For memoranda, transient bookkeeping, and daily business, these tablets were excellent. Several of them bound together by thongs made something that was not at all unlike our notion of a small book.[7]

Somewhere in the first centuries of the common era, the notion of making a formal literary medium out of bound pages on the model of the wax tablet suddenly caught on. Though the *codex*, for such is the name given to the form in antiquity, may comprise pages of either papyrus or animal skins, in practice parchment and vellum (skin of sheep and calf, respectively), began to be widely used.[8] The evidence strongly suggests that the popularity of the codex form may be attributed to the habits of early Christians, but it must be emphasized that when we say that we are working inferentially from the statistics of surviving manuscripts, and there is not one shred of direct evidence to tell us where or when someone first made the case for this form of textual preservation.[9] The first appreciable use of the codex form for literary texts is noticeable in the second century, but it is in the third century (one of the darkest and least documented periods of antiquity) that the corner was turned; by the fourth century, an age of relatively settled prosperity and (for the Christians) triumphant consolidation, the codex had won the day. Of surviving second century Greek manuscripts, 99 percent are rolls; of surviving fifth century manuscripts, 90 percent are codices.[10]

One implication must be emphasized from this vital historical event. If you were a very farsighted citizen of the second century and you had a book on a papyrus roll, the thing you most wanted to do was see to it that it was copied into a codex format. Bluntly speaking, books that made that transition successfully had a reasonable chance of surviving and being read in the centuries to come; books that did not make that transition were more likely to be orphans in one form or another. The Greek plays of Menander, for example, were almost entirely lost to us until modern discoveries in the Egyptian sands began to restore them. The Latin plays of Plautus and Terence, on the other hand, some of them no more than ham-handed translations of Menander, had a long and lively history of medieval and modern readership. They had been rescued from the roll and saved for the codex at an early and timely date.[11]

The manuscripts of the Christian Bible are predominantly transmitted to us in the codex form, and there is much discussion of the reasons for this particular focus. Was the codex form chosen for its ease of reference and cross-reference? That is a hard question, and scholarship at present declines to affirm what was once a commonplace truth. The problem is that none of the traces of such reference systems (whose western origins I will speak of below) can be found in those earliest manuscripts. Even the notion of a "Bible" as such is slow-forming. "Scripture" is transmitted for the most part in separate manuscripts containing parts of the whole. The Greeks had larger comprehensive volumes earlier, but the Latins waited very late, probably until the sixth century, before drawing all the books of their scripture together in one set of covers.

For a variety of reasons, we in the western world are the heirs of Greece, chiefly at one remove, through Roman and Latin hands. The living tradition of Greek culture in the middle ages withdrew (from our point of view) to the Aegean shores and the Bosporus, a veil of Islamic and Slavic settlement fell between east and west and closed the Mediterranean to the free commerce and intercourse of antiquity, and "western civilization" was left to create itself north of the Mediterranean and west of the Vistula.

Within those realms, a remarkable culture came into existence. I have chosen St. Augustine (A.D. 354-430) as the patron saint of this paper, because he does stand predominant at the head of the line of that new culture. When Augustine set out on his literary career, which has left five million words still surviving today, there was little substantial library of Christian literature for him to work with outside of the Bible. In his own generation, the first Christian bibliographic literature was being written, and within the following century, library management became a new and pressing topic for many Latin writers.[12] Augustine appeared to his community as a mediator of the written word from the large and handsome gospel book that stood in his church sanctuary,[13] but it was a book that inspired his own production in great abundance.

The making of the medieval library and with it medieval culture is a subject that still repays study.[14] Cassiodorus, a statesman, monk, and man of letters of the sixth century, is associated with the most ambitious single project we know of, that to create first a Christian university at Rome (but that project fell apart in time of war) and later a model Christian library on his estates near Squillace on the Ionian Sea (on the instep, so to speak, of the boot of Italy).[15] We can still, we surmise, see him as he appeared to his monks. A portrait of the Hebrew scribe Ezra, who was praised for restoring the books of the Law after the Babylonian captivity, was made in his library for a bible manuscript, and it was probably at least implicitly a flattering portrait of the scholar and librarian who commissioned the book in question–the bookshelves in the background show an arrangement of books that matches what Cassiodorus himself describes for his own library at that time.[16] By this time, the arrangement of bound codex volumes in an *armarium* (where they usually lay flat on the shelves, already with titles on the spines), was a de facto standard.

The codex had several advantages over the roll. First, its size was limited only by the strength of the user (or the user's furniture); much more material could be contained in a single unit. Second, the codex could be taken apart, put together, and rearranged at will. This meant that several different authors and titles could be combined and recombined with minimal difficulty. Third, and of greatest importance, non-linear access to the material in the volume was possible; by this I mean simply that the reader did not need to shuffle through every page of information from beginning to end to find what she was looking for–with appropriate indexing or dumb luck she could pop the book open in the middle and find what she was looking for quickly. It is that third feature that offers the genesis of the revolution for which the codex stood and that offers the most important key to the reflections I will make below about our present situation.

It is a useful rule promulgated by Marshall McLuhan, that the content of a new medium is always an old medium. When we invent the motion picture, the first thing we do is put a camera in front of actors performing a "play" and let it run; it takes a while before we even begin to take advantage of the possibilities of the new medium, and it takes a long while before the conventionalities of the old medium can be forgotten–some are never forgotten. So it was in antiquity with the written word. The manuscript was first conceived to be no more than a prompt script for the spoken word, a place to look to find out what to say. The arrangement of words on the page, without punctuation and word-division, was as user-hostile as any DOS operating system could ever hope to be and was meant for the technician, who knew how to read, to use, to produce the audible word.[17] In many ways, then, the mere introduction of writing did little to change the way people used words, at least at first.

And so there grew up a whole literature and culture of memory substitutes. Early medieval manuscripts feature diagrams accompanied by illustrations chosen because their allegorical meanings offered mnemonic keys to accompany the scheme outlining, say, the nine kinds of syllogism or the twelve types of definition possible in the school taxonomies of the time.[18] The people who produced those manuscripts seem still to have expected the reader to manage his own private non-linear information access system–what we might call liveware memory. The real advantage of the written word, that the non-linear system it offers is one that anyone can use and that the user needs to know very little to get a great deal of use out of it, had not yet been fully exploited. In the age of memory, in order to know something, it was necessary to know it–or to know personally someone who already knew it; in the age of writing, it is possible to know things without knowing them, and that is a very great revolution indeed.

But the history of medieval manuscripts[19] is the history of the exploitation of the possibilities of the codex page. Arrangement of material on the page found increasing ways to make information more accessible and to facilitate cross-movements of various kinds. The simplest kind of non-linear access facilitation that we use all the time is the alphabet, and increasing facility with alphabetization, coming with agonizing slowness to our taste, is an important part of the history.[20] Two examples show the resourcefulness of the times. First I need to digress briefly to speak of Cassiodorus again and his intellectual obsessions. When the statesman had retired and not yet become a monk, he spent a decade in Constantinople, where he wrote a complete commentary on the Psalter, running to more than 1000 pages in its printed editions. Cassiodorus was an enthusiast for the application of the secular sciences to religion, not because he thought them superior but precisely because he thought them inferior. The secular sciences, he argued, had been re-invented superfluously by "pagan" philosophers when all the wisdom those sciences contained was already implicitly contained in divine revelation. Accordingly, his argument went on, the proper study of divine revelation included identification of all the parts of speech and forms of argument and styles of rhetoric that holy writ contained. Good monks could be better ones by being trained to detect the privileged forms of pseudo-secular (and in fact authentically Christian) wisdom in the Bible.[21]

All this is background for his practice. The manuscripts of his Psalm commentary are prefaced with an index of abbreviations, two and three letter acronyms, which are then found scattered through the margins of the whole commentary. So RT stands for "Rhetoric" and GEO for "Geometry." Each abbreviation marks some point in the text where the teachings of that science are to be found (and they are almost always explicitly commented on there). Another abbreviation, the standard Christian chi-rho symbol, marks particular points of high dogma worth attending. The function of these marks is thus *not* primarily to be used while reading the commentary straight through in a linear way, but to facilitate non-linear access from a variety of user-defined perspectives–that is to say, one can imagine but need not prescribe the reasons that might drive someone to the text looking for one or the other of the marginal abbreviations; but what is certain is that their presence made the text potentially far more useful than it would have been without them; and made for experiences of the text that were anything but linear and consecutive.

Perhaps a clearer example is that of the Eusebian canon tables. One of the commonest early medieval Christian books is the gospel book; and of course one of the most obvious features of the gospel book is that it contains four narratives of the same life of Jesus, all different. Much modern ink is spilled on the 'synoptic question' (how Matthew, Mark, and Luke are related, and why John seems so unrelated to the other three), but the topic is not new. In the second century already the Christian writer Tatian had produced a work he called the *Diatessaron* (roughly: "Four-in-One") in which he reduced the four accounts to a single linear narrative–the idea was attractive but it is interesting that it did not catch on. In the early fifth century, Augustine had written at length on "The Agreement of the Evangelists," by which he meant their essential agreement in spite of all the appearance of disagreement. But the gospel manuscripts themselves generally have a simple reader's help. Each of the gospels is marked with a running series of marginal numbers in sequence, with each gospel starting over at the number one. Then in the front of the manuscript are pages in which architectural ornament highlights columns of parallel numbers. The technique is to list first passages in which, say, Matthew, Mark, and Luke all have the same story. The marginal numbers from Matthew appear in the first column, with those of the corresponding elements in the corresponding stories from Mark and Luke in columns two and three. There are as many sets of these parallel columns as there are possible combinations of stories, so that there is a separate comparison for stories in Mark and Luke but not Matthew, and so forth.[22]

An arrangement like this, not so much common as standard in the early gospel books and traditionally attributed to Eusebius of Caesarea, the great Greek church historian of the fourth century, is designed to be a form of non-linear access for both the linear reader of the text (who strikes a story in Luke and cannot quite remember where the parallels are in Matthew and Mark) and for the external consulter, who wishes to analyze overall patterns of coincidence and opposition. My point is that such an arrangement of information at the front of the handsome formal gospel book positively cries out for a style of reading that does not simply start on page one and work through the end.[23]

I do not think that I need at this point to say more than that the resourcefulness and the range of possibilities suggested by these examples demonstrate that the codex page format was one that lent itself admirably to non-linear access; and that the reader's own imagination and memory can now begin to fill in many of the other ways in which these techniques have advanced and refined themselves since that time. The index, the concordance, the running head: all of these have medieval antecedents and modern application. Ever since the time of Cassiodorus, we have been at work in Latin and post-Latin culture building a common tree of knowledge, an invisible but powerful structure by which we agree together to organize what we know and to make it accessible. The institutions we call libraries and the catalogues they contain (in whatever form, from old bound books through the familiar cards, and down to our Online Public Access Catalog [OPAC] systems of today) are all only manifestations of a larger cultural project: to make knowledge available to non-linear access in as many ways as possible.

II. AFTER THE CODEX

If we reflect for a moment, we will find that a very high percentage of the forms of the printed word we consult most often are not traditional linear books at all. Look around you: tour guides, textbooks, *The World Almanac*, encyclopedias, dictionaries, phone books, the *Physicians' Desk Reference*, cookbooks, atlases, *Books in Print, Ulrich's International Periodical Directory*,[24] the *National Union Catalogue.*

The learned journal, our "serial," belongs properly to the history of the printed rather than the written word, and there are many members of NASIG far more expert than I on that phase of cultural history. I would like to suggest that what I have said already indicates that the history of the journal needs to be considered under two aspects if we are to catch sight of its future with any confidence:

> First, as a material convenience: clumping together small items and presenting them together makes for ease of access of one kind that is limited to the technology of the print world. The distinction between the "article" and the "monograph" is an artificial one that belongs in this category–it is crude but effective to say that a monograph is an article that is too long for any journal to accept it, and so it must be printed and bound separately. In *this* form the journal is a relic of the age of print.
>
> Second, as a part of the larger cultural project. Where the earliest journals had a unity of place and time (that is, they represented a wide range of observations about the world of learning reported to and from a particular location, say Paris or

London, at the date of issue), the modern journal has gradually been specialized by its place on the invisible tree of knowledge. I read the *Journal of Roman Studies* or *Behavioral and Brain Sciences* because I know that in those pages I will find a range of related but still focused studies that appeal to me. It is possible to imagine that assigning each article a Library of Congress (LC) catalogue number would *improve* access (and short of that, we surround ourselves with indexes of various kinds), but it must be admitted that as a first cut on sorting information, the readers of *Behavioral and Brain Sciences* are mightily relieved *not* to find studies of the philosophical inconsistencies of Seneca or the poetics of self-pity in Ovid in *those* pages, just as I am happy not to find B.F. Skinner's ideas extensively ventilated in the *Journal of Roman Studies*. This function of the scholarly journal is one of its most valuable (the other, peer review, I will mention shortly), and this is a function which is not tied to the technology used to create and distribute the "issues" of the printed journal.

Seen in this light, the journal's possibilities for enduring contributions are clear. What is equally clear is that the reigning monarch of scholarly publication, the eminent monograph from a distinguished press, is in serious jeopardy. Look at it how you will, the traditional monograph, with its sustained linear argument, its extraordinary high costs of publication and distribution, and its numerous inefficiencies of access only partly retrieved by the assignment of an LC call number, is beginning to look more and more like a great lumbering dinosaur, feeling a bit poorly and looking around for a place to lie down. As library buying habits change and fewer and fewer copies of each title are printed and distributed, the difference between a university press and a vanity press is going to become a finer and finer point of ethereal argument.

This is not to say that the traditional book will disappear overnight; but surely its presence will fade from the scene.[25] It will survive if only for its prestige, rather the way the leather bound edition of the classics now survives, not at all to be read but to make a statement about the book and about the owner of the book. For a time, academics will be unable to think of another ready way of delegating the responsibility for tenure decisions to anyone else the way they have of late delegated it to university press editorial boards; but even that will pass, new techniques for arbitrariness and avoidance will emerge, and young scholars will no longer speak with such misplaced reverence and awe of the publishing process.

Other aspects of our learned publishing will fade soon as well. Those aspects of the learned journal that depend on the physical media of printing and binding are evanescent. The "issue," which for convenience yokes together forever items whose only commonality is usually their date of submission, need not any longer govern association.[26] We will no longer refer to published material by page number, and so surrender what is a remarkably imprecise and error-prone form of indexing. Better news is yet to come. Storage of and access to learned journals is one of the principal preoccupations of NASIG. At the moment one touchy point is quantitative: how many copies of an article will be printed, and when? Publishers would like them all printed at once and sold to subscribers; users have no objection to seeing fewer copies printed and sold, and more copies photo- or electro-reproduced and distributed by ILL and other document delivery systems. *That* is a controversy whose life will be short. Initial 'printing' will disappear and any production of hard copy that occurs will be incidental and for the convenience of single end users only.

It is easy to prognosticate that changes will come to the division of labors among the many journals that exist. The proliferation of journals reflects both the crowded submission lists of the most popular ones and at the same time an urge to provide more specialized information through more narrowly focused collections. Both of those needs and pressures can persist and be met more cheerfully in a post-print world. A popular journal need not, in principal, limit itself by cost and number of pages any longer, but can instead use the time and talents of its editors as the measure of its capacity: how much can *they* stand? Similarly, the subject association of articles is no longer going to be determined forever by their place of publication. No longer will it be necessary to agonize over whether to put an article in the *Journal of Roman Studies* or the *Journal of Hellenic Studies*; in fact, there will be no reason why both labels could not appear a single article.

For the likeliest development (and here I am *merely* guessing) is that the association of articles in a given "journal" will no longer be a physical association and no longer be a condition for publication and distribution. The rest of the world will soon follow the scientific practice of publishing by distribution of something like pre-prints. The "journal" peer reviewing and stamp of approval will come after the fact of distribution, and will exist as a way of helping identify high quality work and work of interest to specific audiences. In that world, the "journal" title will be something like a *Good Housekeeping* seal of approval, applied after the fact; and there will be no reason, intellectual or economic, to deny a single article as many different such seals as editorial boards see fit. Indeed, we can already see articles that would reach different audiences if only they could be published twice in different places. We frown on this because trees and ink and shelf space are scarce resources. But if instead of multiple publication it were a matter merely of multiple electronic tags, then the form of indexing and access-enhancement that comes from identifying an article with the approval given it by a specific editorial board could be made much more valuable.

If peer reviewing and editorial identity survive, what else in the current world of journals will survive? Here I will make only one suggestion: many learned journals now publish a variety of forms of communication that I will call para-articles. *Not* learned contributions, peer reviewed and path-breaking, but notices of appointments, reports of meetings, calls for papers, necrologies, forums for discussion of current pedagogical practices related to the journal's subject. That is a form of communication that has been increasingly relegated to association newsletters and the like, and restricted even there, essentially for economic reasons. There is a limit to how much we can print, and so we must print only what is pressing. But the para-article has the important function of providing widespread access to information of a kind that otherwise flourishes mainly in common rooms at well-connected universities; to *publish* it is a democratic gesture, increasing access for a wider audience. As long as there are LISTSERV discussion groups, I think it unlikely that "journals" will be overrun by mere gossip and chat (but vigilance will be necessary), but they can become even more valuable than they are now as media of genuinely current news. In so doing they will recover some of their earlier function, when delays in publication were slower and press dates closer to the actual date of appearance.

So what will be new? What can the "journal" do in the electronic world that it could not do in the age of the codex? I began to pull together these remarks expecting to offer bright new and unprecedented hopes. I have surprised myself in finding that this paper comes full circle to where it began, to the possibilities already inherent in the codex, but still not fully exploited. If I return to them now, and sketch how they may more vividly be realized in electronic form, the reader should bear in mind the McLuhanite principle about the content of a new medium being an old medium. These suggestions, by their very rootedness in the past, condemn themselves out of hand as timid, limited, and unimaginative. If they do not seem that way, the reader should bear in mind that a true prophet would be seeing things far stranger than these.

The first obvious development is that the quality of our non-linear access to information will increase exponentially. To give only a hint of this, consider the difference between using LC subject headings for a subject search on an OPAC and pursuit of the same inquiry using keyword searching. In a world in which the library will cease to be a warehouse and become instead a software system, the value of the institution will lie in the sophistication, versatility, and power of its indexing and searching capacities. We need not wait for the possibilities of artificial intelligence (AI) to manifest themselves to take advantage of intellectually simpler but nonetheless amazingly powerful systems of investigation to lead us through a mass of material to information that suits our needs. If the criteria are a search that reveals a very high percentage of the material we might want if we knew it was all there and that at the same time leads us to relatively few irrelevancies, then we are not far from great advances. The secret is that the end-user's intelligence remains a powerful tool. If a system leads me only *close* to the information I am looking for, I will recognize it and begin processing it in ways that no machine could. Artificial intelligence someday may begin to do some of the processing that I would do, but as long as my own liveware is available, I need much less than a machine does to make sense of my world.

But one corollary of that style of searching is that I will not care where I find information, so long as I find it. A graphical display of the arrangement of information on a hard disk reveals that a computer is far less fastidious than a librarian. The information stored so carefully is in fact mashed together in a mighty jumble, pieces of files interleaved with pieces of other files, and bits of erased files (not really erased but merely ignored) strewn between. In that world, preservation of the boundaries separating one package of information from another is necessary only if the end-user needs it, and search strategies that concentrate on the information rather than the source are far more efficient and will thus be more successful. One way to describe this phenomenon is to say that what we call "hyperlinks" between data will become dominant lines of travel from one item to another; but of course, that is already true now and was already true in the medieval codex–the real user would move from one manuscript to another, and from the indexing canon tables at the front of the gospel book now to one gospel passage, now to another, and back and forth–if the computer makes it possible to do more of that, and faster, in some way the world is not really changed, but its possibilities are realized.

But another way of describing this phenomenon is to say that the boundaries that separate one information source from another are of variable value. Users for centuries have been ignoring them when convenient–consider yourself trying to remember whether you read that book review in the *New York Times*, the *New York Review of Books*, or *TLS*, and realize how little the difference often means. When I have a hundred books on my shelf and I want to know when Cosmas Indicopleustes wrote his marvelous treatise in defense of a biblical doctrine of a flat earth, I little care where I find the information, until I have to come back and footnote it–that is, provide a form of non-linear access for *others*! And of course any experience at all tells the learned writer how hard it can be to track down again an item once found before in your own library.

There are other boundaries that will blur as well, but here I think I begin to run beyond the limits of both the reader's patience and my expertise. I will only suggest that, for example, information that is gathered collectively, over time, with minimal consultation and organization but with equal zeal and care by people who have never met each other may wind up making up large and important databases. Here we will encounter what may be the fundamental conflict of interest in scholarly publishing: that between the freedom to speak one's mind and the responsibility to produce information that is assuredly valid and re-usable by others. Freedom of inquiry and speech demands a world in which we can all say what we think, but the need for quality control speaks to a world in which we give power to people who are editors when we like them and censors when we do not. But however that plays out, an important but flawed or preliminary treatment of some vital subject will, by the time it has been worked over, discussed, revised, enhanced, and reworked by as many hands as care to turn to the job will become the ultimate post-modern authorless creation. Keeping the cooks from spoiling the broth will be important, but bringing together all the world's available talent to solve a given problem is a luxury we rarely have today.

Here I will conclude. A world in which it is not quite clear who is the author of a collective, cumulative, and collaborative work of scholarship may sound very novel, but it is also very old. The late middle ages had already created such books, like the famous *Glossa Ordinaria*,[27] the common and widely disseminated Bible commentary whose origins are still shrouded in much mystery (no two of whose versions were exactly alike) and which continued to grow and live for centuries. We have come since that time to relish and rely upon the fixity of printed information, and that is a fixity that will soon seem suddenly vulnerable. I have every confidence in our collective neurotic ability to cling to the value of that fixity, but at the same time I look forward eagerly to the flexibility and vitality of a medium that, as it plunges forward to the cutting technical edge, still pursues the enthusiasms and uses the technique of the medium that it leaves behind.

Assiduous study of cultural changes of the kinds we are now living through convinces me of one thing: a determinist reading is only after the fact. It is not possible at this point to say who will succeed in imposing a vision on the future, or how. I accepted NASIG's kind invitation to address this meeting because I believe that the learned journal and its friends offer the forum that has the most opportunities to shape that future in the most exciting ways. But it need not happen that way; I will say only that if the learned journal follows the saber-toothed tiger into the La Brea pits, we will all be the poorer for a loss that need not happen. What is needed is a combination of vision and creativity, with a willingness to take a few risks. My experience tells me that this is a good place to look for those qualities.

NOTES

1. Wordsworth on the French Revolution in the *Prelude*:
   Bliss was it in that dawn to be alive,
   But to be young was very heaven.
2. I have tried to supply notes that will lead the interested reader to the next higher level of sophistication and detail of treatment; and I have tried to give several titles in the same vein wherever possible, to make it easier for the reader to find *something* of interest in pursuing these matters further.

For the coming of writing in the Greco-Roman world, see now W.V. Harris, *Ancient Literacy* (Cambridge: Harvard University Press, 1989), with substantial response and discussion in J.H. Humphrey (ed.), *Literacy in the Roman World*, Journal of Roman Archaeology Supplementary Series, no. 3 (Ann Arbor, Mich.: University of Michigan, 1992); there are numerous more theoretical and controversial works by the late Eric Havelock, notably *Preface to Plato*; for the invention of printing, the tendentious classic is Marshall McLuhan, *The Gutenberg Galaxy: The Making of Typographic Man* (Toronto: University of Toronto Press, 1962); McLuhan is excellent at the broad strokes and the defining insights, though weak on details. Work since that date has reacted against him, most notably the two volumes of Elizabeth Eisenstein, *The Printing Press as an Agent of Change: Communications and Cultural Transformations in Early Modern Europe* (Cambridge: Cambridge University Press, 1979), but she shares the McLuhan weakness of working mainly from the secondary literature. A classic in another vein is Lucien Febvre and H. -J. Martin, *The Coming of the Book: The Impact of Printing, 1450-1800* (Atlantic Highlands, N.J.: Humanities Press, 1976 [and later imprints; originally in French, 1958]). Work continues apace: see recently Sandra L. Hindman, ed., *Printing the Written Word: The Social History of Books, circa 1450-1520* (Ithaca: Cornell University Press, 1991). Of great interest is the collection of essays edited by Roger Chartier, *The Culture of Print: Power and the Uses of Print in Early Modern Europe* (Princeton: Princeton University Press, 1989). One inspiration of my remarks today here is worth special mention: R. H. Rouse, "Backgrounds to print: aspects of the manuscript book in Northern Europe of the fifteenth century," *Proceedings of the PMR Conference* 6 (1981), 37-50. In this stimulating lecture, Professor Rouse showed (against Eisenstein) how late medieval manuscripts were already beginning to do things that print would make technically easier.

3. It is not irrational to confine a discussion of this sort to Greek and Roman culture and their heirs: the "western" tradition that creates itself around the accomplishments of those two ancient societies has many common features to justify such a polite fiction, especially features regarding the ways in which texts are created, distributed, and consumed. For a stimulating view of the originality and distinctiveness of this line of cultural history, see now Jacquiline de Romilly, *The Great Sophists in Periclean Athens* (Oxford: Clarendon Press, 1992). She argues that Athens's contribution was to create in the threatening and vast world of physical nature a mental and social community on a human scale, setting human values at a premium. Attendants at the particular NASIG conference where this paper was delivered will recall striking evidence that modern architecture abandons that sense of scale and creates a moonscape on which human beings are as insects waiting to be crushed. For a controversial alternate view of the past, see the two volumes (so far) of Martin Bernal, *Black Athena* (New Brunswick: Rutgers University Press, 1987-); Bernal is wrong about many things, but he is right that our choice of the Greek and Roman past to canonize was deliberate and made within recoverable historical time, and was not the only choice we could have made.

4. Very stimulating and venturesome on the way the inscribed stone itself was imagined to speak aloud to the viewer (and about to appear in English translation) is J. Svenbro, *Phrasikleia: anthropologie de la lecture en Grèce ancienne* (Paris: Editions La Découverte, 1988).

5. When did this happen? Linear A and Linear B memorialize a proto-Greek culture of the late second millennium B.C., but writing as a more-than-utilitarian instrument comes later. Current scholarship still argues when "Homer" and the written word first met, and a recent book, Barry B. Powell, *Homer and the Origin of the Greek Alphabet* (Cambridge: Cambridge University Press, 1991), has forcefully argued that the Greek alphabet took shape precisely to give written form to Homer, in the eighth century B.C.

6. Luciano Canfora, *The Vanished Library: A Wonder of the Ancient World* (Berkeley: University of California Press, 1989) is stimulating and readable, though not especially scholarly. For a different approach, see R. Blum, *Kallimachos: The Alexandrian Library and the Origins of Bibliography* (Madison, Wis.: University of Wisconsin Press, 1991).

7. Some of these ancient tablets survive, preserved in such unlikely locations as an Irish peat bog, derelict when a schoolboy threw them down to play on the way home perhaps.

8. There is a large and, for our purposes, irrelevant debate about the end of the use of papyrus in late antiquity. Henri Pirenne, a Belgian historian early in this century, argued that the disuse of papyrus (which had to be imported from Egypt) was one of the marks of the true "decline and fall" of the Roman empire; there is some truth to that, but no close correlation may be made, for the economics of the situation are complex indeed. Suffice it here to say that a parchment or vellum

manuscript was always a remarkably expensive artifact: the earliest surviving manuscript of the whole Bible in Latin, the Codex Amiatinus now in Florence, whose pages are roughly the size of our typing paper, cost over 500 calves their hides and weighed in its original form about ninety pounds.

9. The standard study on origins is the slender monograph of Colin H. Roberts and T.C Skeat, *The Birth of the Codex* (London: Published for The British Academy of Oxford University Press, 1983), revising a lecture originally published in the *Proceedings of the British Academy* 40 (1954), 169-204.

10. Roberts and Skeat, 37.

11. Transference did not guarantee survival, of course, far from it, but it was a necessary condition. It is worth bearing in mind that when we think of scanning our libraries into machine-readable form, we are making a similarly Solomonic judgment about their fates.

12. I concentrate here now on Christian late antiquity for purposes of simplicity of narrative. There was still an appreciable non-Christian literature being produced, and it had apparently made the transition from roll to codex by now as well; but it was an elite literature, little influenced in substance by the novelties of the world in which it found itself, and it was destined to have little success, narrow readership, and a difficult time transmitting itself to later ages.

13. Thus he appears to us, seated on his episcopal throne before the open book, in the earliest surviving portrait, which appeared in one of the earliest ecclesiastical libraries, that of the Lateran at Rome in the sixth century. The portrait is reproduced widely, perhaps best with accompanying discussion at *Miscellanea Agostiniana* (Rome: Typografia Poliglotta Vaticana, 1931), vol. 2, facing p. 1.

14. I have treated the subject in a very limited way in my *Cassiodorus* (Berkeley and Los Angeles: University of California Press, 1979), but much remains to be done. Cassiodorus' own *Institutiones lectionum divinarum et humanarum* (ed. R. Mynors, Oxford, 1937), is the earliest substantial annotated bibliography produced by a library manager that we have.

15. Cassiodorus is the best-known such entrepreneur, but there were doubtless others working in the same vein. Another monk named Eugippius, working at Naples in the sixth century, felt so strongly the superabundance of the new literature, that he produced the first digest of Augustine's works, a thousand page anthology of quotations that was widely read in after years. The church authorities at Rome, just beginning to feel their way to their medieval eminence, were beginning to manage and arrange their library in this period as well; but it was probably not the papal court but an unspecified north Italian library that produced the first version of the ecclesiastical *Index of Forbidden Books*, the so-called pseudo-Gelasaian *Decretum de libris recipiendis et non recipiendis*, a list of works both good and bad that Christians might encounter.

16. The portrait was copied in the eighth century Codex Amiatinus mentioned above, and reproductions may be seen in many standard works; see, e.g., D.T. Rice, *The Dark Ages* (New York: McGraw-Hill, 1965), 243, but almost any collection of plates of illuminated western manuscripts or surveys of paleography will have some reproduction.

17. Many of those technicians were probably reading slaves; we must always remember of antiquity that when reading and writing were technical skills as difficult and enviable as computer literacy was a decade ago, there was no shame, and indeed sometimes a perverse pride, in leaving those skills to others, menials, to perform at your direction. The transformation of the written page led in turn to the internalization of the word: the real rise of silent reading, reading "without moving your lips," has now been shown to be a late medieval development associated with the introduction of word divisions, punctuation, and other forms of user-friendly graphical user interface: see Paul Saenger, "Silent Reading: Its Impact on Late Medieval Script and Literacy," *Viator* 13(1982), 367-414.

18. F. Troncarelli, "'Con la mano del cuore.' L'arte della memoria nei codici di Cassiodoro," *Quaderni medievali* 22 (December 1986), 22-58, is fascinating beyond words but a bit recondite, on the way the manuscript page was organized to facilitate memorization; the more recent book of M.J. Carruthers, *The Book of Memory: a Study of Memory in Medieval Culture* (Cambridge: Cambridge University Press, 1990), is stimulating and venturesome, but imperfect.

19. There are many good books with ample illustrations for the general reader wishing to know a little more about this vital phase of our cultural history. A few of my favorites are: L.D. Reynolds and N.G. Wilson, *Scribes & Scholars: A Guide to the Transmission of Greek and Latin Literature*, 3rd ed. (Oxford: Oxford University Press, 1991); Stanley Morison, *Politics and Script* (Oxford: Clarendon Press, 1972); Leila Avrin, *Scribes, Script and Books: The Book Arts from Antiquity to the Renaissance* (Chicago: American Library Association; and London: The British Library, 1991); J. Glenisson, ed. *Le Livre au moyen age* (Paris: Presses du CNRS, 1988); H.-J. Martin and J. Vezin, eds., *Mise en page et mise en texte du livre manuscrit* (Paris: Éditions du Cercle de la Librairie-Promodis, 1990)–this last volume offers hundreds of pages of fascinating examples of the ways in which medieval texts were organized on the page, often with startling sophistication and anticipation of modern developments.

20. My late Penn colleague Lloyd Daly wrote the authoritative but not definitive study, *Contributions to a History of Alphabetization in Antiquity and the Middle Ages* (Brussels: Latomus, 1967). Some form of the technique went back to the Alexandrian library, but had been forgotten long before the western Middle Ages.

21. This style of argument of the priority of Christian to secular wisdom goes back at least to Clément of Alexandria in the third century, but Cassiodorus made a particular hobby-horse of it.

22. The tables are still printed in some modern editions of the Greek New Testament. In a 1958 printing by the British and Foreign Bible Society, there are 9 tables of concordances, followed by lists of passages in each gospel that have no parallels in the others. So, for example, the fourth table compares Matthew, Mark, and John thus

	Canon IV, of Three Gospels	
Mt	Mk	Jn
18	8	26
117	26	93
117	26	95
150	67	51
161	77	23
161	77	53
204	115	91
204	115	135
216	125	128

... (through another twenty lines of parallel figures).

The most abundant comparison, linking the three synoptic authors themselves, has about 100 sets of figures. (Matthew and Luke are divided for these purposes each into about 350 separate units, Mark and John run to slightly over two hundred.) The tedium of the arrangement was partly alleviated in medieval manuscripts by a commonly-seen architectural arrangement, where the three columns of numbers on a page between columns of a classical arcade, with two or three or four openings as the individual canon table required. Almost any medieval gospel book will show a good example, but perhaps the Book of Kells, often reproduced (see e.g., *The Book of Kells: Reproductions from the Manuscript in Trinity College Dublin, with a study of the manuscript by Françoise Henry* (New York: Alfred A. Knopf, 1974), is most accessible: ten pages of the front matter to that manuscript contain the canon tables.

23. Of course, we know that the real use of those texts had distinct non-linear features as well. Pieces of gospel text were read aloud in church at all services, *not* following the original narrative order. There quickly grew up a practice of producing "lectionaries," that is, anthologies of gospel passages arranged according to the Sundays and feasts of the year. Though in the Latin west, full gospel manuscripts remain common (a twelfth century monastic library catalog from Italy being studied by one of my students shows that they owned, in fact, one full gospel book and one lectionary), in the Greek east lectionaries eventually become much more common than gospel manuscripts, to the point where the lectionary evidence is regularly cited as ancient and authoritative in our modern editions of the Greek New Testament.

24. To exemplify non-linear access and its rich serendipitous possibilities: at 11:35 pm., checking the form of the title of this reference from my home desk by dialing up the university library OPAC eight miles away, I find this fascinating bit of additional information: "Summary: Vol. for 1947 includes 'A list of clandestine periodicals of World War II, Adrienne Florence Muzzy'." I make a note to myself to have a look at that list, the very need for which had never dawned on me until I saw this screen–before the availability of the OPAC, of course, I would never have gotten to that card in the catalog or read so far were I pursuing merely a title verification, and at the same time I never would have gotten the verification so easily and so much at my own convenience.

25. It is easier to be confident that some form of the overtly narrative codex book will survive, if only for airplane reading; but even there it is to be noted that experimental literature is already playing with "hypertext" forms (see, for example, M. Pavic, *Dictionary of the Khazars: a Lexicon Novel in 100,000 Words* (New York: Knopf, 1988), distributed in marginally differing "male" and "female" editions, and with the alphabetical arrangement of entries differing sharply between the English translation and the original Serbo-Croatian). It is only a matter of time before someone publishes a murder mystery that *must* be consumed as a self-constructing hypertext of labyrinthine proportions. (Two days after I delivered this paper at the NASIG conference, the *New York Times Book Review* of 22 June 1992 featured a front-page survey article by novelist Robert Coover, treating in detail current experiments and venues for hyperfiction of various kinds.)

26. Already PSYCOLOQUY, one of the first and most ambitious e-journals, is struggling to dispense with "volume" and issue" numbering; recent interesting dialogue on this subject on the network shows, first, that it is hard to do without what we have become used to, and second, that what we no longer need can, in fact, be dispensed with if adequate thought and patience are taken. This note is a self-exemplifying artifact: I regret that it is not possible to provide a convenient and transparent form of citation to these discussions; I can do no better than refer the reader (who must have specialized knowledge not yet universally held in order to follow these instructions) to the e-archives of lists known by their acronyms such as AESJ-L, VPIE-L, and Arachnet, and rely on the foresight of the listowners to have arranged those archives in a way that will lead to results. In fact, the easier form of reference would be to send the reader of this paper back to pursue the original author of that discussion, Stevan Harnad of PSYCOLOQUY, in person: and so far as that goes, it shows that we are back (for the moment and, I think, only for the moment) to a medieval kind of search for authoritative information.

27. See on this fascinating heffalump of a compendious book, which took shape in the course of the eleventh and twelfth centuries (and an expensive Brepols reprint, causing fits of indecision among acquisitions librarians around the world just at this writing), Bevy Smalley, *The Study of the Bible in the Middle Ages*, 2nd ed. (Oxford: Blackwell, 1951), 46-66.

Webs That Link Libraries, Librarians, and Information: Evolving Technical Standards for a Networking Age

Julia C. Blixrud

SUMMARY. A strong, but flexible infrastructure is fundamental to the process of building the library information delivery systems that will support scholarly communications in the future. Technical standards are an integral part of our current information infrastructure and must be a part of our future field of dreams. Like a web, standards provide support and flexibility. Like a grid, standards can provide structure, links, and direction. Technical standards are also a good way to level the playing field among participating groups.

Although the complexity of systems and rapid evolution of technology makes it difficult to develop standards for the networking age, specific needs are identifiable. Those needs include standards for data content, structure, display, and transfer. Standards are also needed in the areas of access, connectivity, navigation, and tracking.

INTRODUCTORY REMARKS

The title of my talk was developed with Ann Okerson's help and my reaction to that title today is a quote from Sir Walter Scott: Oh what tangled webs we weave, when first we practice to deceive.

Julia Blixrud is Program Officer, Council on Library Resources, 1785 Massachusetts Ave., NW, Washington, DC 20036.

If you listened carefully to Minna's introduction, you might have noticed I stand before you with no specific credentials in electronics, or computers, or communications. I also doubt that anyone who knows me well would consider me a "scholar." My Scandinavian ancestors (the Vikings) plundered and pillaged their way across Europe and the Atlantic Ocean, establishing their base and then taking whatever they needed. During the past few years, I have been doing my own plundering by accumulating data and little bits of knowledge about standards and networking from around the information world. Perhaps at the end of my talk you will consider my collected wisdom not worth saving and will suggest I discard it, or at the very least, leave it here in Chicago. But instead, I hope that I can pique your interest and perhaps prompt some action from you as we consider together the topic of technical standards for networking.

At a committee meeting on bibliographic issues, hosted recently by the Council on Library Resources, one participant made the perceptive observation that much of our agenda could have been dealt with quickly if only we could come up with the perfect metaphor. (We were discussing the new catalog or library information system, and we decided that a major stumbling block in the discussion was the lack of a good metaphor for "it".)

The theme for this NASIG conference is "If We Build It: Scholarly Communications and Networking Technologies." What is IT? What is it that we are trying to build? Let me suggest that for the purpose of this talk, "it" is infrastructure, and what we use to build it is standards.

CLR PROGRAM AREA OF INFRASTRUCTURE

In the past year, at the Council on Library Resources (CLR), under the direction of President W. David Penniman, we have begun to articulate our new program areas. One of those areas we call infrastructure. We identified it as an area where there is work to be done and an area to which CLR could usefully direct some of its influence and energies. Infrastructure is an umbrella term for the systems, services and facilities that are, as Dave says, "drawn upon to help libraries and other information services operate more efficiently and effectively."[1] Under this umbrella we include communication networks, bibliographic utilities, software and hardware vendor communities, and the scholarly communication process. In addition, we consider the current physical structures (i.e., the buildings where users and equipment are located) essential to the delivery of information and an important component of the infrastructure.

In shorthand terms, I tell those who call or write me at the Council on Library Resources, that infrastructure includes information delivery, either within one building or group of buildings, or through a wider "internet." And it deals with the people and policies (or, if you will, the politics) of cooperation and collaboration.

The audience in this room today, the NASIG community, is an important part of the infrastructure for serials. Represented here are librarians, publishers, subscription services, vendors, technical experts, scholars, etc. We are not the entire infrastructure, but we are an excellent representation of it.

We are interested in finding ways to strengthen information infrastructures. Answers to the following questions may help us to find those ways:

- What experiments can be done by publishers, libraries, and service providers working together that demonstrate processes of change that are beneficial to all participants, including the end users?
- What alternative designs for library facilities demonstrate a focus on service rather than physical structure and illustrate that form can follow function when the goal of service has been clearly understood and articulated?[2]

Standards will be very important as we find answers to these questions.

METAPHORS FOR THE INFRASTRUCTURE

As I mentioned, there is a need for appropriate metaphors. Several years ago I spoke at an ALCTS Serials Section Program on the standards for linking serials information and used a metaphor of webs. This web metaphor was validated recently when I read an instructional workshop package on networked information prepared for use at Syracuse University. The video and script ended with the quote, "It all feels a bit like being a spider in the center of a vast electronic web."[3]

If I had a good slide collection, I could have brought with me a picture of a web. Instead, I ask you to close your eyes and use your imagination. Think of any of the following images for infrastructure:

- Spider web
- Beehive with its honeycomb structure
- Woven tapestry
- Girders in a skyscraper under construction
- Trellis or latticework
- Eiffel Tower
- Webbing on a baseball glove
- Webbed membrane between duck toes

There are many types of webs. Some have a simple and repeating pattern, while others are composed of intricate designs. Webs can be strong, they can be fragile, and they can be flexible While they are often entangling and may become a trap, webs can also provide a means for mobility.

A strong, flexible infrastructure is indispensable for building the networks and information delivery systems that will support scholarly communications in the future. Technical standards are integral to our current information infrastructure, like a common thread of a tapestry or a center pile at a construction site. (And I didn't know I was going to find a construction site set up outside my dorm window!)

No matter what we build, no matter how it looks, or even what we call it, we do need a foundation and structure for our future field of dreams. Technical standards provide you with that foundation. I'll even go so far as to suggest that standards could be considered the nucleus of any structure built in the cosmos. In the hyperspace environment of the electronic world, we need some sort of solid footing or solid core.

Sports metaphors are usually good for a U.S. audience and, given the conference theme, I did consider baseball. The team must work together to succeed and needs an even playing field. A networked environment presupposes a variety of participants or players. Technical standards are a means for establishing reliable links among the participants. Every one of us should recognize that we have a vested interest in the subject of standards. Given the increasing availability and demand for information, no one individual or institution can go it alone. The increasing complexity of options for technologies and the limitations imposed by our lack of resources encourage us to work together. Standards give us a commonly shared base, a strategy for simplification, and opportunities to share resources and expertise.

CHARACTERISTICS OF STANDARDS

Standards can be described characterized in several ways. They can be short or long, simple or complex. They can be easily attained or impossible to reach. They can be formally developed, required, and regulated; or they can be de-facto, generally accepted, and self-imposed. Standards are often interdependent.

Dictionary definitions of "standard" include: an acknowledged measure of comparison for quantitative or qualitative value; a criterion; or a norm. Standards indicate levels of requirement, excellence, or attainment. Standards also are our rules. They provide us with a framework in which to operate.

I will not talk about the process of technical standards development. Pat Harris, Executive Director of NISO, has given excellent presentations on that topic, most recently at the annual meeting of NFAIS (National Federation of Abstracting and Information Services). If you are not familiar with the acronyms ANSI, NISO, ISO, SISAC, CNI, etc., leave me a card and I will see that you get some information.

TECHNICAL STANDARDS NEEDED FOR NETWORKING

What kind of standards are needed to develop scholarly communication tools and networks? Over the past few months, while reading countless articles and LISTSERV messages, I have been creating my own list of general categories for standards that will need our attention as we build our dream of a networked environment. I'm sure others of you have seen or created your own lists. In broad terms, all our lists would probably agree on the need for data and system standards.

My list, which I will share with you shortly, has a dozen categories. There is no significance to my categories other than they are mine; any of you could take these same categories and rearrange, subdivide, or combine them. There is also no particular significance to the order of my list. Some categories lead naturally into others, which demonstrates their interdependence. My attempts to prioritize the list resulted only in a different order, not necessarily a better one. Separating applications from standards themselves can be difficult. Often an application is the best explanation or description of a standard.

When examining standards development or even the more general topic of building networks, we also need to consider carefully those who will be using those networks. That is the unspoken "they will come" in our baseball theme. Who are they and how will they use our networks? The systems we build, the access mechanisms we develop, and the information we provide, should be user-driven. With over a million people worldwide using the Internet daily through hundreds of thousands of host computers, we could just sit back and assume things will happen without our intervention. Unfortunately we already know that not all of the people who have electronic access to networks use them and there are many (and I include myself) who are not making effective use of the systems and networks already developed. Why? The simple answer is that what exists does not meet those users' needs.

In order to provide a user perspective to my standards categories, I will begin each category with the kinds of questions our users would ask. What is the purpose of these standards for the non-technical person? Technical standards should meet users' needs, and in this conference our users are the scholars and those who need access to scholarly information. In a recent article, Mary Stewart makes the point that we need to base our standards development on "observable user behavior and potential user needs in the library community." While we cannot define a "standard user," still we do have the responsibility to know who will be using our networked systems and how they will use them.[4]

Standards are a hot topic these days and time is too short for a complete laundry list and detailed analysis of all the current activities. Let me now instead just describe the categories of standards, ask some of the questions our scholarly information community is asking, provide some familiar examples of current standards, applications, and projects, and suggest areas that need further work. Not all of the categories require our active participation, but we should be aware of general trends in each of them because they will affect our infrastructure web.

1. Data Creation–Content

The scholar asks questions such as: What data should I include in this networked environment? Is that data different from what I already have? How do I turn my current material into networked electronic data? How do I mix text and images?

There are many ways to represent text, images, multimedia, tables, and graphs electronically. We have already heard today about the great number of typefaces and fonts now available from PC packages. Our hardware and software manufacturers are building and expanding their businesses by developing systems and programs that will enable the scholar and lay person to create millions of bits of data.

Perhaps instead of asking what standards are needed in this area, we need to ask ourselves what kind of data should be included in our networked environment. Since the answer will likely be any kind of data, our professional challenge then is not necessarily how to create the data, but how to access, manage, and transfer that data most efficiently.

2. Data Structure–Storage–Handling

The scholar or user asks us: What is the most efficient way for me to store data? How do I distinguish different types of data in my system? Does it matter how my data is stored?

This is another area in which there is already technical and development work being done, especially for bit-mapped images and data compression. Most of us will be observers rather than participants in this work. One standard we can encourage and make use of ourselves is SGML (Standard Generalized Mark-up Language). This standard is becoming increasingly important as a means for encoding document information that will be shared or exchanged among systems.

3. Data Identification–Representation–Display

Our researchers and users ask: How do I present different types of data? What is the best way to show information on a screen? (As I heard recently, we spent years perfecting the printed page, let's not forget what we learned when we now design displays for electronic data.) The scholar is also asking us how to avoid duplication and redundancy in data displays.

This third category should be an area of active interest for those of us here today. Standards that currently exist for data identification in our environment include our traditional cataloging standards, ISBD and AACR. One of the projects currently undertaken by the Coalition for Networked Information is described as "Bibliographic Description and Control for the Internet." The OCLC Office of Research, with funding from the U.S. Dept. of Education Library Programs and staff support from the Library of Congress, is examining bibliographic description on the Internet and have already published a list of document categories located in their test file.

What standards are needed? Cliff Lynch called for work on a Universal Document Identifier (UDI) Proposal and Tim Berners-Lee describes a draft discussion paper on UDI's in an April 1992 article in *Information Standards Quarterly*. Standard identifiers become increasingly important in a networked world because of their ability to represent information in a unique and economic way. Some familiar identifiers (ISSN, ISBN, SICI, BIBLID, etc.) may even take on a new life. Librarians, especially, have both expertise and experience in describing information and should take an active role in the development of standards for the description of data in a networked environment.

4. Data Transfer–Distribution–Production

The scholar asks: How can I share information with my colleagues? How will we transfer our data back and forth? What communication formats do I need?

What standards currently exist? ASCII is our least common denominator for text transfer, MARC for bibliographic data transfer (and UNIMARC in the international arena). Serials also have the ISDS format and our business transactions are beginning to make good use of EDI (electronic data interchange) and the X12 communications formats.

The TIFF (Tagged Image File Format) is being used for image transfers and the FDDI (Fiber Distributed Data Interface) is being developed to move graphics and multimedia over local and wide area networks. Many of us use an FTP command, which allows us to remotely log in to a computer for the purpose of file transfer.

What standards are needed? While we can continue to use many of our current standards, we will probably have to revise them as our needs change. A good example of change is the revision to ANSI/NISO Z39.2, Bibliographic Information Interchange. We may even find it necessary to take a fresh look at the way our bibliographic data is distributed as we learn more about how our scholars and users share information with each other in an electronic environment.

5. Data Integrity

All of us who use computer systems have many concerns about data integrity. Our questions include: If I add data to the network, how can I be sure my data is safe? How can I be sure the data I get hasn't been corrupted? When I send messages in a network, who is responding and what are their credentials?

What standards currently exist? At the very elementary level, we have mechanisms to save our data. Our word processing packages have timed backups and we have other software packages that back up our systems regularly.

But we need standards for encryption, redundancy, and system integrity; and we need protection for breaches of access. There are software packages that provide us with a means to check for viruses, but we need better controls for ensuring the reliability of data as it is transferred from one system to another.

6. Operating Systems

The user asks: Does it matter if I use a Mac to create data and talk to my colleagues? My data has outgrown my PC; can you recommend a different platform for my project? Can we transport these files to another system?

There are proprietary platforms for operating systems such as Mac, NeXt, PC DOS, OS/2, Unix, VMS, CMS, Windows, CD-I. These are local or manufacturer specific, and I don't think our profession will have as much influence in the development of standards in this area as will business or government. However, we do need expertise to make good decisions on the most effective platforms for the nature of our work. And we need experience in transferring data from one platform to another.

7. Access Systems–User Interface

The researcher or scholar asks: How can I find what I am looking for? How do I get to the data? How does my system help me find and organize data?

There is a difference between opening a book and driving a car, but operating a computer should not require an advanced degree in electronics. I am looking forward to the time in which we only need talk to our computer (which I do now but it does not answer me). We need to have adequate online help programmed into our systems so that users won't have to ask questions like: How come this system is so complicated? What does this error message mean?

What standards currently exist? There are already many applications that can make computer programs easy to use: Graphical User Interfaces (GUIs), icons, light pens, touch screens, etc. The up-and-coming personal digital interactive appliances (Apple's Newton) or information appliances promise even easier ways to use a computer.

Our profession has developed some of its own user interfaces and librarians have become quite interested in expert systems. We know there is much to be done. Even the best interface today is still lacking. The "telnet" command allows us to login to a remote host to use a service, such as an online catalog, but unfortunately it still presents the user with a wide variety of interfaces.

Developing interface standards is one of the most important areas of work for our profession. We have the familiarity with our systems, we know our data, and we have done the research that provides us with the knowledge of how users retrieve information. We should be out there defining the systems and developing the standards.

(I can't help but comment on our own version of a user interface that was demonstrated this morning. It took a librarian to provide the necessary interpretation that allowed the scholar to communicate with the technician who was handling the lights. This demonstrates once again the importance of the librarian as a bridge between the user and the technology.)

8. Communication Systems–Protocols

The communication questions are simple ones: Can I talk to you? How do I send you a message?

The answers are complex, but communication standards and protocols are a well-developed area of standardization. Keeping up with developments may be the challenge for most of us. Active participation by the library and information community has led to significant work in these standards. They include the suite under OSI/LSP (Open Systems Interconnection/Linked Systems Protocol), TCP/IP (Transmission Control Protocol/Internet Protocol), and Z39.50 (Information Retrieval Protocol). CCITT X.400 (for mail systems) and X.500 (for directory services) are standards to monitor.

9. Connectivity

Along with communications comes connection. The scholar questions: Who can be connected to whom? What can I be connected to? How do I connect?

There are many ways to provide physical and electronic connections. They include copper wire, ISDN, fiber optics, broadband, packet radio, switches, microwave, cellular phones, LANs, WANs, etc. The standards in this category are also an area in which we need expertise in application because development and implementation costs are high.

10. Navigation (and Directory Services)

The scholar asks: Where is the answer to my question? How do I get from here to there? How do I find my way home? Where am I now? How can I find out what is out in the electronic network? What types of directories are available? How can I find an electronic address? How can I find my colleagues? What is the number for directory assistance?

What standards currently exist? Jean Polly describes navigational aids in the Internet as "travel agents."[5] Some popular travel agents include:

- Wide Area Information Servers (WAIS) from Thinking Machines. WAIS is a natural language search and retrieval system. The search is initiated by a question rather than a key word and uses relevancy to shape results.
- Archie (developed out of McGill University) provides an electronic information directory service. It is an index of software available over the Internet through anonymous ftp.
- Gopher (from the University of Minnesota) is another navigation tool that can be used to publish and search for information held on distributed networks. Navigation can be through a hierarchy of directories or by asking an index server to return a list of documents.

Other utilities include WorldWide Web and HYTELNET (a hypertext system).

The Coalition for Networked Information is very active in the area of navigation. The June 1992 issue of C&RL News details some of the current projects and asks readers to supply them with additional examples. Active participation by librarians and other information professionals is especially necessary in this category. As with data representation, libraries have vast experience in providing access to information. How a scholar will get at the information in the network is a responsibility tailor-made to the information professional. Directory services, catalogs, addressing conventions, and the development of "Knowbots" are all tools and standards waiting to be developed for an electronic world.

11. Tracking

The user in our networked environment asks: How will you tell me how I am doing? What are my obligations? What do I owe?

Computers count very accurately and very quickly. While the accounting mechanisms for use of a network are as many as there are systems, the need for standardized means of accountability is being reflected in the literature. As an example, we will soon need formulas for royalties and the means for collection. The recent double issue of *Serials Review*[6] on "Economic models for networked information" includes articles that speak more eloquently than I can about the "accounting" needs for a networking age.

12. Archiving–Preservation

The scholar asks: Will my information or data be there the next time I need it? If I don't save it, who will? Who has the responsibility for saving the data? As was true with other types of materials, preservation matters are of concern more to librarians than any other group. Very little has been done in this area of standardization and it will be up to us to see that work gets done.

I think you will agree that there is already more than a little interest in standards for a networked environment; while much work is already being done, opportunities exist for increased participation. No matter what level of participation you might choose, at the very least I urge you to stay informed about the general directions taken by standards developers. Your future jobs will depend on it.

USING EXISTING STANDARDS IN A NETWORKED WORLD

Now that I have addressed the categories where standards are needed, I would like to expand on my point of using existing standards in a networked world. When working towards developing new electronic standards, we must not forget good work that has gone before. Before we jump in and say we need to write rules for the electronic age or to develop brand-new standards, we should look carefully at the standards in existence. It may be that much of the foundation has already been established. Granted, there are many new and different functions and actions that are possible in an electronic world that were not possible in our former print-based world, but that does not mean we should disregard past successes or re-invent the wheel.

How resilient are existing standards? Let me describe for you two familiar serials examples.

The first technical standard that should be known by everyone in the serial information community is ANSI/NISO Z39.9-1992, International Standard Serial Number. This is the eight-digit number that uniquely identifies a serial publication. It was developed twenty years ago for the primarily print-based publishing environment, but even in the electronic world, we continue to see "serials." We have started to call them e-journals (Ann Okerson called them the new debutantes), and they have similar characteristics to print-based products. They have familiar basic bibliographic information: a title, a publisher, dates of publication, issue designations; and they contain articles (some peer-reviewed), columns, letters to the editor, etc. The ISSN applies to these publications just as well as it does to print publications. While descriptive bibliographic records may be different, even complicated, the standard's purpose was and is identification; identification is still needed in the electronic age, probably more so. Since I don't see that basic journal structure going away, I also don't envision the demise of the ISSN. In fact, the work on universal document identifiers suggests to me that the ISSN (and its extension for item and contribution identifiers, ANSI/NISO Z39.56-1991) will continue to have a role in identification in a networked environment.

A second familiar standards example is ANSI Z39.2, known to most of you as the basic structure underlying the MARC communications format. It was originally prepared in 1966 and is currently in revision. The revision is significant in that the principal change to the format is the removal of a bibliographic bias, a change of name to "Information Interchange Format," and increased flexibility by the addition of an implementation defined specification. The revision is a reaffirmation of the standard's utility as a format for the exchange of records.

CONCERNS ABOUT STANDARDS DEVELOPMENT

The curve ball in this litany on standards is the difficulties that arise in standards development. The development of technical standards for information, communications, and computers in this country has been generally either a democratic or de-facto process. For example, NISO (the National Information Standards Organization) develops its standards through consensus. Like the democratic process for elections in this country, a vote counts. If you have not participated in the process or have not cast a vote, you have only yourself to blame if your needs are not met by the standard developed. Unfortunately, the process is cumbersome, tedious, and as someone recently observed, boring. Those of you in the audience with experience in standards development are probably already familiar with the following questions.

When to begin the process? Some argue for beginning early so applications can be easily developed. Others say that developing standards too soon may inhibit creativity and developmental activity. How do you identify that moment when the community is ready for work to be done?

Who should be involved in the standards development process? Including those who have vested interests could result in a standard that might be considered proprietary. If you include too many people, the standard becomes a lowest common denominator and does not serve anyone effectively.

How much should be included in the standard? If too much is included then it is difficult to follow. If too little is in and several standards are developed to cover a set of functions, then you have to worry both about keeping the various standards in sync and about the interconnection among the standards themselves.

How long should it take to develop a standard? Sometimes it seems standards development takes forever–kind of like an extra innings baseball game. Building consensus is time-consuming. But standards are a base upon which to build and there is value in many minds contributing to a task.

Who pays the costs? The major costs for standards development is in the people time. People to develop, people to test, people to implement, and people to review and comment. It is not cheap, and we need to find good ways to measure the value. For example, how much check-in time has been saved by libraries across the nation through use of the ISSN? How many cataloging dollars were saved because of the MARC communications format and its applications?

How often should standards be revised? The revision process like standards development itself, is cumbersome, and frankly boring. Once the basic work is done, revisions become tedious.

CONCLUSION

Obviously my underlying pitch is that the standards game is for everyone. Even if we only watch the game, it is good to know the players, the rules, and the umps. We and the players are all a part of the team, or to continue the web metaphor, we all have a thread that helps to make the design complete. If we want our networked future to work, we need effective standards development for networking technologies.

A scary prospect for these new information systems is that if we build them to meet user needs, "they" will come and come in droves. Our resources in the immediate future are not likely to be increased even if the demand for our services is great. We need to strengthen our structures and work together to meet future challenges. We need to make sure that the infrastructures we build are based on a solid foundation and a center piece of that foundation is standards.

Thank you for your attention this morning. I hope I have woven together a few threads for you about standards, entangled you with the need for a strong and flexible infrastructure, and trapped you into playing ball.

NOTES

1. "New CLR Program Areas," *CLR Reports* 5, no.1:6 (Dec. 1991).

2. W. David Penniman, "Libraries and the Future: Critical Research Needs" (Lazerow Lecture given at Simmons College, Sept. 13, 1991)16-17.

3. "Beyond the Walls: The World of Networked Information: An Instructional Workshop Package" (A workshop package prepared for use at Syracuse University, 1991).

4. Mary R. Stewart, "Users, Standards, and Access: In Search of the Standard User," *CD-ROM Librarian* 7, no.2 (Feb. 1992): 17.

5. Jean Armour Polly, "Surfing the Internet: An Introduction," *Wilson Library Bulletin* 66, no. 10 (June 1992): 40.

6. *Serials Review* 18, no.1/2.

Landlords and Tenants: Who Owns Information, Who Pays for It, and How?

Anita Lowry

I grew up in a small town in the Midwest, but I've spent most of my adult life in New York City, so the central metaphor of my title–landlords and tenants–carries some rather conflicting connotations for me. When I was growing up, renting was just something that you did until you could afford to buy; but now in New York, and especially in Manhattan, I live in a city of renters–perhaps the last place in the country impervious to the American dream of owning a house with a two-car garage and the vehicles to go in it. In New York we tenants live in uneasy symbiosis with the landlords who own the roofs over our heads and determine anew each year the prices we will pay for them.

Is it possible that libraries are gradually becoming "tenants" rather than "landlords" in the world of information? What, exactly, might that mean, and does it matter?

Today I'd like to take a look at some of the ways in which the creation and distribution of information in electronic forms is contributing to the shift in libraries from "ownership" to "access," from "landlord" to "tenant," if you will. In particular, I would like to examine some of the conditions under which libraries currently acquire electronic resources–conditions that typically involve a loss

---

Anita Lowry is Deputy Head, Butler Reference Department and Director, Electronic Text Service, Columbia University Libraries, 325 Butler Library, 525 West 114th Street, New York, NY 10027.

© 1993 by The Haworth Press, Inc. All rights reserved.

of rights to and control over those resources—and how, in turn, that loss of control may threaten the service and curatorial missions of libraries.

We must look first at copyright, because copyright has traditionally provided the framework for establishing and defending the rights of authors, publishers, libraries, and users.

Copyright law, and the court decisions that clarify it, have sought to strike a balance between the "exclusive rights" of authors to control and thus to profit from the distribution of their works (so as to encourage the creation and distribution of additional works) and the non-exclusive rights granted to the users of those works. These "users' rights" have generally been justified by the need to mitigate the inherent monopoly of the author's rights and thus to ensure the widespread access to information for the public good.[1] What are some of the ways in which this fragile balance has been struck?

On the author's side of the scale, the current copyright law extends copyright protection to a wide range of "original works of authorship fixed in any tangible medium of expression, now known or later developed, from which they can be perceived, reproduced, or otherwise communicated, either directly or with the aid of a machine or device."[2] You can see how Congress struggled back in 1976 to make the wording of the law technologically neutral! The author, or other copyright holder in lieu of the author, has the exclusive right to control, and by implication to profit from, all copying, distribution, performance, display, or preparation of derivative works for his or her lifetime plus a period of fifty years.

If the law had stopped there, the scale would have been heavily tilted in favor of monopolistic rights for authors and toward a concept of information as commodity whose disposition could be governed solely by economic considerations.

But the law also incorporated a number of explicit limitations on the exclusive control of authors—exceptions designed to encourage the non-commercial and educational uses of information deemed necessary to the cultural, social, political, and economic well-being of the nation. Most importantly for academic and public libraries and their patrons, the copyright law embraced the "doctrine of fair use" and the "doctrine of first sale," and included an entire section devoted to reproduction rights in libraries and archives.

As you know, it is, in part, the doctrine of fair use that allows our students and faculty to keep library photocopy machines humming from morning to night. While people tend to think that any copying for research or educational purposes is protected by fair use, there are limits on the applicability of fair use in those situations where the copying is significantly commercial in purpose or would have a negative impact on the sales or economic value of a copyrighted work–as Kinko's Copy Centers recently found out when the courts decided that Kinko's production and sale of photocopied anthologies of readings for students did *not* constitute fair use. Nevertheless, the assumption that the doctrine of fair use permits photocopying by individuals for private use is widespread and does not seem likely to be challenged.

Section 108 of the Copyright Act grants libraries and archives considerable leeway in photocopying single copies of parts of works and even whole works when that reproduction is not so extensive or systematic as to substitute for acquiring the work itself. Under the guidelines developed by the National Commission on New Technological Uses of Copyrighted Works, libraries may request up to five photocopies of articles published in the previous five years in a given periodical before having to pay royalties to the publisher for copies of subsequent articles.

And finally, weighing in on the side of users' rights is the doctrine of first sale, codified in Section 109 of the Copyright Act. The right of first sale *limits* the control of the copyright holder over the physical copies of a work once they have been legally sold. The doctrine of first sale allows the owner of a copyrighted work–including a library–to lend the work, resell it, or give it away.

So in academic and public libraries we have traditionally exercised considerable control over the printed materials we buy for our collections. We lend books, periodicals, and microforms freely to our patrons and to other libraries. We allow people from outside our institutions to use them. Libraries provide photocopies to their patrons and to other libraries. Librarians weed materials from their collections and frequently offer them for sale or as gifts to other libraries. And last, but certainly not least, we preserve them for the use of future generations. As librarians we take this kind of control for granted as fundamental to our mission of collecting, organizing, managing, preserving, and providing access to information.

But we can no longer take these activities for granted when we deal with information in electronic forms. The Copyright Act of 1976 and subsequent amendments prevent libraries from making any copies other than archival backup copies of computer software.

In addition, many publishers of electronic materials have sought to strengthen and augment the control they exercise over their publications by refusing to sell them outright. Instead they lease them to individuals and libraries.[3] For example, most CD-ROMs are licensed rather than sold. As a result, the library is no longer actually buying and acquiring title to the CD-ROM, so it no longer enjoys those rights–such as the right to lend it, or sell it, or keep it in perpetuity–that it would normally enjoy as an owner under the doctrine of first sale. As many of you know, most producers of bibliographic CD-ROMs require a library to return the superseded disks, and many require the library to return the last disk it received if the library should decide not to renew the contract–so you are left with nothing to show for all the annual subscription fees you have paid. And finally, online databases accessible over networks from remote hosts have obliterated the last semblance of a library's control over the physical object, since there is no physical object to control!

Focusing primarily on the experiences of the Electronic Text Service in the Columbia University Libraries, I would now like to take a look at some of the practical implications of copyright, licensing, and online dissemination of electronic information.[4]

However, before I get into the fine print let me give you some background on the Electronic Text Service (ETS), which was established in 1988 to provide access to advanced computer-based source materials in the humanities and history. The resources in the ETS come in all electronic shapes and sizes: on magnetic media, on optical media, and online, though CD-ROM seems to be emerging as the medium of choice for the publication of large databases. ETS resources contain text, images, numeric data, and various combinations thereof; many come with special software for sophisticated search and retrieval and for textual analysis. Here are a few examples of the kinds of materials that the Electronic Text Service makes available to students and faculty:

- the works of literary authors, philosophers, and religious figures: St. Augustine, Shakespeare, Milton, Austen, Goethe, Melville, Kant, Hegel, and Machiavelli to name only a few;
- ancient and modern texts of the world's great religions;
- the *ARTFL: American and French Research on the Treasury of the French Language* database with over 2000 French literary, philosophical, religious, political, and scientific works from the 17th through the 20th centuries;
- the surviving works of ancient and classical Greece and Rome on the *Thesaurus Linguae Graecae (TLG)* and *Packard Humanities Institute (PHI)* CD-ROMs, respectively;
- and *Perseus,* a brand new interactive multi-media database of textual and visual primary sources, reference works, and studies on ancient Greece, published on CD-ROM and laser disk.

In dealing with these and other resources in the Electronic Text Service, I have essentially two forms of evidence that I use to determine the status and restrictions of a particular database or software program. First, there is the full copyright statement that usually appears somewhere in the printed manual. Second, I look to see if there is also a separate license agreement or contract. Some publishers require an "authorized" signature on the contract before they will send you the product. But most licenses are of the "shrink wrap" variety; once you've read the license and then opened the package you've agreed to abide by whatever fine print the license contains. Needless to say, it is very important that licenses not accidently get separated from the product by acquisitions, cataloging, or processing staff.

After you've found the copyright and licensing statements, what do you look for? First of all, you look for answers to the question: "Am I a landlord or a tenant?" In other words, have I bought a copy of the database or am I merely leasing it?

In general, only monographic electronic materials (and relatively few of those) are actually sold outright to libraries or users, granting them rights of first sale such as the right to: keep it forever; lend it; sell it; or give it away. But even for electronic materials you own you may *not* make full copies, except for archival backups, and, by extension, you probably can't network the electronic materials since that would effectively make or display multiple copies. The "AnyText Scholar's Package" of software and ancient biblical texts from Linguist's Software, Inc. (Edmonds, WA) provides one of the rare examples of a product that is "sold." The copyright statement clearly states that Linguist's Software is selling this item and that while the buyer may not make copies for others, the buyer *may* sell, give away, or lend his/her copy plus all backups to another person.

It is much more likely that the electronic materials in your library have been leased rather than sold, especially if they are serials, and have come not only with copyright statements but also with license agreements stipulating what you may do with these materials. When a contract for an Electronic Text Service or Butler Reference Department title requires an "authorized" signature, I usually sign on the assumption that the person who is actually going to have to abide by and enforce the rules, and who is most knowledgeable about similar licenses in the collection, should be the signatory. And of course, all licenses should be filed in a safe place, preferably close at hand for convenient referral.

Given the fact that so many electronic publications carry licenses, it behooves us to scrutinize them, not only in order to know what we can and can't do with particular materials, but also in order to get a better sense of what rights and control libraries are forfeiting with regard to electronic materials. The following categories are covered by most licenses:

1. Copying
2. Printing and downloading
3. Disposition of the physical copy
4. Purpose of use
5. Categories of users
6. Access

Let's look at each in turn.

1. *Copying* of program software or data, except for archival backup copies of floppy disks, is forbidden in all cases. Occasionally in the Electronic Text Service someone wants to copy an entire text or texts from a multi-text CD-ROM database to take home for

analysis on his or her own computer. I tell the patrons to write to the publisher requesting written permission. And sometimes they even get it!

2. *Printing and downloading.* Most licenses address this from the standpoint of fair use; in other words, an individual can print or download limited portions of an electronic work for personal research use. Some licenses spell out exactly how much printing or downloading constitutes an acceptable "limited portion," and some publishers have built safeguards into their software so that the text can easily be downloaded only in relatively small chunks. Printing or downloading in order to produce multiple copies for classroom use is a little stickier; taking their cue from the Kinko's decision, some publishers specifically prohibit printing that would be used "for the creation and dissemination of course materials in lieu of purchasing the relevant books."[5]

3. *Disposition of the physical copy.* There are essentially two kinds of licenses, which we can call "perpetual" and "temporary."[6] A perpetual license is one that says you may keep the item, so long as you don't do something to violate the license agreement. Temporary licenses are just that–you may keep the disk only so long as you keep paying the licensing fee. Many serial CD-ROMs from SilverPlatter and other commercial publishers are available under temporary licenses. Even though a library may pay hundreds, even thousands, of dollars each year for an electronic subscription, the library must send each superseded disk back to the producer (or destroy it) and often must return all disks and software if canceling the subscription. The H.W. Wilson Company, which allows you to keep *all* the Wilsondisc CD-ROMs you have paid for, including superseded copies, is a blessed exception. Fortunately, only two CD-ROMs in the Electronic Text Service are supplied under temporary, as opposed to perpetual, licenses; unfortunately, they are two of our most important: the *TLG* and *PHI* CD-ROMs, containing the classical Greek and Latin texts. In the case of most temporary licenses, it seems to me that we are paying owner's rates for renter's rights, under conditions that may be fundamentally at odds with our mission to ensure long-term availability of information.

4. *Purpose of use.* "Educational," "Academic research," "noncommercial"–these are the words that crop up again and again in

licensing agreements to define how the materials may be used. Frankly, I've often wondered what possible non-academic or commercial use there could be for a database of ancient Greek papyri, for example! But this can be a significant issue for librarians with electronic resources other fields. For example, the licenses for the CD-ROMs and end-user online systems in the Columbia University Business Library stipulate that they may only be used for "academic research," since that is the basis on which the library receives an educational discount. Since our Business Library is heavily used by our alumni, who may or may not be doing "academic" research, the librarians there have unhappily felt constrained to prohibit alumni and non-affiliates from using the resources; yet another example of how libraries have lost control over electronic materials in a way that compromises traditional service values.

5. *Categories of users.* Few of the Electronic Text Service resources carry serious restrictions on who may use them; even those that limit users to the licensing institutions faculty, students, and staff usually have a loophole for visiting scholars and other "temporary patrons of the institution while such individuals are on the institutional premises."[7] But once again, librarians who deal with products from the commercial world, the LEXIS database for example, may find that their licenses limit usage to students of a particular department or school. Would we have tolerated such restrictions imposed by publishers on our print collections?

6. *Access.* And finally, when we look at how license agreements permit access to electronic materials we see the curious paradox that is at the heart of electronic publishing today. On the one hand, the producers of electronic resources are seeking to exploit as fully as possible the computer's wonderful potential for sophisticated organization, retrieval, and analysis of information. On the other hand, they are extremely nervous about the equally wonderful potential of the computer for widespread access to and dissemination of information, because they fear loss of control and revenue. And so they seek to keep the genie of electronic access stuffed *inside* the bottle, with licenses that limit use to a single user on a single machine at a time. Of course, you can often obtain other network and multi-user licenses for electronic materials, but they usually come at a fairly stiff price. For example, the *New Oxford English*

Dictionary, 2nd. ed., on CD-ROM costs $895 for a single-user license; a campus-wide network license costs $10,000.

I hope that I haven't lost you in the fine print, but in case I have, just let me summarize some major practical points:

1. Look closely at the full copyright statement and the licensing agreement, if there is one, to figure out whether you're a landlord or a tenant of the information in hand.
2. If you're a tenant, read the fine print on the license to see if you're a permanent steward or just a transient boarder.
3. Read more of the fine print to see exactly what the limitations are on access and use.
4. Make sure your patrons get written permission for any copying or large-scale printing or downloading.
5. If you want to offer multi-user or network access, talk to the publisher who may or may not already have figured out what to charge; after all, publishers are still feeling their way in this new environment, too. You may find a fair amount of negotiating room and price flexibility, depending on whether you want campus-wide, simultaneous multi-user access; more limited simultaneous multi-user access on a local area network; or just want to provide access to a single user at a time but from various sites. For example, the complete works of Kierkegaard–in Danish–spring to mind as something that I might like to deliver over the campus network to different places in the library or in Philosophy Hall without paying lots of money for the probably unnecessary privilege of having hundreds of people searching them at once.

At present nearly all electronic publishers of primary source materials in the humanities distribute their texts and hypermedia resources on CD-ROM, laser disk, or floppy diskette. There are only a few scholarly online source databases in the humanities, among them: the aforementioned *ARTFL* database, available online from the University of Chicago; the *Dartmouth Dante Project Database*, freely accessible over the Internet from Dartmouth College; and the *Responsa Project/Global Jewish Database*, available online from Bar-Ilan University in Israel. For the future, the new Center for Electronic Texts in the Humanities (CETH), established last year by Princeton and Rutgers universities, has as one of its goals "the acquisition and dissemination of text files . . . concentrating on a selection of good quality texts which can be made available over the Internet with suitable retrieval software and with appropriate copyright permission."[8] This Center is an exciting development for humanities research, and I wish it great success in working with publishers and authors to forge partnerships that will satisfy the copyright holders' economic interests and desire to protect the integrity of their texts while satisfying scholars' needs for ready and reasonably priced access to quality resources for research and teaching. I would also like to applaud the Center's emphasis on "quality texts" since many of the electronic texts currently floating freely around the Internet would not meet that standard by any stretch of the imagination. In one sense, the *ARTFL, Dante*, and proposed CETH online databases represent for libraries the ultimate in lack of control–how can you catch the wind, or the ephemeral stream of electrons speeding over the networks? However, I guess I have some faith that the non-profit producers and distributors of these databases will strive to make them affordable to users and to keep them viable and available for scholarly investigations well into the future. In other words, I hope that control of these resources is reasonably safe, if not in library hands, then in the hands of institutions that share many of our goals and values and with whom we can negotiate reasonable bargains and even cooperative ventures.

I wish I could be so sanguine about electronic resources controlled by commercial publishers and information services. Earlier this year (1992), after failing to reach an agreement on contract renewal with the Modern Language Association, DIALOG Information Services, Inc. abruptly dropped the renowned *Modern Language Association International Bibliography* database from its online services. At present (June 1992) the full MLA database is not available from any source. One can't help but wonder which of the scholarly databases in the humanities might be next. Can we rely on the information industry to preserve access to specialized or historical data that is no longer deemed economically viable? I doubt it. Does this imply ever greater roles for libraries and library consortia or utilities in regaining control over specialized and scholarly databases and database back files that the information industry will not support? I think so.

Utopian dreams notwithstanding, *somebody* is going to own and control the rights to the most desirable information published in electronic form. In some cases, academic and non-profit institutions, even libraries, will be the "landlords" of that information; in many cases, they will merely be the "tenants" of information controlled by other institutions or by the information industry.

There is a book in the Columbia University Libraries entitled: *Super Tenant; New York City Tenant Handbook–Your Legal Rights and How to Use Them.*[9] Now I don't want to push this "landlord-tenant" metaphor too far, but I know one thing: in cases where I'm going to be a "tenant," I want to be a "super tenant," knowing my rights and how to use them to realize fundamental goals of service and preservation.

NOTES

1. For my overview of copyright I have drawn heavily on *Intellectual Property Rights in an Age of Electronics and Information* (Washington, DC: U.S. Congress, Office of Technology Assessment; distributed by U.S. Government Printing Office, 1986); and Robert L. Oakley, "Copyright Issues for the Creators and Users of Information in the Electronic Environment," *Electronic Networking* 1.1 (Fall 1991): 23-30.

2. 17 U.S.C. §102(a).

3. Cf., Mary Brandt Jensen, "CD-ROM Licenses: What's in the Fine or Nonexistent Print May Surprise You," *CD-ROM Professional* 4 (March 1991): 13-16.

4. See also, Joyce L. Ogburn, "Electronic Resources and Copyright Issues: Consequences for Libraries," *Library Acquisitions: Practice and Theory* 14.3(1990):257-264.

5. InteLex Corporation. *Past Masters Institution License Agreement.* (Clayton, GA: InteLex Corp., [1991]), p.[1]. *Past Masters* is an ongoing series of databases of major philosophical texts with search software.

6. Jensen, "CD-ROM Licenses,"13.

7. Thesaurus Linguae Graecae. *Thesaurus Linguae Graecae License Agreement* (Irvine, CA: Thesaurus Linguae Graecae, University of California at Irvine, 1992), p.[1].

8. "The Center [for Electronic Texts in the Humanities]." Message on CETH LISTSERV distribution list (network addresses: CETH@PUCC.BITNET and CETH@PUCC.PRINCETON.EDU). May 18,1992.

9. Striker, John M. and Andrew O. Shapiro. *Super Tenant: New York City Tenant Handbook–Your Legal Rights and How to Use Them* (New York: Holt, Rinehart and Winston, 1978).

JOINT PLENARY SESSION, NASIG AND SSP (SOCIETY FOR SCHOLARLY PUBLISHING), JUNE 20, 1992

Higher Education in the 90s: Growth, Regression or Status Quo

Charles B. Reed

Twenty-five years ago, when I was finishing my doctorate, the faculty at George Washington University told me to be sure to keep up with the literature in my field after graduation. They cautioned me that everything I had learned would be obsolete by the end of my career. Today, the flow of information is so fast that sometimes I wonder if what students learn at the beginning of their graduate programs isn't obsolete by the time they receive their degrees.

We come together in a time of exciting possibilities and great anxiety. Throughout the world, economies are being transformed. Social values are up for grabs. Political walls are falling. In the middle of this whirling change, no institution is immune. Not the Presidency, certainly. Ask President Bush how *he* feels. Prior to 1992, when has the notion of replacing one rich, white male Presi-

---

Charles B. Reed is Chancellor, State University System of Florida, 325 W. Gaines St., Tallahassee, FL 32399.

© 1993 by The Haworth Press, Inc. All rights reserved.

dent from Texas with another rich, white male President from Texas ever been considered fundamental change?

Universities, too, are feeling the pressure. Some universities have been accused–with an unfortunately high degree of accuracy–of abusing grant funds, charging off luxury items to the taxpayers in a way that would make the designer of the $500 toilet seat blush. Some leading academics have been accused of committing fraud in research or plagiarism in publications.

Scholars, or in some cases their offspring, have published bitter critiques of higher education. Some of them present faculty as more interested in their golf scores than their teaching. Others describe our campuses as straightjackets for the mind, demanding strict ideological conformity to this season's fashion in the politically correct.

Make a list of the Presidencies available this year at major universities: the University of Chicago, Yale, Duke, Columbia. Add two more with newly minted CEOs–Harvard and Stanford–and you have six of the most prestigious universities with new leadership or looking for it. Let me add to that the ongoing experience of a marathon legislative session in America's fourth-largest state–Florida. Our nine state universities today command greater academic respect than at any time in their history. In part this is due to our new National High Magnetic Field Laboratory, the first new national laboratory in America in a generation. Last weekend the Pentagon gave the University of Florida $18 million for a brain research center.

We educate more people than ever, to a higher degree than ever. Twenty years ago, half of Florida's population were high school dropouts and only ten percent had college diplomas. Per capita income trailed the national average. Today three out of four have at least a high school diploma and a fourth have college degrees. And per capita income exceeds the national average significantly. And yet we have not been able to translate all that success into a decent budget. Why? What do all of the above have in common?

I submit that American universities today have a problem. It is not a crisis. It is not a cataclysm. It is not the end of universities as we have known them. But it is a low point–a valley of relatively low public esteem and confidence. I'll return to this point as I conclude these remarks, to suggest to you that every one of us in this room can be part of the solution, even if we've never been part of the problem.

Let me turn, for a moment, to a major engine driving university costs upward, as our institutions try to maintain not their prestige, but their ability to do their institutional jobs. I doubt if anyone in this joint meeting of the Society for Scholarly Publishing and the North American Serials Interest Group doesn't already know what I'm about to say. So I'll keep it tight.

Library budgets aren't growing fast enough, if they're growing at all. Publishers face rising costs of production and in all other facets of their business. This forces them to raise prices, which forces libraries to choose between new books or additional journals–or sometimes, between new books and renewing their existing journals–with the net result that some books go unbought, the subscription base for some journals shrinks, and revenues for publishers of both books and journals drop. The outcome is still higher prices, renewing the cost cycle.

What are possible ways out? First, technology offers some relief. Today there are a few journals which publish electronically and are accessed by modem. Others may adopt CD-ROM or floppy disk publication. And the second solution? We need more money for libraries, which, due to new technology, now face users who demand everything in both paper and electronic form. It is not an easy situation.

The bottom line, it seems to me, is that there are now so many research publications that non-academic people wonder if there aren't too many and if paying for them all is necessary. We see examples of this attitude in items such as the one in the June 16, 1992 edition of *The Wall Street Journal*, criticizing the dubious research topics of some recent dissertations. "Ph.D. may mean Doctor of Clambakes and Slumber Parties," the headline read. The article discussed, in mildly satirical terms, such recent dissertation topics as back swing techniques for golfers, rock climbers' behavioral characteristics, the influence of Mardi Gras on theater, and–yes–clam bakes and slumber parties.

Is it anti-intellectual to raise questions about the value of such research topics? Yes and no. In earlier years, Sen. William Proxmire of Wisconsin used to bestow his "golden fleece" awards on research that seemed to have little, if any, practical value. We all ought to remember that his awards frequently received wide media attention.

Perhaps, when our publishers and librarians are caught in a cost spiral that seems out of control, that ought to tell us something. Perhaps it ought to tell us that we are not only producing more research every year than any one person could ever hope to read. That has been true since the 1950s. Perhaps we are simply publishing more research in more fields than the society which surrounds and supports us is willing to pay for. Perhaps their reluctance to provide the funds to acquire and store all this information is their mute way of telling us that they wish we hadn't produced so much of it in the first place.

So what are we to make of this? First, I think we need to recognize that a crunch is coming. In fact, it's here. In the past in the State University System of Florida, out faculty have become more productive in the teaching area. While our real appropriations per full-time equivalent student dropped by more than 15 percent, the number of course sections taught by faculty rose more than 8 percent, and the number of student credit hours rose by 4.7 percent. That's more teaching for less money. If this trend is valid across the entire country, and it probably is, then our publishing houses, journals and libraries may find some relief–because at least some of our faculty will be too busy teaching to publish.

More seriously, I think the relief we seek will come in two forms: bigger budgets and a permanent technological shift away from print and toward electronics. Bigger budgets will come because, as *The New York Times* reported this past week, housing starts are up, *Dun & Bradstreet* says business confidence is up, and the Federal Reserve's latest "beige book" reports bullish conditions in all twelve of its regions. If the economy drove us into this hole, it's the economy that will lift us out.

In the longer term, however, I see the following trends. If, for now, you need to maintain both print and electronic journals, still you won't have to do so forever. I am more and more convinced technology will help solve the current problems–although it clearly can't do everything.

In the future, the measure of a library's capability will be *less* how many volumes it keeps from crumbling and *more* how much information, in whatever form, it can put in front of a reader in a short time. I think the concept of velocity is the important idea for the future of information. In the years ahead, we'll rank universities according to how fast they can move information to where they need it. We'll gradually stop ranking institutions according to how much data they can store in any one place. Interlibrary loan, microforms, and particularly electronics will all increase the velocity with which information moves.

Specifically, electronics can help through remote computing–using modems, through fax technology, through increased use of CD-ROM, and the expansion of electronic publishing. In fact, I would expect that within ten years, there may well be one or more journals in every technical discipline, and even some of the humanities, which appear in paper only when a user-subscriber hits the print button.

Frankly, I don't see an alternative. And if I were in the publishing business, I would remember that less then ninety years ago, livery stables were as common as gas stations are today. In other words, get in on the ground floor. This is a case in which we need to go with the direction of change, not against it. Don't hold on too tight or you'll miss an opportunity.

I promised at the beginning of my talk that I would return to the big problem of universities today, and what we can all do to solve it. I said the American universities today have a problem–not a crisis. If we are at a low point of public esteem and confidence, what can we do about it? We can talk about it. Tell our neighbors where we work and how proud we are of what we do. Let people know how valuable scholarly endeavor is. Write letters to the editor of *The Wall Street Journal* when it makes fun of dissertation topics. Communicate with legislators about their golden fleece-type awards. When they're off base, tell them.

But also, we have some work of our own to do. We in academic life have to clean up our own house. We can restore and enhance our credibility, but it takes time. You can lose it in a flash, and it takes years to build it back up.

In conclusion, let me offer both sympathy and empathy to all of you who are involved in the process of recording permanently the work of scholars published in America. What they do, and therefore what you do, is critically important. If I offer the reflection that the public does not appreciate everything we do, it is not that I share that opinion so much as that I have to take it into account.

Not since the destruction of the Alexandria library has such a wealth of knowledge existed as that which you and your predecessors have helped America and the world to accumulate. As you ponder the best path to our common future, let me add my respect and my good wishes for your outstanding efforts.

A Potency of Life: Scholarship in an Electronic Age

Willard McCarty

1. INTRODUCTION

In the third book of the Roman mythological compendium, the *Metamorphoses* of Ovid, the poet tells how, before establishing the city of Thebes, Cadmus killed a rampaging dragon and sowed its teeth in the ground (*Met.* 3.50ff). From these teeth sprang armed men. No less lively and vigorously productive than the dragon's teeth, John Milton declared sixteen centuries later, are books: "for books are not absolutely dead things, but do contain a potency of life in them to be as active as that soul whose progeny they are; nay, they do preserve as in a vial the purest efficacy and extraction of that living intellect that bred them" (*Areopagitica*).

The medieval book, sturdily bound to protect its contents from the ravages of time, sometimes richly encrusted with jewels like a saint's reliquary, suggests a different but analogous metaphor: not the alchemist's distillation but a sarcophagus containing a treasured body of dormant knowledge that awaits an intellectual resurrection. In contrast, the modern volume is a common thing, produced in great quantities and variety but clearly not intended to survive the centuries; it suggests a rapidly changing, widely disseminated knowledge–to use another medieval figure of speech, like the nut whose shell you discard once you have eaten the nutritious kernel.[1] Economic and ecological realities are bringing this way of distribut-

---

Willard McCarty is Assistant Director, Centre for Computing in the Humanities, University of Toronto, The Library Building, Toronto, Ontario M5S 1A5, Canada.

ing knowledge into question, however. Faced with a crisis in scholarly publishing, we look anxiously to electronic media, yet here too there are hard problems, particularly with the instability of data and immaturity of the technology needed to access and maintain them. We may, as long as language carries that seminal "potency of life," remain a "people of the book," but once again since the invention of the printing press, an innovation in the technology of publication forces us to reexamine the book, how it may change, and what it may be capable of doing.

My brief here is to explore the implications of this change for the nature of scholarship. Since I can speak only about what I know, I will focus on the two forms of electronic scholarly publishing with which I am involved: first, a form of computer-mediated communication called the "electronic seminar," which because its conversation occurs as text may be considered an alternative kind of publication; second, a particular kind of electronic book, which I call the "edition," that allows us to publish the processes of research rather than the final product. Let me stress at the outset the tentativeness of everything that I say. Not only must I raise large questions beyond my capacity to answer, but I must also describe things so new that their basic properties are as yet unclear.

2. FUNDAMENTALS

My subject has two aspects: the forms and effects of technology on the one hand; and on the other, our conception of the scholarly life. So pervasive is the computer today, and so necessary scholarship to understand its implications, that neither can be ignored in a discussion of the other.

Because the social and intellectual assimilation of technology is a slow and uncertain process, however, the impact of the computer on scholarship and scholarly publishing is difficult to grasp. Amidst the high hopes, little attention has been paid to the basic characteristics of the electronic medium, and how these might be used to direct its application.[2] What we can observe so far suggests that the assimilation of the computer is following what I take to be a common path for new technology: first, in the imitative phase, it tends to be used as if it were merely an improvement upon and replacement for what is already known; then, after some time, we begin to see it as genuinely new, and to realize that its newness alters how we think about the world.[3]

In contrast, our difficulties with the idea of the scholarly life stem from the fact that it is so old, and seemingly the product of social conditions that no longer obtain. It comes to us as an inherited cultural form, like an old manuscript written in an archaic dialect; the crisis of its institutional home, the university, indicates without doubt that it is in urgent need of translation, i.e., renewal or reaffirmation in terms that can be widely understood and accepted. The problem is not trivial. As Benno Schmidt, former President of Yale, has commented on Jaroslav Pelikan's recent book, *The Idea of the University: A Reexamination* (1992), "The true crisis of the university today lies not in financial exigencies, political assaults from the left and right, or the myopia of modern life; it lies in the crisis of confidence within the university itself about its abiding nature and purpose." In his book Pelikan has only a little to say about technology as such, but by probing what we are about as scholars and publishers of scholarship, his book sheds considerable light on the intellectual and social context of human technology. I will draw upon it significantly throughout my discussion.

I wish to proceed first by reasoning from the apparent nature of electronic data to its most important characteristics for scholarly communication. Then, relying on Pelikan's argument, I will consider briefly the role of communication in the university, focussing in particular on how the new medium might allow us to respond to its needs. As working examples, I will cite the two forms of publication I have already mentioned, the electronic seminar and the electronic book.

3. NATURE OF ELECTRONIC DATA

The dynamic, changeable nature of electronic data seems most basic of all. This changeableness is implied in the term itself, which suggests the representation of something, in patterns of energy, that must be transformed before it can be used or even sensed. Hence, I argue, the new medium is fundamentally mutable. From mutability follow two other characteristics: ease of reproduction, and speed of transmission. Thus, electronic data–the text of a book, for example–may be reproduced in any number of electronic copies and sent around the world as easily as a single copy may be sent to a geographical neighbor. Of course, these characteristics spell trouble, especially when integrity and security of data are a primary concern. Once we stop imposing wholly imitative terms on the medium, however, these characteristics also translate into a revolutionary potential. As my examples will show, I am not referring to the incremental improvements computers bring to the conventional machinery of editing, printing, and communication, however much money these save; rather to the ways electronic publication allows us to address the fundamental problems of which Pelikan speaks.

The electronic medium, that is, may serve as a means of producing conventional publications, but we do not begin to understand it until we think of it as a primary vehicle of scholarly work. Assuming, then, that it could be primary, and that it is *essentially*, not accidentally, mutable, reproducible, and transmittable, what kind of a vehicle might it be? How might it affect scholarly communication?

4. COMMUNICATION IN THE UNIVERSITY

Pelikan remarks that "a consideration of the intellectual virtues"–by which he means free inquiry, intellectual honesty, trust in reason, and the readiness to communicate–"suggests that among the many cliches about the university, perhaps none is more worth keeping than the definition of it as a 'community of scholars'" (57). Hence, he observes, for scholars "there is an imperative of communicating that corresponds to the indicative of knowing" (cf. 51; 123). Simply, we communicate–genuinely, as best we can–or we cease being scholars. Thus, a discussion of scholarship in an electronic age is not just or even principally about private matters, as research is usually conceived in the humanities, but necessarily about scholarly communication, publishing in the etymological sense of "making public," through the electronic media.

Communication may seem so obvious a scholarly activity as not to need much comment. Yet experience suggests that the crisis in universities today has to do with our failure to communicate both amongst ourselves and with society at large, despite the fact that we publish more every year. The pressure to publish obviously gets results, but we may be excused for wondering if the cost is not too high. This cost has several aspects–economic, intellectual, psychological, and moral–of which we usually hear only about the first. The rest, however, are more severe, if more subtle: witness those colleagues who write because they must, whether or not they have something to say; those who are too busy taking theoretical positions or striking fashionable postures to communicate anything else; or those who have fallen silent in despair.

It may seem odd that a discussion of new means for publishing should begin with the observation that more is not better, implying that less would be beautiful. Indeed, in many cases it might. My subject, however, is not directly concerned with quantities–if we were wanting merely to increase the volume of communicated words cheaply, we would have no subject worth discussing–rather with the quality of scholarship and the qualities of the new medium. I have suggested that the medium has certain rather abstract characteristics. To know what effects these are having or might have, we need to examine them in the context of scholarly communication, which we can divide into three interrelated activities: collaboration; publication, including public lectures; and, of course, classroom and tutorial instruction. I wish to consider these in order.

For several reasons, Pelikan argues, collaboration is bound to increase across the disciplines, amongst colleagues wherever they happen to be located (63f). Indeed, common usage of the word "colleague" suggests that professors already prefer to think in terms of geographically distributed communities (64), or what sociologists have called "invisible colleges."[4] Highly specialized inquiry, with its necessarily small community of researchers, is in part responsible, but so is wide-ranging interdisciplinary study, which, as Pelikan observes, has produced "some of the most important scientific and scholarly discoveries" of the last few decades. Notable also are those scholars in less economically developed countries, and the euphemistically dubbed "private scholars" in our own, who lack basic materials–including, perhaps, the non-networked tools I will discuss later–and so of necessity are in need of collaboration; they not only add to the pool of intelligence but also bring different points of view, with practical benefits all around.

Historically, invisible colleges have not been characteristic of the humanities, where the primary instrument is the book and "results" are normally complex arguments, ideally the mature product of solitary meditation on source materials that may take many years to master. As I will explain, however, the computer–in the form of large electronic textbases, the tools with which to experiment with them, and new means for scholarly dialogue–encourages interdisciplinary work in the humanities, although it is still too early to tell to what degree. In my own experience, incursions into fields other than one's own certainly tends to result in exchanges with congenial specialists, if not collaboration in the usual sense, wherever one can find them. Again in my case, these exchanges–beginning with electronic mail, then involving visits and lectures–have led to sharing of approaches, bibliographies, articles, and the like. Whether such experiences will become typical, and so lead to a significant amount of collaboration, remains to be seen.

Publication in the usual sense is far more vexed an issue than productive interchange, for it is here that we are faced with the severe economic and academic pressures, the crisis in scholarly publishing, of which I have already spoken. The economic aspects of this crisis have, in part, driven the numerous ongoing experiments in online publishing, some of which are quite interesting. These, however, have yet to gain wide acceptance, especially from publishers, librarians, and university committees for hiring, tenure, and promotion. Apart from the pragmatic considerations of access to the medium, resistance seems to point back to the fundamental mutability of electronic text and its consequences for the maintenance, security, and dependability of data. I take this resistance, as well as the struggle to make the new medium fully "respectable," to indicate, again, how poor a replacement for print it can be. I am certainly not saying that in specific cases electronic publication of traditional materials cannot be superior, just that thoughtlessly imitative applications are not. As positive example, take *The Bryn Mawr Classical Review*,[5] which circulates timely reports on current books to classicists around the world via the academic research networks. It performs a conventional service, but for its recipients does so more conveniently and cheaply than a comparable printed journal possibly could. We can learn much from its success as well as from the failures or uninspired persistence of other such ventures. What we learn is, I think, indicated by Pelikan's statement that we need to give more attention "to the question of *how we are to publish* lest we perish" (124, emphasis mine). There need be no question, I think, of less publishing, at least not of constraining or improving it in any way other than by the self-governance of authors in vigorous argument with each other. Thus, with John Milton, "I cannot praise a fugitive and cloistered virtue, unexercised and unbreathed, that never sallies out and sees her adversary, but slinks out of the race where that immortal garland is to be run for, not without dust and heat" (*Areopagitica*). The real questions of this crisis in scholarly publishing concern the forum that we provide for ourselves in which to discover, through exercise, what truth we have: "*how* we are to publish lest we perish." Obviously, neither the prison cell of solitary despair, nor the prison yard of enforced exercise, can be our model.

My experience suggests that the electronic medium, essentially ephemeral as it is, has the potential to support just such a forum, in which received but unrenewed knowledge and new but immature ideas can get the needed exercise–and then be gone–without having to memorialize them expensively in print. This is not to say that the "abiding nature and purpose" of the university need not be reexamined, rather that we have the technology in hand to solve rather than to postpone or exacerbate the extrinsic problems.

The electronic medium can also help directly in that reexamination by providing a world-wide forum, or many such forums, where we can develop a consensus, not only for ourselves but also, very importantly, for the world at large (Pelikan 124,145). This "consensus about what seem almost unavoidably to be called 'values' [may be] beyond our grasp," as Pelikan suggests, but "the methodology of teasing out such presuppositions and values from the concrete life of the university . . . and of then asking whether they are defensible, carries the promise . . . of defining a set of 'intellectual virtues'" (48)–and in these discovering our purpose. Such 'teasing out' implies an activity not unlike panning for gold, in which much dirt and worthless gravel must be sifted through to find the nugget for assaying.[6] The electronic bitstream fits the job description well.

5. ELECTRONIC DISCUSSION GROUPS

Both collaboration and publication have conversational aspects that are already well served by electronic networks. For the humanities, widespread use of electronic networks had its beginning barely more than five years ago. Since then e-mail has become increasingly commonplace throughout North America and most countries of Europe. For all academic subjects, principally in the humanities and social sciences, electronic seminars of the kind with which I am most familiar now number well over 750. Because of the ease with which messages are redistributed, it is impossible to know how many people are involved, but certainly the number is in the tens of thousands.

My experience with these seminars began in 1987, when I founded *Humanist*, a worldwide seminar for computing humanists, that I edited until Spring 1990.[7] Within the past three years, a number of more specialized groups have sprung up, many of them begun by members of *Humanist*. Their emergence illustrates the general trend for electronic discussion to conform ever more closely to what scholars are ordinarily concerned with, if not formally to become part of the university itself. Happily, for several reasons–including the unofficial nature of these groups–interdisciplinary discussions still predominate.

I use the word 'seminar' to describe these discussion groups because of the form to which the best of them tend. Like the conventional seminar, they constitute a kind of long conversation, which may be convened by a single person but ideally is conducted by everyone for mutual enlightenment. Its purpose, I take it, is not so much to convey facts and information as to further understanding of its subject, to train the minds of its participants, and so to help create a genuine community of scholars. It is a pedagogical structure in which every member is both teacher and student.

How is this done electronically? The basic mechanism is e-mail, a general understanding of which I will assume, but allow me to point out one important aspect of communication it renders irrelevant. Since only words are transmitted, and names can be abbreviated however one wishes, what the sociologists call "social-context cues"[8] are radically attenuated. Thus one's institutional status, age, sex, race, corporeal features, and so forth are irrelevant; indeed, the blind and those with other physical disabilities "appear" on equal footing with everyone else. In brief, what counts is not where or who you are, rather *only what you say*. The effect can be quite liberating, especially when, as with *Humanist*, it occurs in the intellectual context of a seminar.

Early in the evolution of *Humanist*, the pleas of outsiders to be admitted, often accompanied by personal histories, fascinated me so much that I made as the sole requirement for membership the submission of a brief biography. These biographies, gathered into small groups and edited, were then regularly circulated to the membership and stored on *Humanist's* fileserver for reference. In this way, as well as through the daily interchange of messages, a world-wide community was created. Controlled studies of such distributed communities are exceedingly difficult if not impossible to do; much anecdotal evidence suggests, however, that *Humanist* has had profound effects on the emerging field of computing in the humanities, with consequences for all the disciplines involved, and on the applications of computer-mediated communications within the university as a whole.[9]

Even if we cannot measure such effects with complete reliability, we can perhaps see why scholars have taken to the medium with such intelligence and enthusiasm as messages sometimes display. Again, experience suggests the deeply felt need of scholars throughout the world for just the kind of institutional environment that Pelikan has described as "the idea of the university." In the electronic context, the scholarly imperative to communicate has thus often shown itself to be the desire for genuine communication, not principally about status and other extrinsic matters, but about ideas. The attenuation of "social-context cues" helps; so also does the fact that in a world-wide community, local politics can gain no foothold.

Of course no medium guarantees truth, eloquence, cogency, or an end to self-interested deviousness. Noting such technological promise as I have described, Pelikan remarks that the enthusiasts "often seem not to have factored Original Sin and the Fall into their calculations." "There is no guarantee," he continues, "that the university will not, as it has all too often in the past, permit itself to be corrupted also in its cultivation of this technology" (43). I repeat: there are no guarantees. Nevertheless, we have it in our power to do something truly interesting and significant with a potentially powerful medium, and we had better act while we can.

6. ELECTRONIC BOOKS

I would now like to turn from the public and conversational aspects of scholarly work to the more individual and meditative, hence from the electronic seminar to the electronic book.

Much foolishness still surrounds the idea of the electronic book, particularly in speculations that it will replace the printed volume, so rendering conventional libraries obsolete. As I suggested, however, the genius of the electronic medium lies in an entirely different direction. From the few examples we now have, it is clear that the e-book has a much greater potential as a tool with which study and research are conducted, rather than merely reported–a kind of laboratory or workshop for ideas to be developed. My basic point is, again, that by nature the new medium makes a better instrument for those uses that exploit its essential mutability and transformability rather than attempt to work around these characteristics. Here I wish to ask, how might such a "book," conceived so as to realize its own potential, manifest and thus advance the idea of the university and of publishing as a scholarly activity?

Electronic books may now be sorted into a few basic categories:[10] the reference work, such as an encyclopedia, dictionary, or online manual; the "adventure game" short-story; related to it, both the instructional "web" of interrelated material and the scholar's notebook, which may be what is used to construct this web; and the scholarly form I wish to focus on, the electronic edition. These categories are still fluid, since designers have been preoccupied with techniques rather than applications, and it is not yet clear which of the possible applications will prove genuinely useful. Let us, however, proceed by defining the edition broadly as a machine-readable version of an established text together with software designed to assist its study. To understand what impact the edition might have in a scholarly context, let us consider its two logical components–a corpus of material, and the software used to access it–separately, although in practice one is pointless without the other, and often they interpenetrate so as to be nearly indistinguishable.

At the simplest level, textual corpora in electronic form, especially large ones such as the *Thesaurus Linguae Graecae*, the *Dartmouth Dante Database*, or the *Tresor de la Langue Française*,"[11] are truly revolutionary because they allow anyone within reach of the equipment to search bodies of material that once only the most fortunate, privileged, and dedicated scholars could command. Such corpora not only allow the factual basis of magisterial authority and received knowledge to be checked, and for kinds of studies to be undertaken that even the luminaries could not manage; they also foster the interdisciplinary work of outsiders and so quicken traditional disciplines with fresh ideas and approaches. Of course there are still formidable barriers, such as the necessary mastery of languages and critical methods; unhurried time is still required for ideas to be assimilated and to mature. These, however, are barriers that educate; limitations of access may stiffen resolve, but what they teach is largely the inequities of fate and privilege. Because development of these corpora helps to overcome such inequities, it arguably ranks as one of the most promising innovations for the humanities since reliable editions of standard texts became widely available in the Renaissance.

(I say "promising" advisedly, since it is still too early to have much evidence of revolutionary effects on the humanities. The skills of prophecy–not in the sense of predicting the future, but of reading the tendencies of the present–do not need to be prodigious for one to have the courage to act on this promise, however.)

Access to corpora of material is a much more interesting notion than I may seem to suggest because it involves software, the other component of the edition. Like all electronic data, software is changeable; as the word implies, it can take, as it were, the "imprint" of its author's intentions, then be shaped and reshaped to reflect ever more closely his or her idea of the data. Thus it brings about a recursive process of study: the object–let us say a text–gives rise to a theory about how it works; this theory imprints software, software delivers results, and results probe the text, from which comes an improved theory, and so forth. Because the object of the exercise is to formulate a better theory, we value the failures; they show us the difference between information, which comes from the machine, and knowledge, which we get by assimilating information and going beyond it (Pelikan 42).

Actual experience with current software is, however, likely first to teach the scholar how crudely software tools imitate, in their rough mechanical way, the imaginative understanding of a cultural artifact–Vannevar Bush's comparison of such software to "a stone adze in the hands of a cabinetmaker," though spoken nearly 30 years ago, still applies.[12] Nevertheless, raw technological progress is making a difference, first by allowing more complex algorithms– the faster the machine runs, the more can be done in a reasonable time–hence more sophisticated imitation of scholarship; second, by improving what are called 'authoring tools' so that scholars can construct their own models. The dialogue between scholar and programmer has been most useful, but by changing what it means to program a computer, modern systems increasingly allow the scholar to engage directly, interactively with the mechanical realization of his or her own ideas. The machine thus ceases to preserve the old notion of master and slave, with its debilitating consequences both for scholars and for those who support research (Pelikan 62; cf. 42); rather, it shows itself to be essentially a device with which cognitive self-portraits may be realized. In the computer, as in a mirror, we are increasingly able to discover, however darkly, our own mental visage–and to change it, both in the representation and in ourselves.[13]

Heuristic interaction with that visage, or what Pelikan less metaphorically calls "active participation in the processes by which knowledge is advanced" (93), is of course central to education, hence to the university. On it, Pelikan argues, the guarantee of intellectual honesty and the intimate, vitalizing bond between the classroom and the study or laboratory depend. Thus, he comments, "the learning process does not mean simply learning the What of existing knowledge, but learning the How for as yet unknown knowledge" (93). Although teaching in the humanities, at least in theory, concentrates precisely on how and not what to think, nevertheless what we tend to value are the products of solitary work published as finished arguments in a fixed form. As I have suggested, the computer offers us, to a limited but significant degree, a medium for recording, hence communicating the "How" of knowledge, thus involving students and colleagues in it. The electronic edition thus has a pedagogical aspect, although so far we have not heard enough about teaching with such tools.[14]

My current research involves constructing such an electronic edition of the *Metamorphoses* of Ovid,[15] a long, highly complex, and poorly understood mythological compendium of considerable importance to Western literature and culture as a whole. The computer program I use in this edition is more or less fixed in what it can do, but it allows the software to be extended into the text, as it were, through markup.[16] This markup consists of tags, inserted into the text, which allow the program to detect selected textual phenomena and so subject them to analysis. The program can also import lists of word-forms from external files and find all occurrences of these forms in the text; by grouping them thematically, I can thus specify roughly, for example, all the places where the notion of 'ignorance' (which is communicated through dozens of words) are to be found.[17] When my edition is finished, the marked-up text of the poem will thus be accompanied by a kind of thematic thesaurus with which (again roughly) ideas in it may be studied.

Let me draw your attention to two aspects of this edition: first, the mutability and hence status of the editorial meta-text; second, the ability of software to present any one of a number of conflicting views of the original text. Consider that in the conventional edition, the editor's work is usually taken to represent a stable achievement whose function is to settle questions so that work of a different order may proceed on a secure footing. The electronic edition, however, is much more an incorporation of interesting, fruitful possibilities for further work. The mutability of its editorial meta-text means that the editor is providing not final decisions, but cogent examples that may be altered. (Thus, in the edition, the text *must* be provided in a fully modifiable form, not simply as a compiled database.) Furthermore, because the software allows choice now of one conflicting view of a text, now of another, several theories may be entertained on equal footing, tested for their utility, and used as they happen to produce good results. Thus, for example, the editor may encode different schemes for partitioning a text; the user may select amongst these at will, modify one or more of them, or add a new one of his or her own devising. Similarly, the editor may provide, as I am, thematically grouped word-lists; the user is free to use, regroup, or supplement these lists. What results is clearly a new form of publication, logically intermediate between the primary data and the conventional book. When the electronic edition actually plays that role, as it does in my research, then it makes available, to anyone who cares to check, the mechanical aspects of the method used in researching the book. Of course much more goes into a work of scholarship than the results of an experiment, but the edition ensures that what is repeatable can be. Interesting avenues of exploration can be preserved and shared. Collaboration and instruction of a very exciting kind, if the will exists to undertake them, may result.

In the capacity for opening up processes of thought, at least insofar as they can be reflected in a computational mirror, and getting us to think about them, and so be able to teach them, the electronic edition is an instrument of that scholarship which renews our idea of the university and our community along with it.

7. CONCLUSION

In John Milton's *Areopagitica*, the defense of unrestricted publishing from which I have quoted and taken my title, he argues that books contain within them a "potency of life," like a soul within a body. Allow me, by way of conclusion, to think with Milton's imagery, and so to summarize my answer to the fascinating, difficult, and urgent techno-philosophical problem raised by the electronic medium: namely, what happens to the soul of a book when it is manifested within a changeable electronic body?

On the technical side, I have suggested in general that although tools may be used in a wide variety of ways, their most effective use is based on knowledge of inherent characteristics. (Thus, for example, although a wrench can be used as a hammer, it makes a very poor one; it is really much better at dealing with nuts and bolts.) The electronic medium appears, as I said, to be essentially mutable, reproducible, and transmittable; from these characteristics are derived its considerable potential to help us focus on processes rather than products of knowledge, learn and teach how we know what we know, and make our work public in ways that solve rather than exacerbate our publishing problems. Altogether, its genius can be applied greatly to strengthen a community of scholars, or cluster of communities, based on ideas.

The operative words here are the noun "potential" and the modal verb "can," indicating a largely unfulfilled, though not entirely untasted, promise. Despite considerable but, I hope, well hidden trepidation, I have made bold to praise the new medium of scholarship for its capacity to enliven our tired old institutions. Nevertheless, I cannot simply exit without expressing something of the basis for that trepidation, which in fact brings me from the technical to the philosophical side of our problem.

The essential job of the scholar, I take it, is to get as free as possible from the historical and geographical provincialism by which we are all to a degree imprisoned, and so to rescue our cultural heritage from obscurity and anachronistic misunderstanding. Thus, insofar as possible, the scholar must see past the exigencies of the historical moment, the "circumambient noise" of existence,[18] to the enduring and constant. Our Platonic heritage would teach us that, although difficult, the soul of an idea may finally be separated from its historical body. Our Hebraic ancestors condition us, however, to think that historical existence is our only means of knowing, however dimly, what is enduringly human; that there can be no separation of truth from history because we can never know when a more complete vision will show us the relevance of what we thought to be mere noise. Thus St. Paul, speaking about perception and knowledge, proclaimed that "now we see through a glass darkly"–now, while things are as we know them; "then," in the apocalypse his faith revealed to him, only "then face-to-face" (1 Cor 13:12).

The trepidation of which I spoke stems in part from my own

scholarly struggle to understand how the expressive power of written language, its soul if you will, is affected by migration to this new body, the electronic medium. No tool is "just a tool," no medium completely colorless or transparent; all, especially tools of thought, are agents or at least filters of perception. To have the *Metamorphoses* or any other work in the computer, as an electronic edition, means questions will be asked that before wouldn't have been formulated because only now they can be answered. Other questions, perhaps, won't as a result tend to be asked. Furthermore, global communications in the electronic seminar enforces the *lingua franca* of English and brings formerly separate scholarly traditions into intimate contact, with effects we can hardly imagine. Thus, how can we, at this point scarcely a generation into the "electronic age," and just now beginning to discover the genres of electronic publication, understand the implications of what we are doing? Nevertheless we must understand, and then act; the crisis within the university, and its corollary in scholarly publishing, urge us on. Other agendas than our own, considerably better funded, aim to shape the medium in ways we might not find so congenial.

My trepidation also arises from the difficulty of resisting the strong pull of technological and moral determinisms. I have been speaking about the *potential* of the new medium; this potential is all too easily trivialized by thinking that electronic tools must do what they can do, or that what they can do will make no essential difference to scholarship or the academy. To embrace either alternative is to surrender, rather than face the challenge of understanding the two central, interrelated terms of electronic scholarship: on the one hand, the characteristics of the medium, and on the other, the kind of world we want to make for ourselves.

As Jaroslav Pelikan has said, teasing out from our actual behavior what we as scholars think should be done, then seeing if it is defensible, may be the only way of arriving at cogent values. Yet our idea of the university may by circumstance be so obscured as to be hardly detectable in what some of us actually do. Thus, as well as Original Sin and the Fall, we must also factor desire into the equation that navigates us through the electronic age. What is it that we scholars want? I don't mean just larger grants, although they are very desirable indeed; I refer rather to what we may glimpse in those "traces of the divine image [that] still remain in us," as Milton argued *(Christian Doctrine* 1.12; cf. *Paradise Lost* 11:508-10).

Unquestionably it would be desirable to have a pleasant villa in Tuscany where we could get away from the world and think our thoughts in peace, but desire reaches much further than anything money can buy, however pleasant, now or in ancient times. As the literature of philosophical retreat shows, such villas tend to become images of a remade world, a world of desire. From the time of Plato's Academy at least, this has also been the idea of the university: to provide, as Blake said in *The Marriage of Heaven and Hell*, the opposition that is true friendship to the society of which we are inextricably connected.

If we manage things right the electronic medium will continue to grow responsive to desire, a mutable villa of the mind wherein ideas are discovered in dialogue and experiment, become strong through exercise, and are published to communicate their substance and energy–their potency of life, vigorous as dragon's teeth.

NOTES

1. Meister Eckhart, Sermon 11, in *Meister Eckhart: A Modern Translation*, transl. Raymond Bernard Blakney (New York: Harper and Row, 1941), p. 148.

2. See, however, Helmut Schanze, "Writing, Literacy and Word-Processing: Changes in the Concept of Literature in the Framework of New Media." *Literary and Linguistic Computing* 2(1987): 24-9; Willard McCarty, "*Humanist*; Lessons from a Global Electronic Seminar," *Computers and the Humanities* 26.3(1992) [forthcoming].

3. The evolution of the telephone provides one good example out of many; see esp. Ithiel de Sola Pool, ed., *The Social Impact of the Telephone*, MIT Bicentennial Studies, 1 (Cambridge, MA: MIT Press, 1977).

4. Attributed to Derek Price in M.J. Mulkay, "Sociology of the Scientific Research Community," *Science, Technology and Society: A Cross-Disciplinary Perspective*, ed. Ina Spiegel-Rösing and Derek de Solla Price (London: Sage, 1977): 93-148.

5. *BMCR* is edited by Richard Hamilton at Bryn Mawr and James J. O'Donnell at the University of Pennsylvania. Electronic subscriptions are free; to subscribe, send mail to mailserv@cc.brynmawr.edu with no subject line and the text SUBSCRIBE BMCR-L. Inquiries and submissions for the list should be sent to bmcr@cc.brynmawr.edu. Electronic publications is irregular and continual, with individual items published as available; the published material is collected and

published in traditional form five or more times a year. Subscriptions to the hard copy publication cost $10 per year; to subscribe, write, Bryn Mawr Classical Review, Thomas Library, Bryn Mawr College, Bryn Mawr, PA. 19010 USA.

6. See Heraclitus, fr. 22, on philosophical inquiry: "those who seek gold dig up a great deal of earth and find little."

7. For a discussion of the medium and its application to the electronic seminar, with a history of *Humanist* see my forthcoming article as cited in note 2, above. To inquire about subscription to *Humanist*, send e-mail to editors@brownvm.brown.edu.

8. See, e.g., Lee Sproull and Sara Kiesler, "Reducing Social Context Cues: Electronic Mail in Organizational Communication." *Management Science* 32 (1986):1492-512.

9. At the time of writing, a survey of the members of *Humanist* is in progress by Professor Judith Weedman, School of Library and Information Studies, University of California at Berkeley, to determine "the role that the electronic list *Humanist* plays in its subscribers' work."

10. Most speculation about the e-book has involved hypertextual models: see, e.g., Nicole Yankelovich, Norman Meyrowitz, and Andries van Dam, "Reading and Writing the Electronic Book." *IEEE Computer* 18.10 (Oct. 1985): 15-30; George P. Landow, "Hypertext in Literary Education, Criticism, and Scholarship." *Computers and the Humanities* 23(1989): 173-98; Kathryn Sutherland, "A Guide Through the Labyrinth: Dicken's *Little Dorrit* as Hypertext." *Literary and Linguistic Computing* 5(1990): 305-9.

11. For additional information on these and other textual databases, see *The Humanities Computing Yearbook 1989-90*, ed., Ian Lancashire (Oxford: Clarendon Press, 1990).

12. Vannevar Bush, "Memex Revisited," in *Science is not Enough* (New York: William Morrow and Co. 1965): 92.

13. For the cultural background, see Willard McCarty, "The Shape of the Mirror: Metaphorical Catoptrics in Classical Literature," *Arethusa* 22(1989): 161-95.

14. See, however, T. Russon Wooldridge, "A CALL Application in Vocabulary and Grammar," in *A TACT Exemplar, CCH Working Papers* 1(1991): 77-86; Chris Tribble and Glyn Jones, *Concordances in the Classroom: a resource book for teachers* (Harlow: Longman, 1990).

15. For a preliminary prospectus on this research, see Willard McCarty, "Finding Implicit Patterns in Ovid's *Metamorphoses* with *TACT*," *CCH Working Papers* 1(1991): 37-75; the project is currently funded by the Social Sciences and Humanities Research Council of Canada under grant 410–92-0748.

16. The program is *TACT*; see John Bradley, "TACT Design," in *A TACT Exemplar, CCH Working Papers* 1(1991): 7-14, for a brief description of the software.

17. The problems of getting to ideas through specific words should not be underestimated, but neither should the value of making the attempt. I have focused on these problems in a paper given at the joint conference of the Association of Literary and Linguistic Computing and the Association for Computers and the

Humanities, Oxford, UK, April 1992, "Peering through the Skylight: Towards an Idea of the Electronic Edition"; this paper is due to be published in *Research in Humanities Computing* '92 by Oxford University Press.

18. John F. Burrows, "Computers and the Study of Literature," *Computers and Written Texts*, ed. Christopher S. Butler. Applied Language Studies (Oxford: Blackwell, 1992):167.

PLENARY SESSION II:
JUNE 21, 1992

Professionals or Professionless, Information Engineers or ???

Karen A. Schmidt

There is a Sufi folk tale about a wise old woman that seems somehow appropriate to the topic at hand. There was a village that was faced with some terrible unspecified dilemma, and no one knew what to do. Finally, someone remembered the wise old woman who lived outside the town. She was known throughout the land for her wisdom and insight, and so the villagers called her to them to help them with their problem. When she arrived, they explained their situation and asked for her help. She told them, "I can tell you the answer to this problem, but of course you already know what I am going to say, don't you?" Not wishing to offend, the people said, "Yes, of course," to which the wise old woman said, "Fine, then, you don't need me," and went away. The perplexed villagers called her back the next day and restated the problem, to which she said, "Well, I guess you really don't know what I am going to say, do you?" The villagers all agreed that indeed, they

---

Karen A. Schmidt is Acquisitions Librarian and Associate Professor of Library Administration, University of Illinois at Urbana-Champaign, 246 Library, 1408 West Gregory Drive, Urbana, IL 61801.

© 1993 by The Haworth Press, Inc. All rights reserved.

didn't have a clue, to which the wise old woman replied, "Well, since you don't know what I am going to say, you wouldn't understand it anyway if I told it to you," and she went away. The villagers were beside themselves and called her back yet another time, and when she returned and posed her question, half of them said "Yes, we know what you will say," and the other half said "No, we can't imagine what you will say." At this, the wise old woman threw up her hands, walked out of the village and left the people arguing among themselves about how much they knew and didn't know, and she never came back.

I am not a wise woman, and I am not so terribly old, but I do know how this woman must have felt. The challenge here is to talk about the future of librarianship and information science and how technical service librarians will fit into this picture, and is surely as the wise old woman knew it, I know that half of the NASIG group will know what I am saying (to which I tell you, "Go home now!"), and the other half will feel just as strongly the opposite way (to which I tell myself, "Go home now!"). Still, the topic deserves frank and frequent discussion and perhaps these ideas will provoke some good exchange.

Librarianship and technology and information science are the bywords of many discussions today. Far from being happy housemates, however, the concepts seem to be headed for divorce court. From where I stand, it looks like librarianship may be giving up custody of the children, paying child support and alimony, and suffering the scorn of the community at large. Two recent seminal articles illustrate this situation: Ross Atkinson's "The Acquisitions Librarian as Change Agent in the Transition to the Electronic Library,"[1] and Gillian McComb's "Technical Services in the 1990s: A Process of Convergent Evolution."[2] Both of these articles shed light on the topic at hand and are useful vehicles for discussion.

Atkinson divides the library operational world into delivery and mediation, and suggests that online information exchange will serve as a catalyst in synthesizing various library functions into one scholarly information delivery system. Acquisitions' role would be greatly expanded to be the link between information engineering and its by-products and the library. McComb uses the theory of convergent evolution (where two unrelated species begin to act alike and so come to resemble each other) to describe how technical service work can be integrated and streamlined through the vehicle of automation and technology, so that librarianship will become more of a seamless whole. Changes will occur in both the internal operations of the library and the external provision of information to the university at large, and libraries will be strengthened by adapting to the changed universe wrought by technological advances.

While taking different tacks–and sometimes different points of view–towards the same topic, both of these contributions focus on the impact of technology on information transfer in our daily working lives. McComb invites us to a holistic approach to librarianship that has been in place in a number of libraries with varying degrees of success for some years. In fact, as I read this piece, I was reminded of the early jobs of most librarians throughout this country, where the concept of holistic or ecumenical librarianship was a fact of life and not a point of debate. Many of her points are satisfying, but I remain bothered by the idea of technology driving the train.

This is most especially true with Atkinson's article. This has been a widely discussed, even hotly debated, article among acquisitions librarians. I was intrigued to discover that lots of people disagree with his premise, but often in a whisper. No one wants to be the acquisitions librarian that gets left out in the cold with no technology to administer. There is a sense of discomfort out there about his basic premise, and I will suggest that discomfort lies with the notion that our future worth is defined by technology and information engineering. What if he's right? What if our work as acquisitions librarians or serials librarians or catalogers as we know it isn't valuable any more? What if we get stuck in the back room with the paper byproducts that no one wants, while everyone else is out there interfacing with CD-ROMs and schmoozing with the invisible college on the Internet?

Abraham Flexner, a sociologist who devoted a good portion of his time to thinking about what constitutes a profession, noted back in 1915 that "... professional activity [does not] derive its essential character from its instruments; the instrument is an incident..." of the thought processes which control its use.[3] Jesse Shera, who straddled both sides of the librarianship/technology fence at various times during his distinguished career, was much persuaded in his later critical thinking by Flexner's ideas. Shera became convinced, as are many of us, that librarianship is an idea service based on the acquisition, organization, and interpretation of knowledge records.[4] The role of information science and technology is to aid in organizing, arranging, and obtaining knowledge. It does not interpret that knowledge, does not and can not give it body and meaning. I do not mean to suggest that either Atkinson or McComb is planning to toss out librarianship in favor of information science, or that they believe that technology should drive our work entirely. I do find, however, that these articles and many, many others on the same topic, seem to want to move us into a future that does not fully embrace librarianship.

What is librarianship? A colleague, Joe Barker from the University of California at Berkeley, recently expressed his vision of librarianship in a discussion of what he refers to as "information soup" and the "information soup hungry."[5] The idea and its relationship to librarianship so intrigued me that I want to share some if its essence, as I understand it, with you. "Information soup" represents the body of everything we can know about, and the "information soup-hungry" are those who wish to know about these things. Barker notes that libraries are invented realities for coping with these two groups, and, perhaps more importantly, while the library exists in the physical sense, it is not necessary for those seeking information from the library to confront it physically. I was reminded by this of my catechism class that posed the question: "What is the church?" to which, if I remember correctly, the correct response is: "NOT the building, but the thought and spirit."

There are several levels to Barker's presentation that are relevant to this discussion but too lengthy to replicate here. In short he suggests that libraries need to concentrate on how to stay competitive and vital in the interaction between the "information soup" and the "information soup-hungry." Libraries must reinvent themselves so that our response to the chaos of the "information soup" is meaningful to the hungry.

This point of view does not ignore information technology, but rather represents an approach to librarianship and information technology that is at once both pragmatic and idealistic: pragmatic in the sense that it places librarianship, information technology and the body of thought that has developed around these ideas in their proper perspective, and idealistic in that it embraces the best of these two related but not equal approaches to information and knowledge. It directs us to ask the question: What kind of relevance does information science and technology have for librarianship? The answer is that technology has become a requirement of our work, affecting the way in which we acquire, organize and interpret our knowledge records ("information soup," if you will), but has not fundamentally changed the acquiring, organizing and interpreting. This question cannot gracefully be turned on its head. The question "What kind of relevance does librarianship have for information science and technology?" does not invite meaningful answers. Librarianship is not a requirement for information technology.

I would argue that the single most important factor that will have an impact on librarianship in the future is money, not technology. It is money–or lack thereof–that will cause us to seek new and more economical ways in which to conduct our work. It is money that will put a societal value on what we do and help set the parameters for our success. It is money that will develop new technology to help us navigate less chaotically through the "information soup." The marketplace has been and will continue to be the determining factor for much of how our future looks, including the future of information technology.

I want to believe, and I have to believe, however, that librarianship is not solely driven by the marketplace. It is a service-driven, not-for-profit enterprise that enriches our experience in and knowledge of life. Idealistic, perhaps, but one hopes that it is these finer motivations that led most of us to librarianship in the first place. Librarianship is subject to five laws that have stood up to time and technology, laws that, sadly, many students in our newly renamed schools of library and information science do not recognize. These are:

- Books are for use.
- Every reader his book.
- Every book his reader.
- Save the time of the reader.
- The Library is a growing organism.

Since Ranganathan first introduced these principles, little has happened to alter their basic truth. The syntax–"book" for example–may need to be updated, but the laws are still the laws and still represent librarianship. Not information engineering, not information science, not information technology, but librarianship.

Having said this, I am mindful of the quote: "The past is gone, the present is full of confusion, and the future scares the hell out of me." While I am not persuaded that technology will take over my raison d'être as a librarian, I do have a healthy respect for its impact on my work. What will the future of technical services librarianship be like, if it does not turn us into information engineers?

I would count myself more successful among the navel-gazing crowd than the crystal ball-gazing crowd, and also want to avoid, at all costs, the likelihood that someone in 2022 will point out something I predicted in 1992 and have a good laugh. For these reasons, and for the more solid reasons that the future is neither predictable nor predetermined, I will avoid trying to be too specific. There are general trends that should be acknowledged and discussed, however.

Technical service librarians have a wonderful advantage in our relatively long-term, and increasingly close, association with vendors, publishers, and others in the for-profit world where much of the much of the technology we deal with is developed. The alliances we have established here are mutually beneficial and will become more and more critical to our ability to deal with the "information soup." I heard the earlier discussions at this conference that information vendors may become information brokers, and hence one of our competitors for the "information soup hungry." While there are some questions that can be raised about the development of products and services that might compete with libraries, that discussion should not overshadow the heart of this issue, which is the symbiotic relationship between libraries and vendors/publishers that has been and can continue to be so vital.

Certainly the greatest impact of technology on libraries has been and will likely continue to be in automation. In fact, one of my colleagues at the University of Illinois Urbana Library recently observed that, despite all the talk about technology and its impact on our daily working lives, the only impact she had ever seen of any consequence in libraries was the impact of automation on cataloging. I have not settled into my own point of view about the truth of this statement, although it is probably true for technical services work, if not for reference and other public service work. Automation, through the online catalog and its offshoots, has allowed us to rethink our organizational structure and the way we exchange internal information. It has permitted us to share our records among libraries and to interact on a professional level in ways unimagined in earlier times. I will insist, however, that it has not changed the fundamental nature of our work in acquiring, organizing and interpreting knowledge.

Pundits who claim for themselves the title of "futurists" have been brave enough to claim themselves futurists have told us of the demise of the librarian, the demise of the book, and the demise of the library. I suspect that some of these people are cut from the same bolt of cloth as people who suggested that television would destroy radio, although there are always the majority of the more sanguine among the futurists. Throughout the 1980s and into the 1990s we have heard about the impending demise of the book and the mergence of the paperless society, and we have also heard the reports from the field of the increase in paper use as computer and CD-ROM users press the "print" button with total abandon.

There is no denying the growth of the electronic book. Kurzweil's 1992 *Library Journal* articles on the Powerbook and the emergence of the Virtual Library attest to the exciting developments in new forms of paperless reading.[6] As he points out, the virtual book requires that we rethink the concept of buying a book, and this is where changes in our working lives can occur. Certainly there has been, and will continue to be, a niche in our libraries for new forms of communication, requiring that we come up with procedures for–yes, again,–acquiring, organizing and interpreting it. It requires that we stay abreast of new developments in electronic communication, that we work together and not against one another, and that we continue to develop our fruitful relationship with those who represent the research and development end of this new technology.

From where I stand, it looks like we are doing all of these things. In serial publishing, for example, we have already created a medium for communication with publishers on pricing as well as format. In acquisitions work, we are connecting through ALA and other organizations with the creators of new technology to establish new ways of doing business. Catalogers are working to develop ways of describing new forms of communication. Administrators are tackling the problems of ownership, copyright, circulation and use issues for items in electronic formats.

Nattering nabobs of negativism will say that we are soon to be left behind in the fight to serve the "information soup hungry" unless we bow to technology and information science. Bowing indicates subservience, to which, I will hazard, most librarians are not inclined. Librarians have been handling the products of the future long before it became fashionable to rename our schools "information science" centers. Librarianship, which is largely a profession of women, and hence somewhat devalued over the years, has managed to deal maturely and assertively with the for-profit industry and its services and products without a diminution of status. Embracing new technologies is a positive, realistic, and wholly familiar step for us. It is not an enterprise that is enhanced by trying to make our work more "scientific."

Is there going to be a time when researchers turn to places outside the library for information? Of course. They're doing so now, they were doing so before automation and technology became sophisticated, and they will do so in the future. It is what the invisible college and the electronic bulletin boards are all about. Our job as technical service librarians is to stay in touch with the entrepreneurial world and to be the translators of that world to ours. The voice of reason, and in many ways one of the voices of our collective conscience as librarians, Michael Gorman, reminds us that "The future of technical services, and of librarianship as a whole, lies in keeping our eyes on the mission of libraries and adapting our tools and methodology in the light of modem technology ... The first key to successful services in the future ... lies in the judicious use of modem technology to enhance our continuing purpose."[7]

NOTES

1. Ross Atkinson, "The Acquisitions Librarian as Change Agent in the Transition to the Electronic Library," *Library Resources & Technical Services* 36, no. 1 (January 1992): 7-20.

2. Gillian M. McCombs, "Technical Services in the 1990s: A Process of

Convergent Evolution," *Library Resources & Technical Services* 36, no. 2 (April 1992): 135-148.

3. Abraham Flexner, "Is Social Work a Profession," *School and Society* 1 (1915): 902-903.

4. Jesse H. Shera, "Librarianship and Information Science," in *The Study of Information*, ed. by Fritz Machlup and Una Mansfield (New York: Wiley, 1983), 379.

5. Joseph Barker, "Acquisitions Principles and the Future of Acquisitions: Information Soup, The Soup-Hungry, and the Five Dimensions of Library 'Reality'," paper presented at Feather River Institute on Acquisitions and Collection Development, Blairsden, California, May 29, 1992; proceedings to be published in *Library Acquisitions: Practice and Theory*.

6. Raymond Kurzweil, "The Future of Libraries," *Library Journal* 117 (January 1992): 80,82; 117 (February 15, 1992): 140-141; 117 (March 15, 1992): 63-64.

7. Michael Gorman, "Postscriptum: Technical Services Tomorrow," in *Technical Services Today and Tomorrow*, ed. Michael Gorman (Littleton, CO.: Libraries Unlimited, 1990)196.

From Past Imperfects to Future Perfects

Gary J. Brown

I've chosen as the title for our wrap-up "From past imperfects to future perfects," a paradigm in the most literal and original of senses–verb conjugations; and two of them that, as a budding student of language, always gave me trouble–the past imperfect and the future perfect. My simple mind could not fathom why the past, much less the present, and even the future, by golly, had to be divided into imperfect and perfect aspects. (After all, isn't the present world we live in imperfect enough, without having to deal with the past as an imperfect world as well! And why do we need to project a future perfect? Everyone knows the future isn't even here yet. And what makes us think, really, that it's going to be any more perfect than the present!) It finally sank in, however, and realized that there was sense to those verb paradigms–and even more than that, there was complexity and nuance. As speakers, thinkers, writers, planners–we can position ourselves toward the past and the future in different ways. Flexibly filled with nuance and different meaning, and relying upon the past while standing in the present, we could project out into the future–something that not only will be, but from our vantage point of knowledge, something that will have been intimated in our models of the future. Ah the beauty of that paradigm–the future perfect! But let's not jump ahead of ourselves here. One step at a time and without confusion, please.

It was Thomas Kuhn who spoke about paradigms, not as charts of verbs and tenses, but as models or patterns for understanding the process of change. His study of fundamental change in *The Structure of Scientific Revolutions*, alerted us, back in 1962, to shifts in

---

Gary J. Brown is Region Manager, Midwest, The Faxon Company, 2741 Simpson St., Evanston, IL 60201.

paradigms as a mode for conceiving and addressing the nature of fundamental change. My job this morning will be to attempt to throw a little light, or darkness–depending upon your view–on our current transformation of "past imperfects." Perhaps I can begin to focus this attempt by asking some questions: Will the scholarly communication system we are building and transforming for the future discard the imperfections that we so eagerly want to leave behind? What will ease of access, speed of distribution, instant communication and reaction, lead us to? New knowledge, deeper knowledge, more knowledge, more insightful knowledge? Will the system we create allow us to focus more efficiently and readily upon the desired end results of scholarly communication? Obviously it's difficult to answer these questions at this stage, but nevertheless, it is important to keep them in mind as we build coalitions and define new actors and new roles.

In the time we have remaining, I'd like to offer some thoughts on where we are and where we are going; thoughts about our not so necessarily imperfect past and about the not so necessarily future perfect. I'd like to summarize, very briefly, the technological realities we're experiencing, consider the present and future challenges facing us, suggest a model for the process of change and transition, and finally discuss the barriers and impediments to the creation of the future perfect envisioned and implied in our models.

THREE-PHASE SCENARIO

I find us talking about paradigms and shifts, experiencing them and groping with them, in ways not unlike a student of language groping with new verb paradigms. Our challenge however, is to try to forge something that in the ultimate leads to and supports the fundamental processes of knowledge creation and knowledge use in ways that are not merely more efficient than previous modes. If we look at the current phase of innovation, our primary concerns are focused on the delivery and distribution of networked information. In some ways it is undoubtedly more efficient and effective than the distribution and dissemination of our paper system, but in other ways it may be less efficient and maybe even less cost effective.

The simple fact is we don't know what it will cost. (Most of the use we make of the Internet has not been accompanied with a monthly invoice.) We are still at the early stages of proposing economic models, launching projects to gauge use, cost, and expected revenue, and looking for the viable combination of fixed text in a paper environment and digitized text in an electronic environment. As examples, think of the proposed READI Program of the Coalition for Networked Information and Elsevier's TULIP Project. With projects such as these we are signaling a second phase of implementation or modernization (if we use the term suggested by Clifford Lynch) where we are just beginning to address the issues of copyright and cost. I would suggest that eventually we will enter a third phase, a phase of full integration or transformation (appearing at a later date and after much fallout), in which the focus shifts away from the necessary foundations of the network, distribution, copyright, and the cost of information, to the process of how information and knowledge is received and manipulated, how it is read, analyzed, evaluated and transformed in the digitized environment. In short our concern will shift to network tools and applications that will make research procedures and the creation of new knowledge more efficient and effective. We will deal with the psychologies of reading for different purposes–pleasure, information, analysis, criticism, synthesis–and provide intelligent textual software for navigating with these different ends in mind.

THE DIGITIZED AND NETWORKED WORD

Today we are participating in the transformation of concepts and systems that have dominated the communication of scholarly information for centuries. "Paradigms Lost" might be a fitting description of our glance backwards. We are testing the old viability of the library as the physical storehouse of knowledge; of the book as the principal medium for exchanging research; of the paper journal as the most efficient way to communicate new knowledge. In the case of the library, our utilization of technologies that transform the functions of physical storage and physical access into digitized storage and telematic access, allow us to conceive of a "virtual library" with "virtual patrons" who have access without walking through our front doors and security check-points. To many the library is becoming less a building and more a node or an access point on a desktop computer in a home office.

As part of this new reality, we are witnessing the evolution of "fixed text" into "digitized text"; the "paper book" into the "electronic book"; the "paper journal" into the "electronic journal." But the new artifacts of this technological transformation do not augur the complete demise of our Gutenberg-based, paper knowledge system. The book, the journal, and the library to house them, are themselves artifacts of an infrastructure quite sophisticated and complex. We have only to look at the individual links in the information chain to be reminded of this fact.

THE INFORMATION CHAIN

The traditional process of generating new knowledge relies upon an intricate interaction of entities and processes, which have been evolving since the early days of printing in 15th century Europe. The model I am using is a classic conception of the transfer of information (we have Donald King's study on Scientific Journals to thank for it). If we look at it carefully, we will notice the assignment of certain roles: the role of researchers–scientists, engineers or humanists; the role of publishers and vendors; the role of libraries; and the role of A & I services. We could also add the role of ILS vendors. The point to be made here, is that these roles are being radically challenged and altered (See Figure 1).

Let's take a look at the role of publishers, for example. In the construction of a new knowledge infrastructure, digitized and networked words are encouraging new scholarly behaviors–new ways to write, communicate, disseminate, and read. The processes of composition, recording, reproduction and distribution are wrenched from the traditional publisher. The network and digitized communication are changing the way we look at these functions. At the same time publishers are struggling to maintain their role as the conduit and arbiter of what gets published and what does not. And the need for filtered information is perhaps even greater now than

FIGURE 1

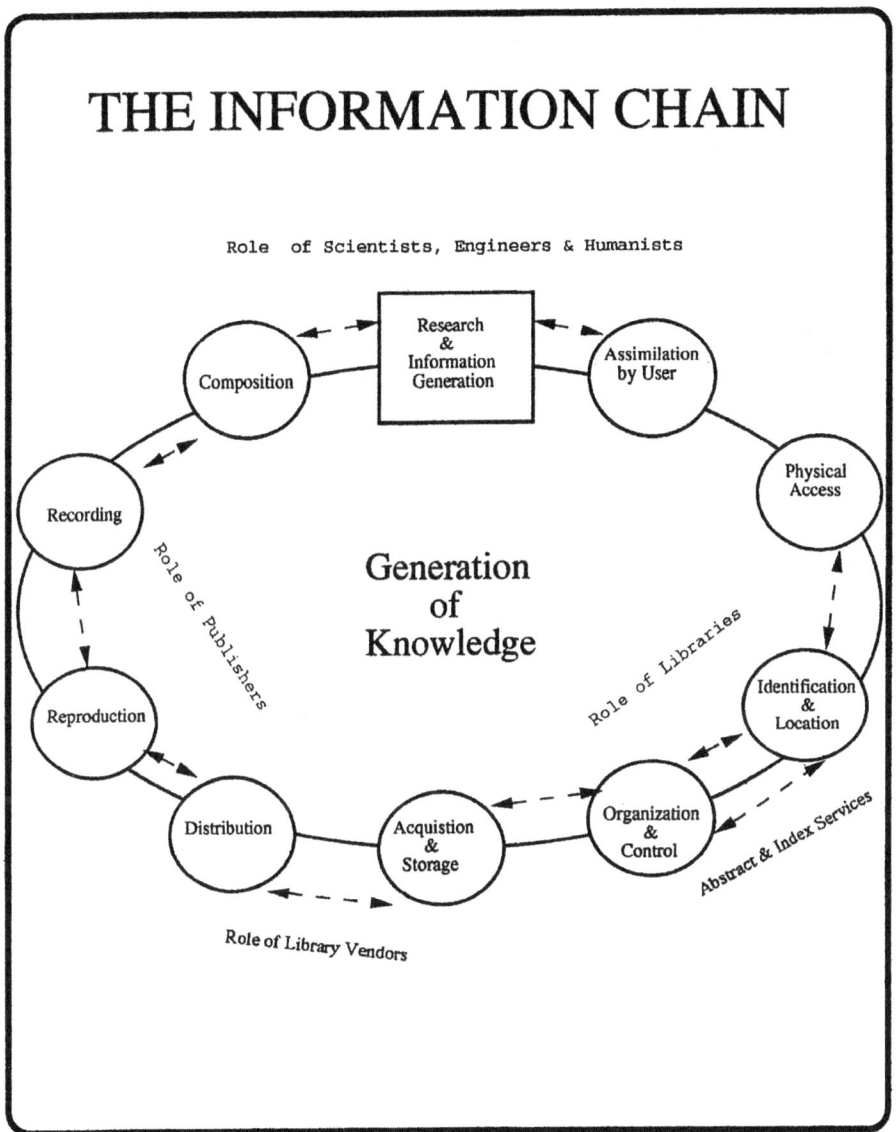

before. Given demands on our time and the superabundance of unevaluated information on the network, we easily become less tolerant of tired, worn-out ideas that incessantly knock on our electronic door. Simply put, the priestly process of peer review provided by the traditional publisher is of high value to a discerning reader. Likewise, the scribal culture of editorial selection, revision and development that has traditionally resided with the publisher takes on a new appreciation.

If we concentrate for a moment on the role of libraries, we see traditional functions: libraries–following the Alexandrian archetype–have acquired and stored, organized and provided control. Libraries also help readers identify and locate information, and of course they provide easy and comfortable physical access to text that is fixed and bound between two covers. The most radical change involves the functions of acquisition, storage and physical access, because the nature of text itself is being altered.

Of course these roles are not going to vanish overnight. More likely, they will gradually be transformed and the actors will rewrite their script as they find themselves performing on a different stage–an altered knowledge-base, where the network, and digitized text reign supreme.

This does not necessarily mean, however, the demise of publishers, or the demise of the library and the librarian, nor for that matter of the vendors who serve those libraries. Nor does it mean that the paper book or journal will disappear. It does mean, however, that certain high-level, high-demand information will only appear in digitized environments–CD-ROM or networked versions. Take as an example the financial marketplace, where high-level, financial decisions are too risk-laden and time-sensitive to be made from data that is paper-based. Information in that environment is old and therefore suspect if it is not electronic.

As the needs of readers and researchers are redefined, the entities that serve them are responding to these needs. This implies a shift from a "possession" model to a "provision" model. I choose not to use the words "ownership" versus "access," because I want to emphasize the redefinition of a dynamic role implied in the word "provision"; it implies a shift from a noun–"access"–to a verb–"provide"; and by so doing, we allude to an immediate collateral support structure that focuses on how access can be achieved, navigated, mapped out, bargained for, influenced, negotiated and funded. "To provide" implies a redefinition of the traditional role; yes, libraries have always "provided" information, but now the network and the digitized environment are becoming a primary access point. Libraries and librarians, publishers, and vendors are looking at ways to become providers, ways to add value to the process of accessing digitized information, ways in which to create consultancy opportunities at the heart of the knowledge and research process itself.

PRESENT AND FUTURE CHALLENGES

So first off, some of our present and future challenges imply an active search for, and embrace of, changing information needs. These challenges, by the way, are not exclusive to any specific actors–publishers, libraries, vendors. They apply to us all. Part of the negotiation we need to conduct involves collaboration with new actors in new roles. But our primary focus in collaborating with these actors should always be to link users with sources of information. In many instances information will be mediated by these new actors, be they publishers, vendors, or libraries. (Witness the developing document delivery arena: ARL libraries and ARIEL, CARL Uncover 2, Faxon Research Services and OCLC, EBSCO, UMI.) As we rewrite the script, I think we will find ourselves forced to become more central to the creation of, formation of, and use of new knowledge. The definition of new tasks and responsibilities will arise from our commitment to "provide" this information rather than merely set up the gateways to access it. Providing this information conveniently means devising opportunities for education, devising software and support mechanisms to help users navigate our systems and perform their bibliographic searches with ease and growing expertise because of our efforts of mediation. The challenge of "provision" requires that we become conversant with the technology of access and the pathways of the network.

MODELING CHANGE

As we indicated, the traditional model of information transfer—the information chain—is being radically challenged. The old model presents roles in a process of exchange and transfer with the different entities relating to each other as brokers of information disengaged from the creation of added value and enhanced service.

An evolving knowledge management matrix focuses on the transfer of information from a different perspective. It presupposes the content-specific nature of the search for information and the building of a knowledge base. This model casts the relationships of the players in very different ways. It considers the interaction of entities as evolutionary and constitutive because these entities become more intimately involved in the knowledge creation process (see Figure 2).

At the institutional level libraries and publishers strive to provide highly mediated services with added values that frame and constitute a body of information; for example, a table of contents database that allows SDI or profiling capability according to individual reader interests; or intelligent software applications that scan digitized and SGML prepared text, providing an outline, headings, paragraph openings, conclusions, and other significant key ideas to the reader.

At the individual level, in this model, readers are writers who create knowledge in the process of consuming it. Their access to information can be mediated or disintermediated. At the extreme form of disintermediation, writers and readers play interchangeable roles in a community of learning, communicating directly in a collaborative working environment where information is created and consumed simultaneously. Here the institutional players do not participate in or mediate the process. An approximate example, could be what Stephen Harnad refers to as "Scholarly Skywriting."

This model helps us focus on the redefinition of roles. It functions most appropriately if we realize that the bottom layer of institutions supports the top layer and is in turn defined by the individual's research content needs and interests. As such, one of the roles of the institutions, it follows, is to discern and develop mediated support for readers and writers in the content field of their interest.

FIGURE 2

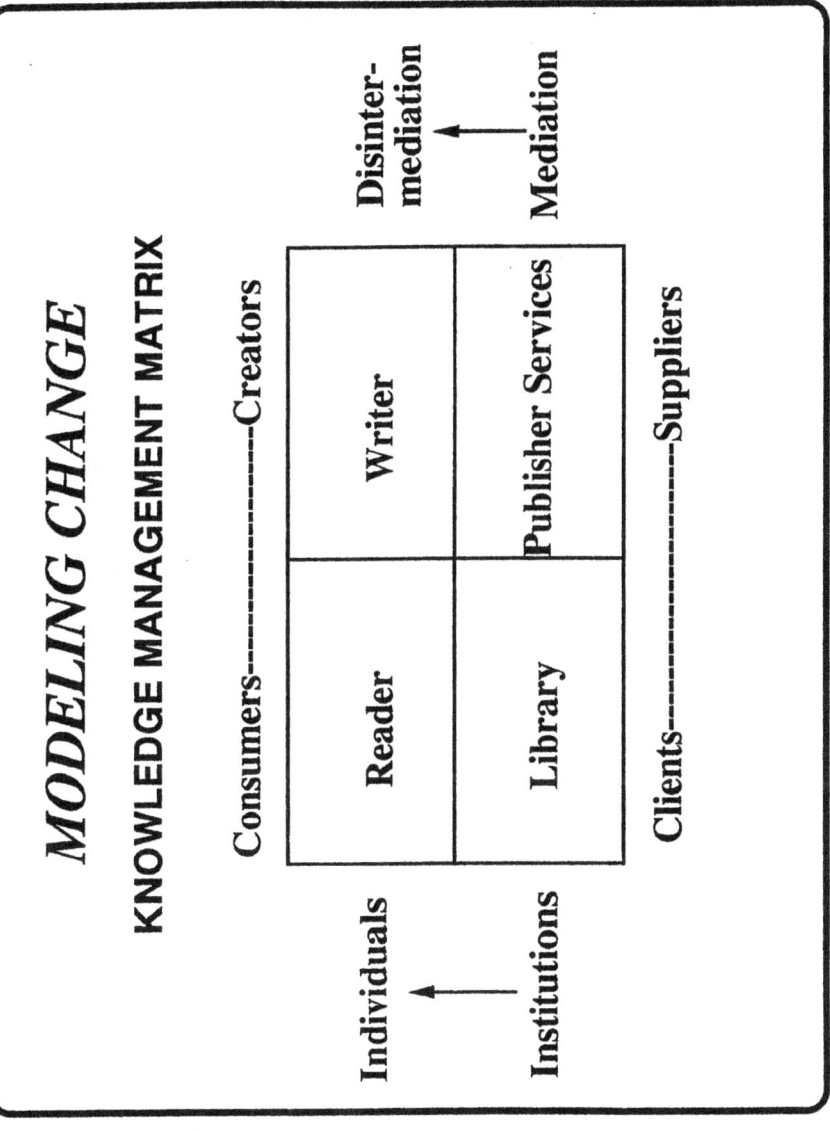

TRANSITION CHALLENGES

If we were to make a "to do" list in order to focus collective interests and move us through the transition challenges, maybe we would come up with something like the following.

As the shift of resources moves away from traditional formats, paper to electronic, we can expect to see information that is high in demand–hot information–increase in cost. Information that is low in demand–cold information–may even become more difficult to produce, or it will very possibly be produced inexpensively through networked capabilities–the electronic journal or the electronic interest group. Fragmentation of formats with only one medium available may also occur.

In attempting to re-define roles for supporting our client-patrons, we will be successful if we help them manage the two worlds–paper and electronic–they will constantly be moving in and out of. Have you noticed that today very few people take handwritten notes from the texts consulted in libraries? The accepted mode is to copy the material and then cite from it in the body of new text that is created. We have reached the stage where it is feasible to speak of readers and writers creating and building their own personal, digitized texts, rather than the traditional mode of creating and building a "personal library" of materials. At one level, in the accomplishment of this reality, I have in mind scanning technologies and the capabilities of uploading digitized text to personal computers. At another, broader level, I am considering the capabilities of the Xerox Docutek, a high speed printer/copier that digitizes text and allows us to manipulate and network it efficiently, or Xerox's new "Paperworks" technology that compresses 25 pages of text into one page of glyph language and can fax this information directly to and from a computer. These are both examples of attempts to manage and traverse the boundaries of paper and electronic environments that we confront as readers and writers.

Another transition challenge, that is becoming a cliche since we know it more than we want to–is how to do more with less. To meet this challenge we will have to define our agendas and eliminate the non-essentials. This means dealing with change both professionally and personally so that we do not allow frustration to debilitate our effectiveness. Doing more with less calls for reorienting ourselves from a time of abundant funds to a time of shrinking funds and increasing service demands. And in the process of managing this transition, we need to deal with acceptance and avoidance behaviors while at the same time devising strategies for recovery from the breakdowns so that we can limit the recurrence of frustration and stress.

BARRIERS AND IMPEDIMENTS

At the 1992 ACRL conference in Salt Lake City, Paul Saffo spoke about information technologies and the future of the library. He cautioned that the future will take longer to arrive than we think. He posited a thirty-year incubation period for all new technology: ten years of doing the same old things with new gadgetry, ten years of "creative chaos" in which we try out new applications with the new technology, and then ten years of maturity, which will turn out to be utterly unexpected in its manifestation (a process parallel in some aspects to what I have referred to as innovation, implementation-modernization and integration-transformation). Saffo offered Gutenberg's printing press as a perfect example: initially it was used as an easier way of producing incunabula, but it ended up revolutionizing society with the explosion of printed text, widely disseminated in small octavo-sized books–convenient enough to slip into a saddle bag and travel across Europe. Change, Saffo maintains, will be late to arrive but when it does, it will be more fundamental than anything we imagined.

I'd like to focus briefly on some of the barriers that may impede the arrival of the radical change we talk about. It may allow us to understand that such change will not necessarily occur the way we think it will and that the results may be entirely different from what we anticipate.

Without a creative or cooperative solution to copyright, the building of a new knowledge infrastructure could be slowed or greatly compromised. In this respect, resolution may ultimately lie in some form of new legislation. If you haven't had a chance to read the contributions regarding copyright in the special issue of *Serials Review (v. 18, no. 1-2, 1992)*, I highly recommend them.

The explosion of information, the disproportion of knowledge being created and knowledge being consumed, outstrips our financial means to acquire it. Highend, expensive information can easily create an intellectual underclass, disenfranchised from the flow of knowledge. Our society and political values imply a democracy of the mind with shared, easy access to information.

Technology lags, however subtle, also contribute to slowing down the rate of change and full acceptance of a new environment. As an example, think of the current delivery of text over the Internet. Aside from the all the discussion about the electronic book or the electronic journal, what we have, in actuality, is a reversion to previous, older technology, a technology that ante-dates the codex–namely the papyrus scroll. The digitized text we read on our terminal screens is but the text of an electronic scroll that forces us to read in serial, sequential fashion from beginning to the end. Although there is a developed hypertext capability which allows us to navigate through text in an intuitive fashion, this technology is yet to be delivered in our current environments. And even when it is delivered, the main question remains that we as readers are not in full control of the reading process.

We are used to reading fixed text in completely random, intuitive ways. Sometimes in reading an article we begin at the conclusion and make our way back to the beginning; or we begin with the footnotes and read through; or we scan paragraph openings and endings throughout the text. A serial presentation of scrolling text does not allow us to read analytically, as we are accustomed to do in fixed text. We struggle with the psychological residues of reading fixed text in a digitized environment.

While we deal with digitized text as if it were fixed text–it looks the same and is presented in the same familiar format–in reality, the text on our terminal screens is more analogous to an oral culture. Words appear and disappear in digitized environments just as words appear and disappear in the oral flow of speech. In our use of electronic mail we have transformed a verbal process into a written process. The medium for communication is not the telephone, but the terminal, where we let our fingers do the talking, remaining mute, while signing to each other electronically. Although we have transformed our customary mode of communicating over the telephone, our new digitized text medium is still grounded in orality and speech.

PROJECTING THE FUTURE

Projecting the future is always condemned to failure. But in our travel down the roadway, if we have no perspective of where we have been, our trip may not be as directed as we would like it to be. Marshal McLuhan's metaphor of the mirror in the roadway is emblematic of the process. My final words are taken from AnnaLee Saxenian, an economist from the University of California at Berkeley. They focus on our need to create new institutions that foster partnership and exchange as we attempt to project the future:

"Our greatest challenge is to transcend our prized individualism and create institutions that foster collaboration and interdependence without sacrificing autonomy and individual initiative."

BREAKOUT SESSION A:
NEW STRATEGIES FOR PUBLISHING

New Strategies for Publishing

Robert Bovenschulte
Maria L. Lebron

Presenters

Michele Crump

Recorder

Lois Smith from the Human Factor Society convened the session with introductions for Robert Bovenschulte, Vice-President for Publishing of the *New England Journal of Medicine* and Maria L. Lebron, Managing Editor of the *Online Journal of Current Clinical Trials*.

Bovenschulte presented his view of the current economic environment and the choices it offers scholars, librarians, and publishers in eleven predictions for the future. The "Eleven Conjectural and Disputable Assertions" or "Eleven Self-Evident and Unremarkable Orthodoxies" are as follows:

Michele Crump is Instructor/Librarian, University of Florida, George A. Smathers Library, Acquisitions Department, Gainesville, FL.

1. The economic base underlying the system of scholarly communication is showing increasing strain, and is not likely to improve.
2. Economic circumstances will force scholars and learned societies representing them either to bear greater financial burden for scholarly communication or to forgo some services.
3. Librarians will be increasingly driven to economize by reducing acquisitions; incentives will grow for them to compete with publishers.
4. Publishers will face declining demand, higher costs, and lower profit margins for print publications.
5. Publishers will feel even greater pressure to justify that what they contribute to the scholarly process is worth what they charge.
6. Technological innovations affecting the scholarly process will alleviate the situation but not remedy it, because funding constraints will retard full utilization.
7. Technological improvements in the efficiency of producing print will delay, but not avoid, the day of economic reckoning for most publications.
8. The demand for document delivery will grow substantially, turning into a sizable business, but the economics of print publishing will be adversely affected.
9. The government will emerge as a greater and more aggressive player, which will be to the detriment of publishers.
10. Copyright issues will be settled eventually–more often in favor of users, not providers.
11. Those seeking to take over the role of publishing from established companies and organizations will find that it looks easier to do from the outside than it is.

Bovenschulte said that, if his predictions come true, scholars, librarians, and publishers may react in several ways. Scholars might respond with a willingness to spend more money to support the current system, or unite with librarians to boost funding, or sidestep librarians and publishers in the communication process, or choose to struggle through with less. Librarians may reply with increased deselection, resource sharing, and document delivery, or force a crisis by refusing to pay increased prices, or work with scholars to solicit more funding, or take on more publishing functions. Publishers could answer by maintaining the status-quo of financial policies and strategies, or cutting profit margins to preserve the system, or employing technological innovations to reduce cost, or incorporating with other businesses.

With his predictions and feasible responses in mind, Bovenschulte offered three scenarios to illustrate the full range of future possibilities. Scenario one, called "Catastrophe," describes a bleak outlook; Scenario two, named "Drift," relates a "more of the same at the same rate"; Scenario three, tagged "Renewal," suggests a "resurgence" in support for all levels of education.

Bovenschulte asked the audience, with a show of hands, to select a scenario which will "most likely happen." The majority chose the "Drift" scenario saying it best describes the future of scholarly publishing and libraries. Bovenschulte concluded that, even though this is a gloomy outlook, hard times offer scholars, librarians, and publishers the opportunity to work together for "transformation." He reminded the audience that a "wild card" scenario is the not yet imagined setting which is always a real possibility.

Maria Lebron offered a real example of new publishing strategies with a preview of the electronic journal *Online Journal of Current Clinical Trial* which begins publication July 1, 1992. This electronic journal of medical research is a cooperative effort between the American Association for the Advancement of Science (AAAS) and OCLC. As stated in the brochure Lebron distributed, AAAS provides "the focus and editorial content" and OCLC supplies "the graphic displays and distribution technology." Subscribers to the journal will access the journal by using a single PC workstation, preferably an IBM 386 or compatible which employs Windows 3.0 or 3.1 software and a modem. The annual subscription fee for unlimited free connect time does not include the telecommunication charges. However, the subscription offers the user tailored search capabilities and subject area notification when an article of interest appears in the journal.

Lebron discussed the advantages to publishing a journal in electronic format highlighting such features as: self-contained format including text and tabular; interactive; easy to use; immediate access to primary medical research; no space limitations. On the other hand, she pointed out that electronic journals still have technical limitations (for instance, they can't handle special characters and complex graphics using half-tones). She added that economic limitations in storage cost and equipment availability further limit user access.

Lebron stressed that this publication is not a bulletin board or an e-mail discussion list, because all articles submitted will undergo peer review before publication. She outlined the journal's rigorous peer review process, which generally takes ten days. The definitive, online copy of an article, in typeset quality, is ready to go within forty-eight hours of acceptance. Thus each article published in the journal receives simultaneous worldwide release and offers the subscriber automatic access. Subscribers may download articles without charge and/or request reprints for a small fee.

Smith led a brief question and answer session following the presentations. The audience wanted to know which scenario Bovenschulte thought would most likely occur. He thought the "Drift" scenario the most probable, because he feels the economic environment "is not bad enough" for the "Catastrophe" scenario to take place. He added that we need to establish a ten year perspective so the scholarly, librarian, and publishing communities may progress eventually to a "Renew/Transformation" scenario.

Lebron answered general questions about peer review, advertising, and site licensing. The journal will not carry advertising nor will it offer, for the time being, any site licensing. She stressed again that the journal is indeed a journal and not a database because it maintains peer review of the information selected for publication.

BREAKOUT SESSION B: PRICE STUDIES: WHY AND HOW

A History of Journal Price Studies

Barbara Meyers

Convener

Barbara Meyers, President, Meyers Consulting Services, began the workshop with a brief overview of the history of journal price studies. Some of the earliest studies were Meyers' efforts at the American Chemical Society, starting in 1978. These were produced annually until 1982 and then biennially ever since. The studies remain an ongoing part of the Society's market research activities.

The American Mathematical Society published their first price study in 1983 with an update in 1987. As consultant to the Optical Society of America, Meyers conducted price studies in optical science and engineering on an every-other-year basis since 1984, all of which have been published. The American Physical Society conducted a single price study, which was published in 1986 and two other societies have published one-time price studies: the American Mineralogical Society in 1988 and the International Union of Crys-

---

Barbara Meyers is President, Meyers Consulting Services, 1836 Metzerott Road, Adelphi, MD 20783.

tallography in the same year. The American Geophysical Union also produced some price studies in the 1970s.

Meyers' is currently preparing a bibliography of published studies based on publishers' research on the costs in cents per thousand words or characters.

Meyers' studies have all been on the micro level, which complements studies by librarians (such as Astle and Hamaker) on the macro level. Since macro level studies compare only the absolute or subscription prices of a serial title they do not present an even playing ground for all journals. The vagaries of trim size, number of pages, typesetting, and the like are only taken into account by the micro level study based on cost per thousand words or characters. Thus, coupling the micro and macro studies provides a complete picture which can be extremely helpful for collection development.

Meyers and Janice Fleming, Director of Publications, Optical Society of America, published an article on serials price analysis in the May 1991 issue of the *Journal of Academic Librarianship* (vol. 17, no. 2, pp. 86-92). The article describes the first application of the micro level price study methodology. Also, the article stresses that price studies (at either level) cannot be used in a vacuum, when evaluating serial retentions and cancellations. Rather, the authors suggest using other quantifiable measures in tandem with price studies; for instance, a serial's impact factor within its subject area, the number of reprints distributed to authors, and the number of articles requested, by serial title, for ILL.

In conclusion, Meyers restated a fundamental point from the article. It is critically important to have all the quantitative data collected through price studies and other research efforts linked to qualitative data collected by serials practitioners from their user community (faculty, technical staff, etc.). Only by combining all these variables can a true assessment of a serial be made in terms of its value to the library serials collection.

Libraries and the Use of Price Studies

Deana L. Astle

SUMMARY. Given the shifting paradigm to access from ownership and the competing demands on the materials budgets from new services within academic libraries, price studies which use a "unit cost" to compare journal titles within a given discipline are becoming a more important component of the review process as libraries determine which serial titles to add and which to delete. Several studies are available from societies, and some librarians have designed their own. Longitudinal studies, which show trends in "unit cost" over time are especially helpful, and several of these are discussed.

Price studies are an important component of the review process for serials when they are added to, or more often, deleted from, the collection of libraries. As librarians have become increasingly savvy consumers bent on getting the best information value for our limited dollars, we have embraced well prepared quantitative analyses of titles to accompany use studies, faculty perceptions of worth, and citation studies in determining what to buy and what to retain in the collections.

The need for price studies becomes readily apparent when we look at the realities facing academic libraries today. Budgets, especially for state supported institutions–or state assisted as many of us call ourselves now–have not increased very rapidly, and the portion of the academic pie allocated for libraries, while never enough to cover the rising cost of materials let alone the growing demand for more services, must often be defended vigorously against competing demands from other campus interests. This is especially true

---

Deana L. Astle is Assistant Dean, Clemson University Libraries, Clemson, SC 29634.

© 1993 by The Haworth Press, Inc. All rights reserved.

when dollars are scarce. When the issue of faculty raises is pitted against the need for increased money for the libraries, salaries tend to win hands down. In addition, given an average of a 10% increase in serials prices in each of the last ten years, a serials list worth $1 million in 1983 would require $2,357,948 in 1992 just to maintain the same titles, let alone add any new ones. The dollars are not there; choices must be made; and titles must be culled which are deemed to be less important or not cost-effective for the institution.

There has also been a major paradigm shift in the attitude towards higher education over the last forty years. A commentator in Newsweek stated that in the 1950s when universities and colleges were suddenly swamped with people taking advantage of the GI bill, educating the populace at this level was seen as a public good and was supported as such by the taxpayers. Today, higher education is seen as a private benefit for the individual for which he or she should pay, rather than as a benefit to society. If more money is to become available for higher education and for libraries this paradigm will have to shift again–an unlikely event given the present climate.

Within libraries themselves, new technologies are competing with the materials budget for funds. As stated in a recent article in the *Chronicle of Higher Education* "when it comes to technology, libraries face even more difficult–and expensive–choices. . . . the desire to stay current sometimes comes at the expense of traditional materials and personnel."[1] Reallocation of resources is a reality, with the budget for acquiring material for permanent retention in the library often taking a cut as more demand arises for online databases, CD-ROMs, and full text delivery; and as more emphasis is placed on providing information just in time rather than just in case. Recent figures from the Association of Research Libraries clearly show this trend; during the period 1985/86 to 1990/91, interlibrary borrowing increased by 47 percent and interlibrary lending by 45 percent while serial titles purchased dropped 2 percent and monograph volumes purchased dropped 15 percent. Identification and subsequent provision of information regardless of its format or where it is held is becoming the major goal of library service and as a consequence journal acquisitions are suffering.

With these challenges to our serials budget, such tools as price studies provide information to allow comparison among journals with similar content. Methods which create a "unit price"–such as cents/1000 characters–can indeed provide for relatively equitable comparisons since they smooth out differences between large and small journals. While such studies cannot measure quality, they can indeed identify trends and raise flags for further investigation of individual titles. For example, if one were using a price study as part of a review process for titles in a discipline such as optics and had on hand a price study such as the one published by the Optical Society of America,[2] the titles with the largest cost/1000 characters would probably be selected for more intensive review since their unit cost is higher than those further down the list. It is important to stress, however, that unit price should never be used as the sole determiner of the value of a given journal to a given collection; it must be used in conjunction with how relevant that title is to the curriculum and research needs of the institution, projected number of uses, whether there are factors in a given journal such as heavy use of photographs and graphics which may legitimately drive up the unit cost and the total dollars expended for the title.

While a title with a high unit cost may prove to be needed in a given collection, it is also true that a title with a low unit cost may not be cost effective in all cases. For example, though Elsevier's Brain Research has a not unreasonable cost per article, we at Clemson found we did not need the huge number of articles generated by this publication for the $5000 we were paying. Though important for the research of many faculty on campus, it was cheaper for us to provide them the articles they really wanted through a document delivery service rather than house the many that they might sometime possibly need.

Because librarians have not had the time or resources–or maybe the inclination–to do cents/1000 character studies, we have tended to look at more easily obtainable cost/page or cost/citable article statistics when trying to determine unit cost for comparison purposes. These measures, while probably not so equitable as the more abstract cents/1000 characters, are more easily comprehended and visualized, and as such are more often used. For example, during a recent study of the list of one publisher, I found one title consisting mostly of straight text that cost $2.35/page for 158 pages in 1990 and increased to $4.31/page for 239 pages in 1991. A similar title went from $2.05 per page for 440 pages in 1990 to $4.25 per page for 292 pages in 1991. While further investigation may be needed to determine the "worth" of these titles, legitimate questions are raised. We must ultimately ask if the value of the information provided warrants the $4.25 or $4.31 per page that is being charged.

The following is part of a letter from a music librarian to a publisher who will remain nameless:

> We have just instructed our [dealer] to cancel our subscription to [blank]. The invoice for the forthcoming volume has the outrageous price of $213 for four scanty, 75 page issues. An issue of *The Musical Quarterly* with almost twice the number of pages, is $8.95. An annual subscription to the fat, beautifully printed *Music and Letters* is $85. Twelve issues of *The Musical Times* are $70. *Music Review* is $85. In the USA, *The Journal of the American Musicological Society* is $36. *Opera Quarterly* $48. *The Journal of Musicology* is $52.
>
> You undoubtedly have reasons for charging so much, such as the lack of advertising, just as I have reasons for canceling, such as we're being overcharged for the product. We have adequate funds to purchase your journal, but it is repugnant to us to be taken advantage of.[3]

Librarians are using price studies and look at unit costs however they are defined. We are making comparisons and are making judgements on comparative worth. We are also communicating our observations over e-mail so that findings may be widely and rapidly distributed.

Longitudinal studies–looking at trends over time–are really the most valuable tools for managing collections. Some libraries have been tracking growth in prices, and some have done studies of their own titles. For example, Utah State University did a retrospective longitudinal study of journal prices for those titles held in their library with the stated purpose of getting "control of their destiny." They wanted quantitative information for decision making instead of relying solely on anecdotal information of perceived use. For a twenty year period from 1967 to 1987 cost/page was determined for each of 370 randomly selected journals in all disciplines. Comparisons were then made and trends charted for discipline, publisher type, country of publication groupings, etc. over this twenty year period. They plan to use this data as a guide for purchase and retention of titles. As Marks and Nielsen state in "A Longitudinal Study of Journal Prices in a Research Library,"[4] a report first presented at the 5th annual NASIG conference:

> Now that we have assembled our database for journals in the sciences, technology and medicine, what will we do with it? As we prepare for the inevitable next round of cancellations, we will be able to examine each title on a title-by-title basis to determine how it has behaved in relationship to the rest of the titles we subscribe to within each of the disciplines we are reviewing.
>
> The process will unfold in this manner. We will calculate the mean and standard deviation for each discipline or subject area within our acquisitions budget.... Against that framework, we will plot the pricing history of each journal to determine how it has behaved. If the journal's prices fall within the +1 standard deviation, we will probably assume that the journal does not need extensive consideration in the cancellation review. If the journal is an outlier, that is, its price falls outside the boundary of +1 standard deviation, then it will be reviewed carefully to determine how valuable it is to the programs of the university.... It is quite possible that, after an extended review of one of these outliers, we might still decide to continue the subscription, but, at least we would have identified the title as one of the culprits causing us a long term problem in handling our serial budget.[5]

Another study presented at the same NASIG conference examines price and compares journals in another way. In "Survey of Cost-Effectiveness of Serials: A Cost-Per-Use Method and its Results,"[6] Milne and Tiffany describe an effort to determine "whether it would cost the library more in the long run to subscribe to the serial rather than to provide library patrons with the information by ILL."[7] With a use study and a formula to generate predicted lifetime uses, a cost-per-use was generated by dividing the subscription cost of a title by the number of projected lifetime uses. Interestingly, they found "no correlation between the opinions expressed by faculty members about the value of a particular serial to their work and the cost effectiveness of the library's subscription" and the "serials generally thought to be the 'core' or to have high prestige were not cost effective."[8] They also found that:

> The serials published by a group of eight major commercial publishers [were] more cost-effective than the average for all the serials in our collection. However, even among these publishers, 44% of the dollar value of their subscriptions was found to be cost-ineffective in our library at the present time.[9]

They conclude:

> If we assume that the cost of subscriptions will continue to increase at a more rapid rate than the number of uses patrons make of them, the cost-per-use of these serials will continue to rise, and an even greater proportion of them will become cost-ineffective in the future.
>
> Some publishers are markedly more competitive than others in this regard. To meet this challenge, publishers need to reduce their page costs and to increase the use made of their serials by exerting greater editorial control over what is published. If the quality and relevance of published articles are improved, use should increase. Increased use would keep the cost-per-use low and would assure that the serials remain cost-effective.[10]

Sandra Moline at the University of Wisconsin-Madison took a cents/1000 character study and added another dimension to it. In her article "Mathematics Journals: Impact Factor and Cents per Thousand characters,"[11] she discusses her attempt to determine if any correlation exists between rankings of title by cost/1000 characters and their rankings by impact factor. For fifty-one of the titles in the American Mathematical Society study for which impact factors were available, she discovered that "a higher unit price is not an indication of greater usefulness. More expensive journals do not, on average, have more highly ranked impact factors than the less expensive. In fact . . . the opposite is true to a slight extent."[12] She concludes:

There is no easy way to select or deselect journal titles. No formula provides a foolproof keep or cancel decision. Each title must be considered individually; cents/1000 characters, impact factor, collecting policies, existing collection strengths and weaknesses, local budget constraints, and the research interests of the local user population are among the factors to be considered in these decisions. While it is likely that no one piece of data about a title will be decisive, each bit of information can contribute to the ongoing evaluation of journals in a collection.[13]

Price studies are important to us, and longitudinal price studies which track journals and disciplines over time are very important. As more studies become available, the more they will be used as part of the serials review process. Because of our stewardship–our need to get the most information to the user for the best price–we must make choices as to how we spend our money. The more information that is available to us to allow quantitative comparisons among titles, the better our choices can be. Publishers and Societies are encouraged to commission price studies of titles within disciplines, and librarians who have created their own are encouraged to share.

NOTES

1. Julie L. Nicklin, "Rising Costs and Dwindling Budgets Force Libraries to Make Damaging Cuts in Collections and Services," *Chronicle of Higher Education* (Feb 19, 1992):A29.
2. Barbara Meyers, "How Much is that Journal on Your Library's Shelf," *Optics and Photonics News* 2 (Nov. 1991): 35.
3. *Newsletter on Serials Pricing Issues*, NS 32 (May 29,1992).
4. Kenneth E. Marks and Steven P. Nichols, "A Longitudinal Study of Journal Prices in a Research Library," *The Future of Serials: Proceedings of the North American Serials Interest Group, Inc.* (New York: The Haworth Press, Inc. 1991), 105-35.
5. Ibid.: 128-29.
6. Dorothy Milne and Bill Tiffany, "A Survey of the Cost-Effectiveness of Serials: A Cost-Per-Use Method and Its Results," *The Future of Serials: Proceedings of the North American Serials Interest Group, Inc.* (New York: The Haworth Press, Inc. 1991), 1 37-49.

7. Ibid.: 137.
8. Ibid.: 143.
9. Ibid.: 148.
10. Ibid.: 149.
11. Sandra R. Moline, "Mathematics Journals: Impact Factors and Cents per Thousand Characters," *Serials Librarian* 20, no. 4(1991): 65-71.
12. Ibid.: 70.
13. Ibid.: 70-71.

Index Medicus™ Price Study

Lynn Fortney

INTRODUCTION

Increases in health sciences journal subscription prices have been a topic of discussion for decades, and there seems to be no solution to what will be, inevitably, a continuing problem. Librarians have responded by becoming more knowledgeable about inflationary trends within specific disciplines in order to provide this information to their constituents and make informed decisions regarding collection development and resource allocation. With the *Index Medicus™ Price Study*, EBSCO Subscription Services provides information to librarians in a way that can be used to illustrate in detail the price of providing information to specific groups of library users. The *Index Medicus™ Price Study* examines biomedical journal publishing trends over a five-year period and analyzes these trends by subject category and country of publication.

This is the third year of the study, and it has been met with very positive reviews. I'd like to give you some background about how EBSCO happened to undertake this project and why we set some of the parameters we did. I'll also tell you about some of the ways it has been used in the collection assessment and development processes of some major medical center libraries.

BACKGROUND

We all have empirical knowledge of price increases in some disciplines and also in non-domestic publications, but librarians haven't

---

Lynn Fortney is Marketing Manager of the Biomedical Division of EBSCO Subscription Services, EBSCO Industries, Inc., International Headquarters, Birmingham, AL 35201.

© 1993 by The Haworth Press, Inc. All rights reserved.

really had any definitive proof that they could use to educate their administrators and faculty. To compile pricing information for various medical specialties every year would be a very labor intensive project.

Because most health sciences libraries do not apply subject classification systems to journals in their collection, it is not easy to analyze journal price increases by discipline. Some librarians do assign broad subject headings to journals for budgetary reasons or to facilitate collection development. Subject assignments are commonly made by using the subject listing of the *List of Journals Indexed in Index Medicus*™ (LJI), or the 49 Conspectus Categories: Medical and Health Sciences developed by the Research Libraries Group (RLG), or by pulling the topical field (subject heading) from the 650 field of the MARC record. However, because the application of these subject authority lists to journals is most often done only for internal library purposes, there is no universally accepted standard to provide consistency.

A list of current journal subscriptions sorted by subject can be a very useful tool in a health science library, but it does little to aid in collection development. Current requirements for collection assessment and development include a methodology to measure the library's collection against standard indexes, accepted bibliographies, and/or expert opinion. I mentioned the RLG Conspectus a moment ago. The RLG Conspectus is a valuable tool for participating libraries to compare and evaluate research collections on a chart arranged by subject. The Collection intensity levels are defined as:

- 0 = out-of-scope
- 1 = minimal
- 2 = basic information
- 3 = instructional support
- 4 = research
- 5 = comprehensive

The Conspectus defines research level collections as containing extensive periodical subscriptions capable of supporting dissertations and independent research. Libraries measure their collections against commonly accepted bibliographic tools or authoritative bibliographies. For instance, participating libraries may agree that at least sixty-five percent of the periodical titles pertinent to a biomedical subject bibliography must be received by a library to constitute research level collection for a Conspectus project. One of the most widely accepted and authoritative bibliographies of medicine is, after all, *Index Medicus*™, so in biomedical libraries, collection strength is evaluated based on the *List of Journal Indexed in Index Medicus*™ (LJI). Library staff record both existing collection strengths and current collecting intensities according to forty-nine health sciences categories based on LC Class. Biomedical libraries must force their unclassified journal collection into these categories. This is a very difficult process.

METHODOLOGY

EBSCO had been asked to provide information on journal titles by medical specialty, but as we all know, a good working knowledge of the structure of medical literature is fairly important for its subject classification. Imagine attempting to do so without the benefit of having the piece in hand, because as a vendor frequently all we see is the rather scanty information sent to us by publishers who are interested only in providing the information necessary to filling an order. I was told by the general manager of our Title Information Department, who is a librarian herself: "Most of my people don't know the difference between gynecology and genealogy; there is no way I can expect them to understand the intricacies of Medical Subject Headings." Well, while you and I might see some general distinctions between genealogy and gynecology, nevertheless, I was horrified at the prospect of anyone attempting to categorize an undefined body of biomedical serials by the thousands of terms available in MESH. Even the National Library of Medicine has a problem with this. However, we could see a very real benefit in providing some sort of biomedical subject and price analysis, so we decided to bite the bullet, and as they say, "Just do it." Our first objective at EBSCO was to settle on definition of "biomedical literature" and our second was to decide upon a manageable subject authority list.

Because the National Library of Medicine (NLM) publication

Index Medicus™ is widely accepted as the authoritative index for the health sciences, we decided to use all active titles in this index for the purposes of this study. Based on information gleaned from online searches of NLM's SERLINE ® database, we identified about 3,000 active titles currently indexed by *Index Medicus*™. This figure excludes ceased titles that are nevertheless included in the 1992 edition of the *List of Journals Indexed in Index Medicus*™ and active titles that NLM discontinued indexing prior to 1992.

It is very difficult to present a year-to-year comparison of *Index Medicus*™ titles as the Indexing Section and the Serials Division of the National Library of Medicine maintain "fluid" databases that are continually changing. Another problem we face is the phenomena of "daughter" journals that can be purchased as separate subscriptions, but can also be included in the subscription to the "mother" journal. The problems encountered in trying to maintain an accurate serials list (e.g., Is this piece really indexed? Is this a new title or a title change? Has this title died or has indexing ceased? How are these titles related?) are the same as those encountered daily by beleaguered serials librarians everywhere.

EBSCO's Title Information Department performs research continuously, and all *Index Medicus*™ titles are researched just prior to running the initial reports to ensure that the title information database used for this analysis contains the most current publishing and price information available. Editing one bibliographic item actually requires updates to several records as many titles have several different price listings: airmail, surface mail, members, individuals, institutions, libraries, and geographic regions or countries. For the purposes of this study, we use EBSCO's main price listing, which is the surface-mail, non-member rate paid by libraries in the United States The subsidiary listings such as airmail, combined titles, and rates for libraries outside the U.S., are not included in this analysis as a title with five or six subsidiary price listings would artificially skew the overall average for a specific subject. About nineteen percent of *Index Medicus*™ titles are either published irregularly, and therefore have no prepriced annual subscription rates, or are free on request, as is the case with many journal supplements. These titles are not included in the calculations.

We developed a list of 114 subject headings for this project. The headings are based primarily on those used in *LJI*, but in order to accommodate the needs of libraries involved in RLG conspectus projects, many *LJI* subject areas were combined or renamed in favor of the RLG health sciences conspectus categories. For the purposes of this ongoing research, we use only one subject heading per title so that the cost of the entire *Index Medicus*™ list can be calculated accurately in a subject sort.

In well over fifty percent of the titles, a single heading is not obvious, e.g., *American Journal of Obstetrics and Gynecology, Biochemica et Biophysica Acta*. As an arbitration device, I use the current MEDLINE® file and assign subject headings according to the predominant theme of the articles in recent issues. Subject headings relating to primary care such as "pediatrics" are favored over medical subspecialties, and consideration is given to the subject discipline of the contributing authors as ascertained by the address field of the MEDLINE® unit record. Subject headings that I've assigned are then added to both the main and subsidiary listings in EBSCO's title information file.

RESULTS

From the information in the title information file, I have our data processing department run two historical price analysis reports covering the past five years. One report lists all *Index Medicus*™ titles sorted by country of origin. We manipulate the information from these two reports in several different ways and use the results to produce the *Index Medicus*™ *Price Study*. Preliminary examination of these reports for 1992 indicate that the average price of an analytical chemistry title is highest ($1,320.75), followed by biochemistry ($970.73), and neurosciences ($793.45). It is costing libraries 330% more in 1992 that it did five years ago to purchase all of the titles on acquired immunodeficiency syndrome, primarily because there are more titles now than there were in 1988. Another area requiring a substantial level of increased support is biotechnology at a 252% increase since 1988. The *Index Medicus*™ *Price Study* also provides an analysis by country of origin, which is particularly important as only about thirty-five percent of the titles indexed by *Index Medicus*™ are published in the United States.

APPLICATION

The primary benefits of *Index Medicus*™ *Price Study* is to help librarians effectively communicate the growth of biomedical literature and the fluctuating costs of the intellectual resources necessary to support their institutions' faculty and research staff. However, beyond the study itself, information used to produce the *Index Medicus*™ *Price Study* enables EBSCO to provide to its client libraries several tailored reports, including a complete list of all *Index Medicus*™ titles sorted by subject. This is one of five statistical analysis reports of subject strengths and weaknesses. Collection intensity is based on the ratio of titles purchased by the library through EBSCO vs. titles indexed by *Index Medicus*™ in any given subject area. These reports have proved to have a direct benefit for many libraries who have used the data to justify budget increases. From the comments we have received in the past year, librarians are using the study and our reports to look at serials collection development in a more systematic way and to make better informed decisions on journal cuts.

BREAKOUT SESSION C: COPYRIGHT AND LICENSING IN THE ELECTRONIC ENVIRONMENT

Copyright and Licensing in the Electronic Environment

Anita Lowry
Sanford Thatcher

Presenters

Laurie Sutherland

Recorder

This NASIG/SSP/AAUP Concurrent Session focused on librarians' and publishers' copyright concerns in the electronic arenas of CD-ROMs, tapes and networking.

Anita Lowry, Deputy Head, Butler Reference Department, and Director, Electronic Text Service, Columbia University, has been involved with integrating computer-based source materials in the humanities and history into Columbia's collections and providing services to support them. From her experience she sees de facto

---

Laurie Sutherland is Serials Acquisitions Librarian, University of Washington Libraries, Serials Division FM-25, Seattle, WA 98195.

© 1993 by The Haworth Press, Inc. All rights reserved.

models emerging in electronic licensing and subscription agreements for control, access, pricing, and payment.

Lowry described the various models for control. The traditional model for printed materials–ownership–has largely been abandoned for electronic publication, apparently because publishers are nervous about the economic implications of ceding these rights to owners. The ownership model is being replaced by a number of access models.

In the perpetual license model the publisher retains all rights of ownership, granting back to the licensee only those rights specified in the contract. In return a library can retain the resource for as long as needed. Most scholarly electronic texts and software published as monographs use this model.

The temporary license model is the standard model for serial electronic publications. Libraries pay to gain temporary use of the electronic resource, but must return the superseded disks. If they cancel the subscription they must send back the last disk received and any accompanying software.

In the online model, access is sold in limited portions of time or quantity, and the public is dependent on an information provider who may be the sole source. Lowry has little faith in the willingness of the information industry to provide access to specialized databases or backfiles when they are no longer deemed economically viable.

Lowry examined two models for access–number of users and classes of users. In the first model, based on the number of users, the standard license for an electronic product says that at any one time the product may be used only by a single user on a single machine. Here electronic publishers are exploiting the computer's potential for sophisticated organization and retrieval, but are nervous about how potential for access might affect the profit margin. Other options include simultaneous, multi-user access over a network and single-user access from a variety of points on a network. But Lowry believes that prices for the use of electronic databases on a campus LAN or WAN are often too high, and that this approach seems problematic in a world that increasingly expects network access.

The second model restricts access to particular categories of users, such as a single department. It strikes at the heart of the academic librarians' perception of mission and service, generates negative feelings, and forces librarians to police users.

Finally, Lowry described models for pricing and payment. Pay-per-use makes a certain sense in theory, but is a deterrent to those interactive information retrieval methods that emphasize browsing (and usually result in a large number of hits).

Paying a single price for unlimited usage is the other major pricing model and is, in her opinion, a major factor in libraries' and users' acceptance of CD-ROMs.

A hybrid model is the flat-rate annual subscription that pre-pays for a specified number of online searches. This model allows the library to budget but opens up the option of charging back costs to users. Lowry believes this model abdicates the library's responsibility to support the use of electronic information and discourages successful searching methods.

The READI program (Rights for Electronic Access to the Delivery of Information), sponsored by the Coalition for Networked Information, is addressing these issues in a comprehensive way. But for specialized electronic materials in the humanities, the non-commercial nature of many of the major players in production will influence the models of control, access and pricing.

Sanford Thatcher, Director, Pennsylvania State University Press, presented the publisher's viewpoint on copyright. He emphasized that copyright is not an obstacle to progress, as it has sometimes been viewed. There are powerful practical and political considerations that make overthrowing copyright an ambitious, even utopian, task. For example, copyright is succeeding internationally as never before; the U.S. copyright industries maintain a positive trade balance; it is doubtful Congress will address the issue soon; and the conservative Supreme Court is unlikely to present a fundamental challenge to property law.

If copyright is here for the foreseeable future, the question is how to adapt it for the new electronic environment. The Copyright Act of 1976 was written with technological change in mind; the "right of public display," for instance, implies that electronic distribution of a text would be legal only if you have the permission of the copyright holder. Thatcher agrees with Ann Okerson that we must reallocate costs. He suggested that her vision of universities retaining control over their faculty's intellectual products can be accomplished within our current copyright system. Legally, universities could argue that faculty's research is work done within the scope of their employment.

Thatcher believes solutions must be sought in technical devices, licensing agreements, reallocation of economic costs (and, associated with that, a restructuring of the publishing industry, at least the scholarly division), and moral education.

Technical solutions could make it more difficult to violate copyright. Journal articles could be encrypted and copyright notices added, or storage or reproduction of copyrighted text in an electronic device could be checked and recorded.

Creative licensing agreements, now in the earliest stages, offer more flexibility than formulaic models and can be written to insure possibilities for experimentation in searching, ease of use, simple processes and procedures, and above all, good faith cooperation among the players.

In the past, journal publishing sustained an even cash flow that made up for the drainage of monograph publishing. But now both kinds of publishing are imperiled–monographs because libraries have reallocated resources to pay for costly scientific journals; and journals (at least the paper variety) because of the competition from faster, cheaper electronic versions. Unless university presses can produce and market electronic products themselves, Thatcher does not see a very long future ahead of them in journal publishing. He does not expect university presses to take over scientific journal publishing, as has been advocated, unless university administrations suddenly plow vast sums of money into press budgets.

University presses will either have to abandon the publication of monographs in some fields, or find some alternative form of publishing. He has proposed a pilot project in which the Big Ten university presses, instead of *printing* monographs, would *deposit* them in an electronic database to be maintained by the Big Ten university libraries.

He offered this scenario for the future. By 2001 presses will abandon much of traditional monograph publishing in print form, since it will have proved to be economically unfeasible. Presses will concentrate more on publishing scholarly works with broader appeal. Those presses that haven't abandoned journal publishing altogether will issue many journals in electronic form only. But a good deal of both monograph and journal publishing will revert to the professional associations. Librarians will have become specialists in facilitating "just in time" access.

Thatcher closed by condemning the moral myopia of academics who only care about their narrow self-interest and by reflecting that many people have yet to learn what is in their own enlightened self interest.

BREAKOUT SESSION D: PRESERVATION: FUTURE STRATEGIES FOR RETAINING THE PAST

New Books from Old: A Proposal

David Cohen

Library work is replete with ironies. My favorite example is the so-called 80/20 rule where no matter what size the library collection is, you can be sure that only 20% of the books will ever circulate. The ironies seem to multiply when you introduce publishers and scholars into the equation. Our universities hire scholars who do research. The universities then provide additional support, stipends, grants and the like, to conduct this research. When the research is finished, the university pays subventions to publishers in the form of page costs so the research can appear as a journal article. The university library then pays to subscribe to the journal, and now the university may pay for the same information in an electronic format. These ironies perhaps are the focus of some of the other NASIG/SSP sessions. This morning, however, I would

---

David Cohen is Director of Libraries, College of Charleston, Charleston, SC 29424.

like to consider yet another irony; preservation, that subset of library work which revolves around old, embrittled books, and the art and craft of book repair and conservation, may offer a new paradigm for library acquisitions and book publishing. This morning I will describe a project, very much in the planning stage, which uses scanning and high speed computer printing technology to produce on demand copies of out-of-print books.

Now I do realize that I am at a NASIG meeting speaking to an audience of serials librarians who believe that monographs acquisitions is a fairly straightforward business–the proverbial "piece of cake." The librarian working with monographs acquisitions buys a title, pays the invoice, and sends the book on to cataloging. Few of the arcane problems of serials librarianship ever emerge. But, serials librarians, let's show some sensitivity here. Monographs acquisitions does have its problems. All too often book orders come back to the acquisition department marked out-of-print, out-of-stock, or indefinitely out-of-stock. While this problem may seem fairly prosaic compared to the difficulties of a serials title change, it can prove quite frustrating. Our library once owned a copy of the *Journals* of the French artist, Eugene Delacroix, but it is now missing. Nevertheless, it is needed for a class assignment. In fact, the professor who teaches the seminar on 19th century art originally planned to ask his students to buy copies of the *Journals*, but a quick check of *BIP* showed that the book was no longer in print. As a last resort, the professor turned to the library. Could we put it on reserve for his class? Like the bookstore, we let him down. Our copy, which I am sure had circulated many times, eventually turned up missing and we were never able to replace it. An angry art historian simply doesn't believe that Delacroix's *Journals*, arguably one of the classics of art history (certainly that is what he is arguing!) is simply unavailable for students.

Traditionally librarians have had few options for purchasing out-of-print material. In our library we work as follows. Our jobber returns on order to us as "op." If the title is less than about fifteen years old, we send it directly to the publisher. Sometimes, perhaps ten to twenty percent of the time, in fact, the publisher fills that order. But most are truly unavailable. We maintain "want lists" which we periodically place with out-of-print dealers. Still, the majority of our titles never make it to the "want list," since they have not been singled out as absolutely necessary to meet curricular or research needs. The situation is improving. Certainly the advances in computing make the maintenance of want lists a relatively straightforward matter. New services are emerging, such as the Faxon service, which complement the work of the traditional out-of-print service.

Nevertheless the failure to obtain important out-of-print items remains a serious problem for librarians. A recent study in the *Journal of Academic Librarianship* revealed that 41% of the books listed in *Books for College Libraries* were out of print. The data from that study is now over two years old and the percentage of key titles from the core collection now out-of-print can only have increased. Another analysis, of a want list from Franklin and Marshall College, revealed that many of the out-of-print books needed by that library were quite new. Some 39% of the titles they needed were published during the 1980s; another 36% were published during the 1970s; 13% were from the 1960s; 4% from the 1950s; and 8% were published before 1950. In other words the vast majority of the out-of-print books that the librarians at Franklin and Marshall need had gone out-of-print very quickly and were still covered by copyright.

Why do books go out of print? Why do they stay out of print? The obvious answer is economics. The publishers do not believe that they can make money by reprinting. One publisher reported to me that his company would reprint any title which he believed would sell 200 copies, but clearly even signalling the importance of a book in a bibliography like *Books for College Libraries* does not guarantee 200 sales.

By now you must see that I believe there is a whole class of material–books, monographs–for which there is some demand but the demand is insufficient to warrant reprinting. Perhaps there are only three of four libraries that need a given title. Should that title be unattainable? Should the 20,000 + BCL IIIs remain unavailable?

Now at this point I would like to shift gears and turn to a discussion of new preservation technologies. In particular, I would like to describe to you a project at Cornell where staff in the library and computer center, working with Xerox Corporation, "have been collaborating... to test a prototype system for recording deteriorating books as digital images and producing, on demand, high quality and archivally sound paper facsimiles."[1] At Cornell, the staff have produced digital images of 1000 math books from the turn of the century and "recast" these images into "new" books which then are returned to the shelves of the library. The project is remarkable, because it yields data and insights on many issues involved with scanning, storing, retrieving, and networking, as well as cost and workflow information.

Production begins in the Preservation Department of Cornell's Olin Library where two technicians take turns operating a high resolution image scanner. The scanning activity includes initial set-up, on-screen inspection, scanning, storing to optical, and transmission for printing; staff have been able to achieve scanning rates in excess of 1500 pages per day. Staff transmit the digital files created in the Preservation Department over Cornell's TCP/IP network for printing to the Xerox Docutech printer located in the computer center. This printer then produces 600 dpi pages from the electronic files at the speed of 135 pages per minute. Note that the printer can print much faster than the books can be scanned. Image scanning rates for other types of documents can be done more quickly, often using an automatic "bin" feeder, but the fragile quality of the paper and the demanding requirements of producing a copy in every way like the original mean that a person must put the individual pages of the original on the platen for scanning. Still, even with faster rates of scanning, the scanning rate will not approach the printing rate of the Docutech:

> The image quality is quite satisfactory. Again I quote from a Cornell report: There is less than 1% variation in print size from the original; skew results only when the edge of the original is not parallel to the page trim: front to back registration is reproduced within 1/100th of an inch of the original; the contrast between text and background is sharp; and the 600 dpi resolution compares favorably with the capture capabilities of photocopy...[2]

The Cornell project is exciting. I think that it is a "peek into the future" of library and information services. The Cornell configuration is the only networked version out of Xerox. They are literally moving images of books all across campus. Another component, local access, where users can access the full digital images of fifty math books, produces on screen images which are quite acceptable for end-users. The 200 dpi images can be enlarged for close reading; the user can select individual pages after browsing through tables of contents or indexes and make a request to print all or part of the book.

With so many dimensions to a project, it will be some time before librarians and others can follow up on all the possibilities. For my purposes, interested as I am in the problem of the out-of-print books, several points about the Cornell project stand out. The image resolution, 600 dpi, is high. The facsimile copies closely resemble the original texts. Except for the quality of paper, which is far better for the facsimile, the two cannot really be distinguished. And the productions rates attained at Cornell, 1500 pages a day seem high enough to indicate that speed of production for on-demand printing may keep overall costs down. In fact, the library staff at Cornell have found that the preliminary cost data approximates $100 per volume.

To summarize, there is a problem. Libraries need many books that are now out-of-print but are still covered by copyright. Publishers do not believe that this demand warrants reprinting these titles. The experience at Cornell provides a model for an on-demand printing process.

Working with a librarian at Amherst College, I have just received a small grant from the Commission on Preservation and Access to explore this idea. Specifically, we would like to determine if it is feasible to establish a not-for-profit corporation, to keep needed, recently published books in print by scanning them and by using the Docutech printer to produce a limited number of copies of the out-of-print books on demand. We call the proposed corporation "IBID." We envision an operation which works along the following lines. Cooperating publishers will forward requests for out-of-print books that they receive to IBID. At the same item, they might assign titles from their out-of-print back lists to IBID. The IBID corporation plans to contract with an experienced reformatting agent, someone like Solinet, Maps, or the people at Cornell, to do the actual printing. As long as books consigned to IBID remain under copyright, IBID will pay the publishers or their representative (i.e., the Copyright Clearance Center) a fee for each book copied and sold. The publisher will continue to be responsible for any royalties due the author. The copyright holder, usually the publisher, will retain the right to withdraw any title at any time to reprint it. IBID will have the right to advertise any book in its electronic library as a publication of the original publisher available through IBID. IBID will distribute the books it produces to dealers, bookstores or individual customers.

As you can see, our project calls for a very special relationship with publishers. We need the publishers to help us in several ways. We want to negotiate agreements with publishers to select titles for IBID from their "op" backlists. We want them to let us know when a title becomes "op" so we can consider it for IBID republishing. And we want them to notify IBID when they receive requests for titles they once had in stock but that are no longer available.

Why should a publisher help us? We see many advantages for publishers:

- The publisher can keep a book in print forever.
- The publisher satisfies a customer who otherwise is unable to obtain the title he or she needs.
- The publisher maintains a positive relationship with an author by keeping the author's book in print.
- The author and the publisher receive additional revenue without making any additional expenditure.
- The publisher has access to and perhaps ownership of an electronic image of a work it owns.
- The publisher receives additional marketing data about whether the demand for a title is sufficient to warrant reprinting that title.
- The publisher can eliminate the costs incurred in storing and distributing books for which there is little demand by declaring these titles out-of-print but available through IBID.
- Lastly, the publisher gains additional knowledge of new technologies for scanning, printing, and distributing information without incurring significant developmental costs, while still maintaining copyright.

Some publishers do have reservations about the project. We do not plan to sell or distribute the electronic images of the books. Many publishers feel that the guarantees are not in place to prevent illegal copying.

Still, the benefits to the library are quite obvious. The library will receive a copy of a book, identical to the original, probably better than the original because it is printed on acid free paper and has a sound library binding. The turn–around time will be much better than it is with the normal out–of–print search and costs should approximate those of a new book, $40 to $50 a copy.

If librarians know that they can count on being able to obtain any book on demand that we have digitized, they may begin thinking in new ways about interlibrary loan, collection development and even the use of space within their buildings. For example, a library might choose to buy a book from IBID rather than request it on interlibrary loan (assuming a reasonable turn around time). Librarians faced with the need for more shelving space may consider buying a book for which they envision little demand beyond the initial request, without necessarily adding it to the collection. A strategy like this makes more and more sense as construction costs reach $150 per square foot. Some librarians might even consider weeding their collection based on a list of books available from IBID.

Frankly this paper is without a conclusion. That is not altogether surprising in view of the fact that I am simply describing a proposal for future action. I hope that I have the opportunity to come back to a NASIG/SSP meeting and report conclusions and findings from the IBID project. In the meantime, I'll just finish by asking for your help. I would like people who are interested in IBID, especially publishers, to give me their ideas and perhaps to volunteer to participate. Thank you.

NOTES

1. Anne R. Kenney and Lynne K. Personius, "Update on Digital Techniques," *The Commission on Preservation and Access Newsletter,* Number 40 (Nov–Dec 1991), Newsletter Insert, p.1 1991.

2. Ibid, p. 3

BREAKOUT SESSION E:
REGIONAL LIBRARY NETWORKING:
NEW OPPORTUNITIES
FOR SERVING SCHOLARSHIP

Regional Library Networking: New Opportunities for Serving Scholarship

Jim Neal

Presenter

Glenda Thornton

Recorder

In this breakout session, Jim Neal, Dean, University Libraries, Indiana University, described the networking efforts of academic libraries in Indiana, identified technological trends encouraging library cooperation, and projected the impact of networking on libraries and scholarly communication.

In 1987 the academic libraries in Indiana met to form SULAN, the State University Library Automation Network. The member

---

Glenda Thornton is Associate Director for Library Services, University of Colorado, Denver, Auraria Library, Lawrence at 11th St., Denver, CO 80204.

© 1993 by The Haworth Press, Inc. All rights reserved.

libraries developed a plan with a list of objectives. Topping the list were full implementation and maintenance of local systems (all of the members are using NOTIS), retrospective conversion of their cataloged collections, and enrichment of the SULAN database by the inclusion of other collections. Another was the ongoing ability to assess system developments in light of changing technologies and network environments. Other goals included providing access to all faculty, students, and citizens in the state; enhanced resource sharing and document delivery; and development of expanded access to networked information on the Internet. Members recognized the need for cooperative collection and resource development, as well as a need for more general cooperative planning among libraries and other agencies in the state. Finally they realized the need for more energetic staff development in technical areas. As these goals have been achieved, the reality of expanded access, enhanced search capabilities and the embellishment of the database has created a challenge for the libraries to keep their users up-to-date. The need for improved student, faculty, and citizen information-literacy has never been greater.

The automated information environment presents technical complexities such as increased functionality and performance, more diverse types of digitized information, high-density storage, downloading capabilities, and artificial intelligence software that creates new possibilities for the retrieval of information. Powerful search tools, round-the-clock remote access, rapid dissemination of new information, and increased awareness of the physical location of resources are all new challenges for libraries and their users.

This enhanced information environment creates computer network issues that, so far, have not been adequately dealt with. At the local campus level most concerns center on the need for a common framework to accommodate expanding interconnectivity, technological diversity among the network's participants, the drive for improved performance, and the need to develop a skilled user population.

At the network level, questions arise such as: Who will have access? Who will pay for development, implementation, use and maintenance? How will development and access be managed? Copyright and security concerns increase when the potential exists for individuals to locate and access almost unlimited sources of information! As the private, for-profit sector gains access to the Internet, the potential for commercialization of this information raises other possible concerns.

Finally, Neal discussed flow these technological developments have added to the current debate over access vs. ownership of information and the creation of the "virtual library." Neal believes that the "virtual library" cannot exist without the "virtuoso library" (the research library which acquires materials comprehensively) and the "virtuous library" (the research library that is willing to give others access to what it has acquired).

The current automated information environment has created enormous expectations among the information literate public, expectations which libraries cannot fulfill. Technological babel is overshadowing the fact that most library users do not currently have the skills required to navigate the information-rich electronic networks successfully.

The concepts driving SULAN--universal access to integrated information via the desktop workstation, high-performance shared resources, and high-speed access to scholarly and institutional information--will also drive the library technology of the future. Indiana University Libraries are committed to the concepts of expanded access, communication, and dissemination of information. SULAN is a step in that direction. More research and development is needed to improve access to and use of information. Better tools for filtering, analyzing, and manipulating information must be forthcoming for automation to truly serve the growing community of scholars around the world.

Regional Library Networking: New Opportunities for Serving Scholarship

Barbara von Wahlde

The State University of New York University Centers located in Albany, Binghamton, and Stony Brook (hereafter referred to as the University Centers) have been working for the last several years on a variety of cooperative projects that support collection development and resource sharing. The purpose of the cooperative endeavors is to improve access to resources for our scholars and students without a proportionate increase in individual library costs. Additionally, we want to maximize the effectiveness of the dollars currently being spent on our collections. Such cooperative endeavors can provide concrete experience and different models for a new vision of the library–a vision based on access to information rather than ownership of enormous, burgeoning collections.

The title of this presentation emphasizes regional library networking. The word "networking" can be used in two distinct senses. The first is cooperation; we "network together," i.e., interact and build on relationships with a variety of players and partners. The second sense is utilizing a physical telecommunications system to support our intellectual and philosophical networking efforts. The regions involved in networking can be small or large, local or state-wide; they can even overlap state boundaries. In Buffalo, for example, we have regional affiliations with libraries in the "3-R's" of Western New York (a system based on the geography of New York State and supporting information-sharing among libraries of

---

Barbara von Wahlde is Associate Vice-President for University Libraries, State University of New York at Buffalo, 433 Capen Hall, Buffalo, NY 14214.

© 1993 by The Haworth Press, Inc. All rights reserved.

all types in a particular region). At the same time, the University Centers are all members of the Research Libraries Group, which has a large constituency in New York State, including several private institutions (Cornell, Syracuse, Rochester, NYU, Columbia) and the New York Public Library. This regional New York network of RLG libraries is integrated into the program of the Research Libraries Group, which has members both in the United States and abroad. Also, the University Centers are members of OCLC and work within New York State through the OCLC Network, which is both national and international in scope. Another regional state network making considerable progress with an elaborate, multifaceted integrated library system is Ohio Link, a group of academic institutions supported by the Ohio State Education system. Yet another model is the University of California system and the California State College system in California. The Florida Library Automation Project is an example of a state system in which one vendor is used as the integrated library system for the universities in the state. As mentioned above, some regions presently cross state boundaries or have different sorts of affiliations that draw like institutions together. An example is the CIC group (the Big 10 plus Chicago), operating in the Midwest and in Pennsylvania.

The focus today, however, is on the University Centers as a subset of the SUNY family of educational institutions. SUNY is composed of a number of institutions, from the University centers to the affiliated Community Colleges, all of which receive some support from the State of New York. The attached map (Exhibit A) shows the locations of the members of the SUNY "family" (four University Centers, four Health Science Centers, thirteen Colleges of Arts and Sciences, four Specialized Colleges, two Statutory Colleges, five Colleges of Technology/Agriculture, and thirty-five Community Colleges). The connections shown on the map are through SUNYNET, the state network for higher education, and NYSERNET, a mid-level, regional network serving as our connector to the NSFnet, which provides the Centers with Internet access. New York State also has a network for school teachers and a network for government agencies. The telecommunications environment in New York is rich and complex.

At a recent invitational RLG meeting in Ypsilanti, Michigan held

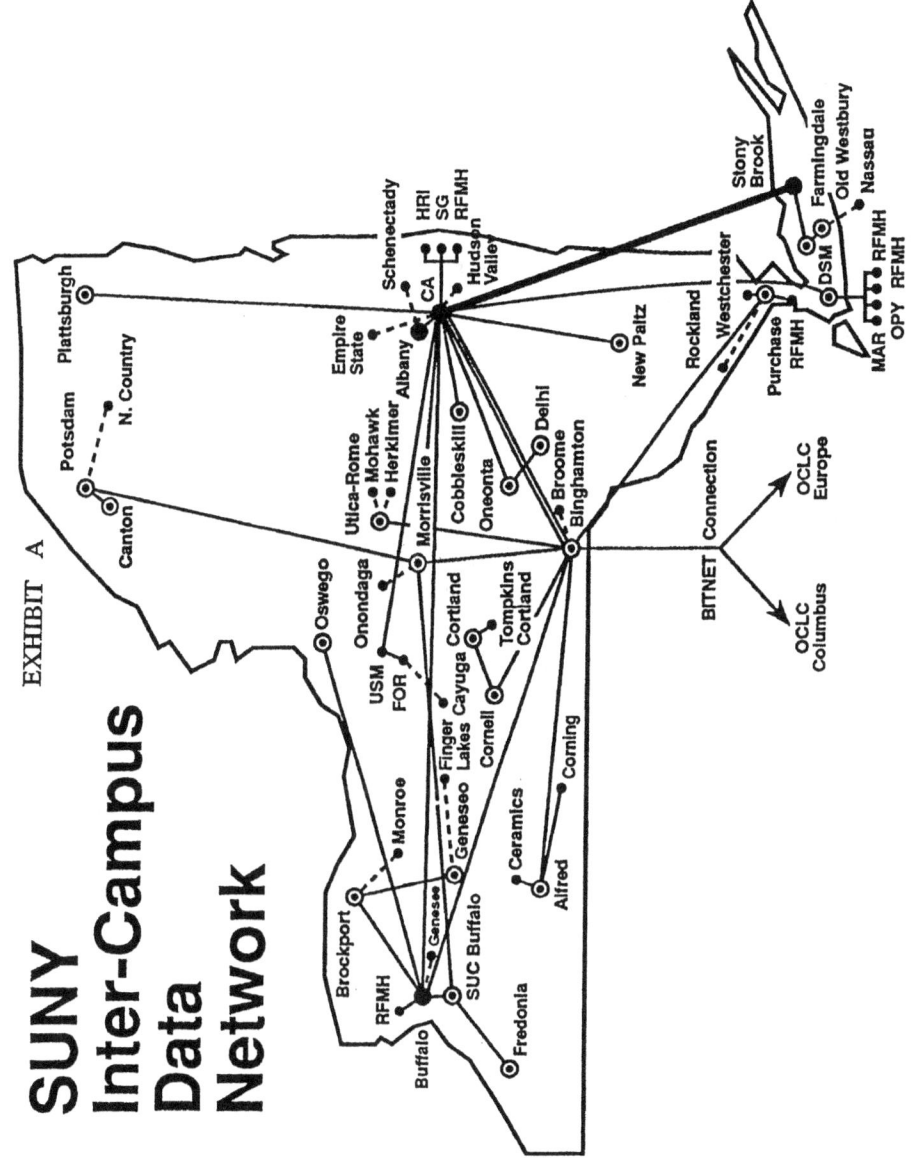

on June 10th, to explore "Preferred Futures" for a variety of stakeholders, definitions of collaboration and cooperation were developed. We often use these two terms interchangeably, but they have distinct meanings. "Collaboration" means working together; "cooperation" means acting together, engaging in activities of mutual benefit and providing active mutual assistance. The difference is important. The University Centers are engaged in both collaboration and cooperation with a heavy emphasis on cooperation.

The University Centers began substantial collaborative efforts in late 1989 with the preparation of the University Centers' "Principals Document." Selected relevant statements from the larger "Principles Document" (Exhibits B & C) illustrate some of the major points where we have agreed to cooperate on resource sharing objectives. The statements focus on our commitment to improving our collections and our services, by viewing the University Centers' collections as a common resource for all Center constituents. The "Principals Document" was prepared by the University Center Directors and staff to solidify our philosophical commitment to work together and to articulate important achievable goals. The "Principals Document" provides a framework for our deliberations and plans, and has served as an effective tool. The creation and use of the "Principals Document" has enabled us to secure outside funding for projects that support our cooperative objectives. We are presently engaged in three specific projects that provide practical experience and, as a result, the basis for further cooperation.

Until recently, most institutions have been striving to build large, stand-alone collections. The University Centers, and Buffalo in particular, recognize that an unreasonable amount of resources would be needed to bring us up to a collection size large enough to achieve our President's goal–to make SUNY one of the top ten public universities. It was unlikely that the additional three to four million dollars needed annually to achieve this kind of collection growth could be provided. The first of two examples of reformatted collection development figures from the Association of Research Libraries (ARL) statistics (Exhibit D) illustrates the unattainable ideal. The second (Exhibit E) more realistically achieves the desired status by pooling the resources of the four Centers. The size of the

EXHIBIT B

STRATEGIC DIRECTIONS FOR COOPERATION AMONG THE SUNY UNIVERSITY CENTER LIBRARIES

Statement of Principles for Cooperative Development, Collection Access, and Resource Sharing

Technological developments are making increased levels of cooperation not only possible but necessary. Collectively, the four Centers will have much more clout negotiating attractive contracts for vendor services, databases, licenses, equipment procurement, etc. Working together, all will benefit.

Cooperative development of automated systems and research collections among the four SUNY University Center Libraries will strengthen public services and increase access to a broader and richer pool of resources. It will make it possible to provide these services and collections more economically and effectively than could one library working alone.

The four University Center Libraries recognize the importance of interconnectivity of automated systems and plan to promote such interconnectivity among themselves and, at least, the libraries of the nine SUNY Liberal Arts Colleges, e.g.: SUC Brockport, Buffalo, Cortland, Fredonia, Geneseo, Oneonta, Oswego, Potsdam, and Plattsburgh.

EXHIBIT C

COOPERATIVE DEVELOPMENT

Sharing information about new serial subscriptions and candidates for cancellation before final action is taken.

Exploring the feasibility, affordability, and cost effectiveness of joint licensing of periodical databases in electronic format and providing coordinated access to selected databases through campus mainframe computing networks.

Exploring the feasibility of developing an efficient, reliable, and affordable electronic delivery system to support a program of resource sharing.

Working jointly to secure the necessary administrative, budgetary, and systems support for jointly sponsored cooperative programs.

Encouraging interaction among the collection development, access, and systems offices of the University Center Libraries.

EXHIBIT D

ARL STATISTICS

	ACQ BUDGET (MILLIONS)	TOT COLL SIZE	VOL ADDED FY87/88	MONO FY87/88	SERIALS FY87/88
UCLA	$ 7.14	5,812,000	207,000	N/A	95,000
BERKELEY	$ 6.67	7,190,000	195,000	N/A	99,000
ILLINOIS	$ 5.24	7,377,000	189,000	124,000	92,500
MICHIGAN	$ 6.84	6,133,000	130,000	N/A	67,500
ALBANY	$ 2.32	1,225,000	38,500	21,600	16,300
BINGHAMTON	$ 2.29	1,328,000	45,200	26,200	11,900
BUFFALO	$ 3.43	2,493,000	59,300	23,400	24,100
STONY BROOK	$ 2.96	1,614,000	48,500	25,400	11,800

EXHIBIT E

	ACQ BUDGET (MILLIONS)	TOT COLL SIZE	VOL ADDED FY87/88	MONO FY87/88	SERIALS FY87/88
UCLA	$ 7.14	5,812,000	207,000	N/A	95,000
BERKELEY	$ 6.67	7,190,000	195,000	N/A	99,000
ILLINOIS	$ 5.24	7,377,000	189,000	124,000	92,500
MICHIGAN	$ 6.84	6,133,000	130,000	N/A	67,500
SUNY CTRS	$11.00	6,660,000	191,500	96,600	64,100

four University Center Libraries compares favorably with major top ten public universities.

The first experimental step in the SUNY Centers' technical and philosophical cooperation was engagement in a Title II-D project from January 1988 through December 1991. A two-phased project was designed to test the quality of faxed and digitized information transmitted from the Buffalo campus and to study the timeliness of document delivery to the different Centers and to the dispersed libraries on our local campus. This project, supported by the U.S. Department of Education, at $175,000 successfully demonstrated our ability to provide high quality copies of journal articles to distant sites. Other data on costs of faxing and on the acceptance of the document delivery experiment will be shared in a final report to the Department of Education. Basically, it was a positive, successful experiment which proved that we could provide acceptable quality and timely delivery in a narrowly focused experiment. The next step for us is to build on the experiences with Title II-D faxing by purchasing better software such as Ariel for our institutions and by designing "real time" experiments in document delivery which require pulling material from the shelves when needed as opposed to operating from a sequestered journal base as in the Department of Education experiment.

Following our collaboration with the Title II-D project, the Centers were awarded a $100,000 grant from the Council on Library Resources to investigate issues and policies related to cooperative resource sharing and viewing the four University Centers collections as a common resource. In connection with this two-year project, which has been underway for a year now, we have held a successful Information Symposium in Albany for staff, faculty, and administrators from the four campuses as a first step to improve awareness of the project and identify issues. Various committees are at work on issues associated with setting policies and designing procedures for improved access to our respective collections. The CLR grant was built on the objectives outline in our "Principals Document" but will require us to explore much more thoroughly a variety of issues and policies associated with becoming more cooperative and interdependent.

When the "Principals Document" was first drafted, the University Centers explored the idea of a common catalog and interface which would allow us to link our collections. Since three of the four University Centers were NOTIS customers, the decision was made to join Indiana in a cooperative software development project with NOTIS that would link our catalogs, allowing users to view collections at a terminal on the local campus and to request interlibrary loan for material from other Centers. While Albany is not a NOTIS customer, they have committed to the project and are supportive of connectivity between the system they use and the NOTIS software. Other SUNY institutions are being supported with a library automation project (LAIP), funded by SUNY Central for the benefit of state colleges, community colleges, and special schools without any library automation. Various nodes that will be part of the LAIP project have been identified and clusters of institutions will receive service from a host. The LAIP project is proceeding slowly, but on schedule. Earlier, the University Centers selected automation vendors and secured local funding; thus, their commitment is to a different form of automation. Within the state, however, there is an awareness that all systems need to be able to communicate with one another and interconnectivity is the ultimate objective.

One goal of PACLink is to improve access so that users do not have to roam the Internet looking at a variety of catalogs and interfaces. PACLink will offer an easy, automatic interlibrary loan process for ordering materials from any of the University Centers. Such technology requires us to start developing new interlibrary loan policies which are based on an interdependent relationship. As a first step Binghamton has drafted a document entitled "PACLink Borrowing Guidelines"; a conservative approach to responsibilities, based on the national interlibrary loan code of 1980. The document has started us thinking about the number of questions that will need to be resolved in an interdependent resource sharing environment.

What will be the impact and the benefits of the PACLink project for the University centers? First, the University Centers have already begun to share information about our serials cancellation projects (there have been many at each institution), but currently it is difficult to coordinate and integrate the separate cancellation lists in the online environment. Paper lists are a cumbersome way to try to keep track of what another campus is canceling. The ability to look at one another's catalogs through PACLink, as well as at our serials holdings and on-order materials, will facilitate collection development decisions and resource sharing. Interlibrary loan activity will doubtlessly increase through PACLink. Policies and procedures for access and delivery will be affected by the PACLink technology and are already under preliminary discussion as mentioned earlier.

In an article on the goals of the Ohio Link Project, Carol Pitts Hawks details the Florida Center for Library Automation's experiences with interlibrary loan borrowing. Sixty-eight per cent of the interlibrary loan borrowing and lending is reciprocal within the state.[1] As a part of our CLR grant activity, several studies are underway or planned. One is a comprehensive journal use study of the University Center's collections. Another relates to interlibrary loan practices. Preliminary information about ownership and availability of materials in our collections indicates the following: about forty-six per cent of all ILL requests submitted by our users at the University Centers could be supplied from one of the other University Centers (Exhibit F). One goal of our CLR grant ILL project is defining the potential for more borrowing between University Centers and outlining the level of support needed for such interdependency. The second study, part of a project scheduled to start in 1992, requires University Centers to borrow more extensively from one another, tracking availability and success rates.

What might be some of the effects on services, staffing, and collections? We would expect that a highly efficient staff and reliable delivery mechanisms will need to be in place to successfully move us toward the access environment. More people may be needed in our interlibrary loan departments, at least temporarily, to meet a twenty four hour turn-around time or whatever delivery time frame is set once PACLink is in place. Improved access to the collections and expanded utilization of our collections may present new service burdens not yet fully understood. No doubt we will spend our collection dollars differently as we strive to stretch our book budgets locally and collectively. The local process of book selection might become more time-consuming in the beginning,

EXHIBIT F

ILL STUDY

AVAILABILITY:

45.54% of all requests (526 of 1155) are available from at least one University Center (NAM,BNG,BUF,SBH,YSM,VZB)

    11.34% available from Albany (131)
    20.52% available from Binghamton (237)
    19.48% available from Buffalo (225)
    7.45% available from Buffalo-Health Sciences (86)
    11.26% available from Stony Brook (130)
    6.75% available from Stony Brook-Health Sciences (78)

SUCCESS RATE:

11.77% of all records in the data base (136 OF 1155) had at least one University Center in the lender string.

The overall success rate - University Centers is 46.32% (63 of 136)

    14.29% success rate - Albany (1 of 7)
    18.18% success rate - Binghamton (8 of 44)
    57.69% success rate - Buffalo (30 of 52)
    12.50% success rate - Buffalo-Health Sciences (2 of 16)
    32.26% success rate - Stony Brook (10 of 31)
    44.44% success rate - Stony Brook-Health Sciences (12 of 27)

because we will need to build relationships and apply and understand new rules and procedures.

What are some of the possible long-term objectives? First, we assume our users will have more access through PACLink and that formerly isolated collections at the University Centers will now be used outside of the local libraries. Another objective is to prove that access, not ownership, is a workable approach. Collections can be viewed as one resource and materials can be supplied more successfully. There are many implications for our collections that need to be analyzed and discussed. One approach might be to build on the strengths of our existing collections; dollars may not need to be shunted to lesser areas of interest and need. Or we might decide to keep high demand items in "the system," as well as programmatic material that would be of narrower interest but needed somewhere within the system. The principals of "just in time" management would be applied; we would no longer collect "just in case" a user might need an item some time in the future. Tracking the usage patterns by the University Centers as a group and individually should help us create more informed and cohesive collection development policies. Issues for discussion include possible copyright obstacles and the possibilities presented by commercial document delivery services. Additionally, we will need to work on ways to speed up delivery of monographs among the institutions. It is easier to focus on faxing articles, but there will also be a need for movement of individual, monographic items. Questions about how we finance our collections will surface. Perhaps we need some sort of a pool for buying materials that need to be held collectively for the Centers, but not in four places. What will be the obligations associated with holding materials jointly? What demands will arise from trying to provide access to a remote as well as local client base? Who will have priority? These issues will require sorting out. We are only now beginning to see some of the problems and pitfalls associated with this interdependency.

What might be some of the implications for publishers and vendors of library material? We may order fewer copies of any single monograph. It is possible there will be fewer subscriptions to a serial so long as it is kept in "the system." On the other hand, as duplication decreases, funds will be freed up for the purchase of more titles. I believe that the purchase of materials will, therefore, more accurately reflect local strengths and responsibilities. Approval plans, blanket orders, and subscriptions will be more closely aligned to the individual programs of the institution, providing better focus. At the same time, some types of lesser-used materials will be acquired and held for the common good. Probably there will be less dramatic shifts in collection development policy. Serial cuts will be decided taking into account the holdings at other Centers. It is difficult to predict the impact of such sharing on the growth and use of commercial document services, but the demand for those services is on the rise. It would be foolish to expect that we would always provide for one another, especially when it may be more economical to purchase material for one-time local use. Valerie Oliver, reporting on the electronic journal and related issues of document delivery, identifies a wide variety of electronic journals and develops some analysis of pro's and con's of document delivery.[2] We need to study the implications and costs of commercial document delivery vs. on-going subscriptions so that the broadest array of choices are made available.

Licensing of software, data bases, and serial subscriptions in electronic format can be considered for group purchase and use by the University Centers. Will there be advantages in terms of service and costs if our resources can be "owned" centrally? Will we be able to offer more variety? At the Society for Scholarly Publishing meeting in Philadelphia in 1991, Emily Fayen, the Director of Information Services at the University of Pennsylvania Libraries, offered an interesting array of models for pricing electronic information. This is a topic not yet fully articulated, and it needs more discussion and debate among the interested parties: libraries, database suppliers, and publishers. Some of our early pricing models have not been rationally designed and do not take into account the scope of expanded cooperative arrangement that is possible in these days of expanding telecommunications. We need more discussion between all the interested stakeholders. I predict that there will be an increased need and demand for electronic information which could be shared via local or national networks. Our budgets now focus on building permanent collections, but gradually we will start spending more dollars for access.

In the *Chronicle of Higher Education's* "Point of View" column on August 14, 1991, Paul German focuses on setting budgets for libraries in an electronic era. He speculates on the evolving world of licensing and how acquisitions work may become more involved with licensing agreements than with individual purchases. Occasionally a publisher will say that as the number of journal subscriptions drop and as fewer copies are produced, the price of the remaining subscriptions will become prohibitively expensive. While a typical view from the perspective of the publisher, this tends to threaten librarians who fear that a journal title will be lost due to outlandish pricing. However, we should not be intimidated by the notion that a journal might be published in a very small quantity and at a very high cost. There may be new ways in which we can continue to access that journal or pay for some share of that subscription in a national setting. Michael Keller, Head of Collection Development at Yale, suggested, at the Center for Research Libraries meeting of April 1992, models of national excellence, with a few institutions providing and keeping material for the country. There is nothing to prohibit the notion of national collections or centers of excellence serving all. However, there would be many issues associated with how they are established, funded, and administered.

In conclusion, the global scholar operating at one of the SUNY University Centers should have better access to the collections of the four Centers, with a correspondingly high level of service. We will be "focusing on the need of our users," as suggested by Richard M. Dougherty in his editorial "Making Resource Sharing Really Work."[3] Service, according to Dougherty, should be focused on the needs of the user and not the needs of the library, and, as he suggests, we may need to reimburse one another to a greater degree than we have in the past for providing interlibrary loans. Over the next decade, cooperation and collaboration, either one or both, will become increasingly important for the University Centers as well as for other libraries. We will be engaged in an expanding series of library partnerships supporting regional and national affiliations. The whole environment will become more complex, involving new players at a variety of levels. The old players–librarians, vendors, and publishers–will be developing new relationships. While the ultimate form of access is ownership, as stated by Judy Quinn and Michael Rogers in an article entitled "Serials Librarians Form Aqueduct Action Group,"[4] there will be tradeoffs that we will have to make Libraries will be looking for collaboration with vendors and publishers on the development, pricing, and purchase of materials and products. PACLink is one example of a venture which sets a direction and tone for future endeavors. New pricing models will need to be developed and allowed to evolve as networking becomes more prominent and reliable on our campuses. We will need to explore the possibilities of providing access with implications for staffing and service.

The outcome will be a rich climate for scholarship, but it will mean layers of complexity for individual libraries. This environment will require the user to become more self-sufficient; users will need better navigational tools. There is a new role for libraries in helping to provide training and interfaces to this expanding electronic environment. We will need transparent approaches so that users can operate with a high degree of independence. We will need to sort out the use of traditional interlibrary loan and the role of commercial document delivery. I believe there will be room for commercial services, but questions about whether the library supports this or whether the user goes directly to the vendor are not resolved yet. Experiments in both areas need to be undertaken and reported; for example, there is a project presently under discussion between the Association of Research Libraries and the National College Bookstores Organization to experiment with digitizing and providing network access to reserve room material formerly held in the library. Finally, experience with PACLink as a tool which supports the University Centers' fundamental commitment to interdependent collections and shared resources will need testing and refinement.

The journey has begun.

NOTES

1. *Library Resources and Technical Services* 36, Issue 1:61-77.
2. Valerie Oliver, unpublished paper, University of Connecticut, Dec. 1991.
3. *The Journal of Academic Librarianship* 18, no. 2 (May 1992): 75.
4. *Library Journal*, May 15, 1992:12-13

BREAKOUT SESSION F: Z39.1– You Just Don't Understand! Librarians and a Publisher Discuss the Standard for Periodicals Format and Arrangement

Z39.1– You Just Don't Understand! Librarians and a Publisher Discuss the Standard for Periodicals Format and Arrangement

Regina Reynolds
Speaker

Nina Kramer
Minna Saxe
Reactors

Daphne Hsueh
Recorder

Daphne Hsueh is Chinese Studies Librarian, Ohio State University, Columbus, OH 43210.

© 1993 by The Haworth Press, Inc. All rights reserved.

This breakout meeting was one of the eight concurrent sessions jointly sponsored by NASIG and the Society for Scholarly Publishing (SSP) with the purpose of bringing librarians and publishers together. Sylvia Martin, Coordinator of General Technical Services Operations, Vanderbilt University, served as the convener.

Throughout her presentation, Regina Reynolds, Acting Head, National Serials Data Program, Library of Congress, injected a humorous tone by equating the understanding (or the lack of it) between publishers and librarians regarding serials with the relations between the sexes.

Reynolds explained that Z39.1, a NISO (National Information Standards Organization) standard, was established by both publishers and librarians working on the same committee. With both sides working together, it was possible to foster a mutual understanding of each other's needs and to agree upon some acceptable practices for periodicals. This could be an important first step leading to future dialog between publishers, who produce the serials, and librarians, who provide bibliographic description, access and control for the same serials.

Specifically, Z39.1 sets forth requirements on format and arrangement of periodicals that would make them easier to identify, catalog, provide access to, and preserve. In stressing the usefulness of standards, especially in cooperative ventures, Reynolds conjured up the image of the well-known ALA poster on the importance of standards that depicts railroad tracks coming from two different directions and failing to join due to differences in size of the tracks. However, Reynolds also pointed out that Z39.1 is unique among NISO standards in that the lack of adherence to it would not have disastrously negative effects, while adherence would have dramatically beneficial consequences: the savings of time and money for libraries, and easier identification, use, and retention of periodicals.

According to Reynolds, Z39.1 is not a new standard. It was first published in 1935 with revisions in 1943, 1967, and 1977, but it is very little known—some people might not have heard of this standard. This is not surprising since it is not even available nowadays and is also woefully out of date. At present there is a committee working on its revision. The current draft was balloted in Dec. 1990 with three "no" votes, twenty-eight "yes's," seven "yes's" with comments, two abstentions, and seven comments from interested parties. The negative votes and conflicting comments have not been resolved and because of other factors, no new draft has been sent out for balloting.

Reynolds emphasized the importance of Z39.1 especially in these days of budget cuts and reduced number of personnel to provide for serial control. She stated that Z39.1 is at present a standard in need of support and it was the purpose of her presentation to bring renewed interest to such an important standard. She wanted to help her audience believe in the need for librarians and publishers to understand how they would help each other, as well as the library users, by agreeing on some basics about serials.

Reynolds demonstrated the current relevancy of having a revised Z39.1 by showing a few examples on how difficult it can be to determine the main title of certain serial publications due, for example, to different typographical arrangements. She also showed how much work is created for the serials librarian by an unintentional title change; for instance when a publisher innocently adds or drops a word or two from the title.

Reynolds then went on to describe the scope of Z39.1, which is limited to conventional paper periodicals, more narrowly defined than in AACR2, because it (Z39.1) excludes newsletters, newspapers, series, and conference reports. Electronic journals are also excluded. Z39.1 provides specifications for overall production of periodicals–regular issues, completed volumes and special issues or sections, errata, abstracting and indexing, and reprints–plus eleven appendices covering topics such as ISSN, copyright, the Copyright Clearance Center, abstracting and indexing services and so forth.

Because Z39.1 has increased in length over the years (from eleven pages in the 1967 edition, with the actual standard starting on page 5, to thirty-seven pages, including the summary and appendices, in the current draft), Reynolds posited some relevant questions for further consideration. Have serials gotten more complicated since 1967 or have librarians become more fond of complexity? Is the standard asking for too much and therefore ending up with very little? Should a handbook be devised, instead of the more authoritative sounding standard, as one response suggested?

Reynolds commented that not all the recommendations in the

standard carry the same weight; there are mandatory provisions alongside suggestions. Some provisions in the standard are for retention and preservation over time. But since not all serial publications are equal (for instance, a research journal vs. a hobby magazine) difficulty arises as to who should decide which provisions of the standard applies to which publications.

The rest of Reynolds' presentation was devoted to outlining the major recommendations and highlighting some of the controversial aspects of the draft. She pointed out important points in areas such as title, frequency, volume and issue numbering, printing and binding considerations for individual issues, ISSN, SISAC code, barcoding, identification of individual articles, volumes, and a section on special considerations that includes anything that did not fit in somewhere else in the draft.

According to Reynolds, Pat Harris of NISO is interested in suggestions and is working on resolving conflicting comments to present a draft for fall balloting. Reynolds concluded by expressing hope that Z39.1 would be a starting point for an ongoing dialog between publishers and librarians. It is hoped that the standard will lay the groundwork for the development of handbooks, manuals, and how-to books on serials publishing, as well as for user-friendly works to assist library users.

Nina Kramer, Manager of "the Journals Publishing Division, American Society of Civil Engineers, was the reactor representing the perspective of the publishers. She affirmed the need for standards and welcomed Z39.1 as a product with input from both librarians and publishers. However, she emphasized that inherent in a standard for periodical format and arrangement there should be sensitivity to the financial restrictions faced by the publishers.

Kramer assured the audience that publishers abhor, just as much as librarians, any title changes because, first and foremost, they entail great expenses, in design as well as in publicity. But there are sometimes compelling reasons for a publication to change its title. Relevancy to trends, changing boundaries of disciplines, survival, and maintaining a leadership role in a field are just a few of the valid reasons. These reasons sometimes also apply to numbering and frequency changes. There is no universal rule that can cover all cases.

In view of the uniqueness of each publication and taking into account the financial considerations faced by all publishers, Kramer then took up specific requirements and changes in the major sections of the draft Z39.1 such as title change, the use of permanent paper, outside margin, and so forth. The recurring point emphasized throughout her comments was that Z39.1 would be more likely to bring about greater compliance if all the mandatory "must's" were changed to less authoritative "should's."

Minna Saxe, Chief Technical Services Librarian, Graduate School, City University of New York, served as a reactor presenting the librarians' point of view. To Saxe, Z39.1 was almost like a Second Coming which may not deliver librarians from all serial woes, but it certainly would help ameliorate the eternal despair felt by most serial librarians nowadays. She wholeheartedly endorsed the revised draft and prayed for its speedy passage. Furthermore, she added a few more requests for the publishers such as making the ISSN a bit larger so that one did not have to search throughout the publication for it and also the adoption of the newly approved SICI (Serial Item and Contribution Identifier) to facilitate access. Though her comments were brief, Saxe's enthusiasm for Z39.1 was contagious and seemed to be shared by most librarians in the audience.

The session was followed by a brief question-and-answer period characterized mostly by questions on specific points of the standard.

BREAKOUT SESSION G: MARKETING TO LIBRARIES: WHAT WORKS?

Marketing to Libraries: What Works? Adapting Marketing Strategy to Changes in the Library Community

Nan Hudes

R. R. Bowker, K. G. Saur, Bowker-Saur, and D. W. Thorpe, under the umbrella of their parent Reed Reference Publishing, have traditionally had the library field–academic, public, and special–as their primary market. With almost two hundred years combined national and international experience, we feel that we have something special to say about the needs of libraries and how to adapt marketing strategy to changes in the library community.

AT BOWKER, WE LISTEN

Bowker Library Advisory Board

Yes, we are a for-profit company. Yes, we must be accountable to the vagaries of the stock market. And, yes, we do report to boards of

---

Nan Hudes is Senior Director of Marketing, R. R. Bowker, 121 Chanlon Road, New Providence, NJ 07974.

© 1993 by The Haworth Press, Inc. All rights reserved.

directors and layers of corporate bureaucracy. But first and foremost, we listen to our customers. We really do care about them; we want to make sure that they are well-served–whether it be product-related or service-related.

As a part of this customer-oriented philosophy, we have instituted the Bowker Library Advisory Board. As stated in our corporate catalog, "This unique group of library professionals advises Bowker on the latest trends in the library industry and suggests directions that should be taken in order to produce the reference products and services [libraries] need." Among its distinguished members are librarians who head large public library systems and major university libraries, as well as directors of library and information studies programs, children's services, serials departments, materials acquisitions, collection development, technical services, and special libraries.

We have asked our Board to:

- describe the technological environment in which libraries are now operating.
- fill us in on the role of publishers in aiding the library community.
- tell us if we're in "information overload," if there is too much to choose from, and what should publishers do regarding product development?
- provide us with information regarding the use of Abstracting & Indexing services, including the criteria for use, the types of services used, and formats being used.

All of these questions are related to publishing and libraries in general. But we also ask Bowker product-specific questions such as:

- Why haven't more libraries acquired certain highly-respected, critically acclaimed, and unique reference resources like the *Bowker Annual Library and Book Trade Almanac*?
- What patron services materials do librarians want us to produce?
- What are the most positive features of Bowker products, i.e., the *American Library Directory*?
- Should we package products together into collections by subject, usage, etc., at a special price; for example, *the Books in Print* family?

The Bowker Library Advisory Board convenes on a regular basis–at ALA Summer there is a meeting and cocktail reception; at ALA Midwinter a cocktail reception; and there is also a yearly meeting held in New Jersey at our corporate headquarters, where board members spend several days working together on product review and overall market research.

Market Research Studies

Bowker also assesses its market through Market Research Studies. We do our research via telephone and the mail. We also use focus groups, and we regularly query attendees who come to our booth at trade shows. Within the last few months we've contacted hundreds of our customers with surveys on:

- *Children's Books in Print*–should it go from one volume to two volumes so that the indexes need not be truncated, and should we change its publication date?
- *Ulrich's*–at what time of year do serials librarians use the book the most; what is the most vital information they get out of *Ulrich's*?
- General Bowker Survey–on diverse aspects of many of our titles like *Literary Market Place, Books in Print, American Library Directory*. And, after we listen, we act. For instance, in response to the Ulrich's survey, we did not change the publication date of *Ulrich's*, and because children's librarians wanted the indexes to remain intact, we will now produce *Children's Books in Print* in two volumes.

AT BOWKER, WE ADAPT TO CHANGING TIMES

Throughout our history we have adapted to the needs and wants of our marketplace. Our products and services have progressed as time and technology have progressed, and we've always been the leader in providing our customers the type of material they need in the formats they want.

Books

We started out as book publishers, and when we started, books were set by hand. As technology progressed so did our book production operations. Now computers do the work for us, and those computers enable us to produce our products in new and innovative ways.

Microfiche

When microfiche technology started to revolutionize the way libraries worked, Bowker immediately put its major products—*Books in Print* and *Ulrich's*—into fiche format. This was the hightech of its day, and with a good reader/printer you could scan the fiche and print out a hard copy of the citation as well.

On line

When we started printing our books from computerized tapes, it was an easy and logical step to strip out the printing codes and put in the codes necessary to disseminate the information via online services like Dialog and BRS. These tapes were mounted on mainframes at the online vendor. Consequently, librarians who were subscribers to a particular service could access the data via their computer, a modem, and a phone line. Very high-tech in the late 1970s and early 1980s, but also costly and not immediately available to all interested parties in a library.

CD-ROM

As soon as this exciting new technological breakthrough was announced (and even before, because we experimented with twelve inch laser discs when they were thought to be the wave of the future), we used that same tape to make the premier library information resource: *Books in Print Plus*, our award-winning CD-ROM product. This 3/4 inch disc works with a CD-ROM reader and a computer. This is a cost-effective, on-site product that lets you find citations in our database in the most unusual and innovative ways–even when you only have fragmentary information. And not just *Books in Print* is on CD-ROM. We have more than ten CD-ROM titles–and that number is growing.

Tape Services

This leads me to the newest Bowker offering, Tape Services. That same computer tape can now be stored on-site at your institution–you now have your own in-house *Books in Print* or *Ulrich's* or *American Library Directory* working for you, with as many users as you want, using it day and night. To-date, the ultimate way to get information to large groups of people simultaneously.

AT BOWKER, WE TALK TO OUR MARKET

Direct Mail

To let you know about all our advances and innovations, we use Direct Mail, and it isn't meant to wind up in the "circular file." We know you receive so-called "junk mail" on a daily basis, but direct mail is the most powerful marketing tool available to us. The objective of Bowker's direct mail is four-fold:

1. To let you know about a new product or new edition, and get you to buy it immediately.
2. To let you know about a new product or new edition, and get you to buy it eventually.
3. To let you know about a new product or new edition, and get you to inquire about it in some fashion–more information, salesperson's call.
4. To let you know ways to use our products and ways to save money buying them.

All the response mechanisms on our mailing pieces are coded, so if an order comes in on our order form, we know immediately what you have responded to, and if the mailing was successful. If you choose to order on what is called "white paper" (your own form), then we must judge that an increase in sales around the time of the mailing has been prompted by that mailing. Naturally, we'd prefer to have our order form returned–even attached to your purchase order or with our mail code noted on your order form–because then we can quantify and qualify each mailing, know its cost-effectiveness, and judge whether we did it right. By the way, look over an order form carefully and you'll usually see tiny little numbers or letters (or both) tucked away in a corner–that's the code–please use it–for all orders for any publisher (most publishers do it, and if they don't they should).

We try to take immediate action when you make an inquiry. Inquiries are usually made for big ticket items, like our CD-ROM products or for new titles. Frequently, we're asked to have a representative call–either in person or on the phone. If we have sent out a detailed, complex, direct mail package, more information can mean a customer service representative's phone call. Our representatives will answer all questions over the phone, and help in any way they can. They'll probably suggest purchasing the product and using it for thirty days with an iron-clad, money-back guarantee. If more information is requested after a mailing of only a simple flyer or letter, we can offer more detailed promotion pieces and our catalog, as well as customer service assistance. CD-ROM inquiries are handled by the CD-ROM sales representative for the inquiry area. The rep will either send more information or suggest a sales call. But whatever we send or do, each inquiry is precious to us, and we make sure that each is courteously and promptly handled. Even though we do market research, your calls, letters, and other forms of inquiry are a vital part of our marketing strategy. We take into account what you've told us, and when we see a trend, or a bona fide issue arise, we take immediate steps to fix the problem, enhance the product, or produce a new book.

We try to help you save money by special pre-publication discounts, dollars off on select titles, standing order prices for annual products, and free book offers when ordering certain titles. And, we offer three-year subscriptions on our CD-ROM products that hold the price for three full-years while at the same time offering a discount.

Advertising

Our advertising goals are very simple:

- Introduce new titles to our marketplace.
- Let the market know that a new edition has been published– and why this new edition should be purchased.
- Sell our products.
- Sell our image.

Our advertising tries not to beat around the bush, but gets straight to the point–giving benefits . . . why buy the product . . . and features . . . what the product contains.

We give all the helpful information we can, but best of all, we try to include reviews. If you know that respected peers like something, you'll probably pay closer attention. And you'll see our ads in conjunction with our direct mail campaigns. It is a "one-two punch" that works very effectively because the ads reinforce the credibility of the direct mail effort. However, we often let our advertising "soften up the market" by coming out before the direct mail program, or we use ads as a reminder of the product long after the direct mail campaign has come and gone.

Telemarketing

Marketers have increasingly turned to telemarketing to get the message out, stimulate leads, or close a sale. We telemarket immediately upon the heels of any direct mail campaign. It not only helps to determine if the mailing was well-received, and if the message was clear and on target (giving valuable research data), but it allows us to follow-up immediately on any problem, to send more information in a very timely fashion, and of course to obtain the sale.

Though telemarketing is often perceived as a nuisance, in reality, it is a quick and efficient means of assisting our customers, as well as an easy way to close sales and prompt other feedback. And for renewals of subscription products, telemarketing is far and away the best way to reach the market. Often one forgets when it's time to renew, and a telemarketer's prompting is all that is needed to make sure that continuity is kept, with no issues missed, and, for CD-ROM, no down-time involved.

Public Relations

We use public relations as an adjunct, but highly important part of the marketing mix. As reference publishers, we usually cannot generate the same kind of publicity as trade publishers can with an especially "hot" title, but we can and do get excellent coverage and high interest for the releases we send to our market's media.

Press releases are sent out for all the products we produce–whether it be an annual book, such as *Books in Print*, a new edition, such as *Magazines for Libraries*, or a brand new product, such as *Topical Reference Books*. We send copies of brand new books with a press release–or if not the book, then the galley or chapters. Something is sent so the reviewer can do the title justice.

Reviews are everything and should be relentlessly pursued. A great review from a respected magazine or journal goes a long way in selling the product, and is used in direct mail as well as advertising.

Other things we publicize include:

- Anything unusual that happens to a title–the Twentieth Silver Anniversary Edition.
- When a milestone is achieved–100,000 copies in print.
- When something unusual occurs either to a product or to the company.

This last tip has been put into overdrive at our company this past year because of our acquisition of other publishing companies. We have worked especially hard to inform our market that Bowker's now responsible for *Broadcasting and Cable Market Place, The Official Catholic Directory, The Official Museum Directory* and the *Annual Register of Grant Support*. We had to let everyone know that we now can provide all information, ordering, billing, and problem solving on these titles at our shop–and through our "800" number.

We've also contacted the press through press conferences. Back in 1986, when we launched our very first CD-ROM, *Books in Print Plus*, we started the ball rolling by inviting the major library and computer press people to see a demonstration and receive literature on the product. Press coverage was terrific, and we received highly favorable reviews because of it.

Following up with the press has also been important for us. We've established good rapport with key media people–and though no one can get a favorable review or mention when a product is not acceptable–a good product can get its "good review" placed at a judicious time or mentioned in an upcoming article in the publication if the press like and respect your work.

We take advantage of all publicity and let it enhance all other marketing efforts. Our direct mail recipients and advertising audience read about our products in their journals and magazines. This secondary exposure enhances the primary penetration and keeps our products in the forefront.

Exhibits and Seminars

Taking the show on the road is not an empty saying with us. Bowker products go to over sixty exhibits and seminars worldwide each year; K. G. Saur, Bowker-Saur, and D. W. Thorpe go to as many as well. At major library exhibits such as ALA (Midwinter and Summer), SLA, ACRL, and important state shows all products are showcased. But a show like the American Booksellers Association would only get Bowker's titles specific to the bookstore market.

We like to send letters to the pre-registrants of a trade show to let those who are coming know about what we'll be offering at our booth and also about our show specials. We've also found it useful to have direct mail campaigns break around the time of major shows. For instance, *Books in Print* and *Ulrich's* come out at the very end of the summer and are heavily promoted at summer ALA. Their direct mail packages arrive in the library around the time of the exhibit letting the exhibit reinforce the direct mail and the direct mail reinforce the exhibit. Additionally, around the time of an exhibit, we advertise in either the sponsoring association's journal or in the conference program itself–and if available in any daily show publication. We have found that advertising's an excellent way to get booth traffic by letting attendees know that we are exhibiting, where they can find us, and what "Show Specials" we are offering. "Show Specials" are a big part of each exhibit and usually take the form of some sort of price reduction:

- Take twenty percent off the price of any title ordered at the show.
- Get a free CD-ROM drive when purchasing a three-year subscription to *Books in Print Plus*.
- Order one of our A & I monthly journals and get three additional months free.

We've enticed attendees to our booth with exciting give-aways, sweepstakes et al. Ultimately, special "one-time only" or buy at the special exhibit price work the best. Exhibits are also a great time to offer further information and get sales leads. We have Product Information Cards if conference attendees are interested in learning more about particular products or areas. These cards are filled out with the name, title, institution, address and phone number of respondents; dropped into a special receptacle; and, immediately upon our return home, responded to. The cards are then given to our sales team. The reps can make a determination on how "hot" the lead is and take it from there. Many attendees use exhibits to formulate "wish lists," which is fine with us. Though they cannot buy on the spot, they can take literature home with them and save it to use later. I have seen order forms from an exhibit make their way back to us as long as twenty-four months later. As stated before, exhibits give us market research opportunities. I have received some of the very best reviews for our products from librarians walking by our booth.

Sales Team

Sales and Marketing work hand in hand at Bowker. Marketing's responsibility is to make sure that the sales team is kept up-to-the-minute on product pricing, enhancements, new product developments, and reviews. Marketing makes sure that Sales has press releases, catalogs, promotional pieces, flyers, newsletters, special fact sheets, and anything else that can help them do their job effectively. They use these pieces as leave-behinds on their sales calls and send them to their customers to provide them with additional information.

But Bowker's sales team does more then just ask for the sale. They work closely with library associations, consortia, networks, and other library groups. We are happy to do special showings and presentations for any or all of our products. We also aid various library special interest groups with either monetary support for a particular occasion, i.e., a cocktail party at an appropriate trade show, or some other tangible assistance. If a main public library and its branches would like to see a demonstration of *Ulrich's Plus* or any *Plus* System product, the area rep would work out a mutually agreed upon location and time, and present a detailed demo of how the CD-ROM product would work for that particular library group. Often we get a local network or consortia to allow us to be the speaker at a scheduled meeting–we provide the cake and coffee. These exercises are used more than just to sell products. They extend a confidence level to the prospective buyer that the programs are easy to use, appropriate, and that we are there to assist in any way we can.

Customer Service

And that leads me into one of the most important parts of Bowker's marketing mix–customer service. Without good customer support a publisher would be hard-pressed to maintain the loyalty of its customers. Customer service keeps customers coming back by offering them: a mechanism to straighten out any problems that arise; a quick and easy way to order; a way to gather information on a title of particular interest; and a way to find out what's new.

At Bowker we offer one general 800 number to get you into the loop, and several specific 800 numbers, if you already know exactly what you are looking for. For example, our Electronic Publishing 800 Hotline offers assistance with loading *Plus* software on your computer, help searching our programs, product hardware requirements, trouble shooting for problem hardware et al. This hotline works from 9:00 a.m. to 7:00 p.m. EST, so that the east coast can get information bright and early while the west coast has until 4:00 p.m., their time, to work with our customer service people.

The general 800 number is the one to call if you're not sure whom you need to talk to, if anything has gone wrong with an order (God forbid), if you want to place a standing order, if you want to cancel a standing order (God forbid)–or anything else you can think of.

Good customer service also gives us valuable feedback. We listen very carefully to what you tell us. If we "goof," it's more than noted–it's acted upon and hopefully it will not happen again.

AT BOWKER, WE MAKE GETTING INFORMATION EASY

Newsletters

At one time, we had four newsletters offering information on several different product lines–CD-ROM, Serials, K. G. Saur, and A & I Publishing–going to those customers who bought products within those specific areas. Recently, we've combined most of the newsletters into one company-wide resource, named it "The Cornerstone"–because our titles are the cornerstone of any good collection–and are mailing it to our entire customer base. The Cornerstone will inform all our customers about what is happening company-wide. Its information will let you make more informed purchasing decisions, provide you with ways to make your work easier and market your library more effectively (we've found out that every library has to justify its existence and has to market itself to both management and patrons alike), and, in general, keep you up-to-date on what's new and hot.

Product Information Cards

Wherever you see us you'll see our blue Product Information Cards. Please use them if you require detailed information on any of our products or services. If you're at an exhibit, drop the card off at our booth. If you take one with you, mail it to us. The cards have postpaid indicia on them, and won't cost anything to mail. We're so committed to giving you the information you need, that we've even had the Product Information Cards bound into a number of our annual titles–although in the books they're beige not blue. You can simply tear out the card at the perforation and pop it in the mail. Tearing out the card will not mar or deface the book in any way.

Catalogs

Finally, we come to our catalogs. We produce three: *The Reed Reference Publishing Catalog, The Bowker Electronic Publishing Catalog,* and *The K. G. Saur/Bowker-Saur Catalog.*

The Reed Reference Publishing Catalog offers more than seventy pages on all Bowker products and almost every product for all other RRP Companies. It's the ultimate reference resource for our titles. It comes out annually to keep you informed of our publishing efforts– and backlist titles–available for the year ahead. Bowker Electronic Publishing Catalog has almost fifty pages of information on our CD-ROM titles, online offerings, and products available for tape leasing. It is so informative and packed with information, many customers use it as the demo for Books in Print Plus, from which they actually buy. And last, but not least, is the K. G. Saur/Bowker-Saur Catalog featuring their entire line-up of industry-standard books and microfiche collections with a more international or highly academic slant.

AT BOWKER, WE PROVIDE ONGOING INFORMATION AND EDUCATION

There are even more marketing elements that we employ including invoice stuffers (information about related titles enclosed with your bill); an exciting renewal authorization program, that lets you automatically order an annual title, even if you don't have a standing order; and computerized letters that come to you twice a year to tell you what you ordered last year, but have not yet ordered this year. These reminders generate business for us it's true, but they also assist you in not letting things you need fall through the cracks.

And very interestingly, we have started producing curriculum guides available to accredited library schools that help introduce Bowker products to students and help them become more familiar with products available throughout the profession. In addition, the guides offer suggestions for developing student assignments for classroom situations. Such exposure in library school can facilitate resolution of important selection decisions facing professional librarians on a regular basis. As you can see we have a pretty complete and complex marketing program, but whenever we plan, or whatever we do, we constantly strive to keep the librarians wants and needs in mind.

CONCLUSION

Technology, changes in life styles, and budget crunches et al., have reshaped and changed libraries over time. Through all that, Bowker has made the commitment to help you to work better and more effectively. As I stated in the beginning, we want you to buy our products, but when you do, we want you happy and coming back to us because you trust us and know that whatever we do, we really want to do it right for you. It's been a great working relationship–Bowker and Libraries–ever since Frederick Leypoldt and Richard Rodgers Bowker started over 120 years ago. You have our commitment to continue it for another 120!

Marketing to Libraries: What Works and What Doesn't

Vicky Reich

INTRODUCTION

How can publishers more effectively market to libraries? In 1975, 1987, and 1991, the AAP/RTSD (ALECTS) committee surveyed publishers and librarians about marketing to libraries. Looking at the results of the three surveys we see that many of the practices of librarians and publishers are unchanged over the last seventeen years. Much of the advice from librarians to publishers about how to do business is the same. Some important pieces of our world are different. Today I hope to reinforce the practical advice that still applies, and point out the changes in libraries which may cause us to question long held beliefs about how to effectively market to libraries.

My experience is in large research libraries. I will give you a look at the way we do business at the Stanford University Libraries (which do not include the Hoover, Medical, Business, or Law Libraries), and I will try to relate our experience to processes in other academic libraries.

This paper addresses the following questions:

- What do librarians need from publishers?
- How is collection development changing?
- How is acquisitions changing?
- What marketing strategies do librarian's like?

Vicky Reich is Chief, Serials and Acquisitions Department, Stanford University Libraries, Stanford, CA 94305-6004.

WHAT DO LIBRARIANS NEED FROM PUBLISHERS?

Typically in large research libraries, two groups are involved in spending money for library materials: the collection development staff and the acquisitions staff.

Collection Development staff choose what materials to buy for collections. They track academic program and build relationships with faculty. They know the details of a particular geographic or subject area's bibliography and publishing patterns.

Acquisition staff place orders, maintain vendor/publisher relationships, choose what vendor to use, and negotiate service fees and discounts. They claim materials ordered but not yet received and they pay the bills.

These two groups have overlapping but *differing* functions and the two groups need different information from publishers. Publishers need to consider two basic marketing issues: how to get the collection development librarian's attention so she selects your company's publications for purchase; and then how to make it easy for the acquisitions librarian to buy the chosen materials.

It's not that easy to get the collection librarian's attention. Increasingly within recent years the once full-time collection development staff are now part-time collection builders. As staff resources shrink, reference librarians, and occasionally other library professionals (for instance, catalogers) have assumed this additional responsibility. Within the Reference Division of ALA (RASD) there is a section called CODES (Collection Development and Evaluation Studies Section). In five years, it has grown from an interest group to a section with twelve committees and two discussion groups. Conversely, at Stanford, staff who were once full-time book and serial selectors now have expanded reference responsibilities. At Stanford, there are about thirty-five bibliographers.

CD decisions are made differently in some non-ARL, special, and public libraries. In these libraries the director usually is in charge of collection development. It is only in public libraries that the head of collection development plays an active role in collection development.[1] To effectively market materials, publishers must get the right information to the right library staff. In 1987, ALECTS ranked publishers' catalogues and flyers as very important in the alerting and selection process of library materials.[2] I believe this may be changing.

Tons of mail flows into the library every day. We need one full-time person just to handle mail opening. On a typical day we fill three book trucks with the mail we receive. Libraries used to routinely distribute blurbs and catalogs to subject bibliographers. Now because of staff cuts, some libraries have begun to throw away this "non-essential" material. Two years ago, my department began to throw away *all* marketing information except the annual serial vendor catalogs and the antiquarian dealer catalogs. Every couple of weeks we throw away about four big cardboard boxes full of marketing material into the dumpster. Most of the blurbs and catalogs Stanford receives are from publishers whose books we receive through approval plans. When we discontinued routing this material we heard no complaints from the bibliographers.

If publishers want to avoid wasting their own and the acquisition librarian's time, effort, and money here are some suggestions:

- DON'T send us unsolicited samples of either books or serial issues; they waste staff time and make us mad.[3]
- DON'T send marketing information to the serials or acquisitions department.
- DON'T waste your time or our time with telemarketing.[4]

We do want to hear from the publishers, after all we are in the business of buying your materials. How to best get our attention?

- DO call: to find out the status of the library budget and staffing, to make contact, and to find out WHO to contact.
- DO call or survey before starting major projects. Solicit advice.
- DO send materials to the most specific collection development person you can identify.
- DO tell us something about the content of a book you're trying to market (particularly details of revisions). Furnish information about the author and point to reviews of the book.

This is difficult advice to follow. It is time consuming to gather information, particularly regarding the internal organization of a library. It is equally difficult to gather and interpret information on libraries as a whole.

October Ivins has reported on a meeting held last summer sponsored by the AAP and ALECTS. The meeting centered around the results of and reactions to the 1991 marketing surveys. One of the speakers was Barbara Colson, deputy director/marketing director, Cambridge University Press. I want to highlight two of the points that October reports from Ms. Colson's presentation:

> Since patron and faculty requests both ranked high, Cambridge will target faculty with direct mailings, exhibit at professional meetings, and use editorial board contacts to market new titles . . . Sample copies ranked high, so Cambridge will expand its policy from supplying samples on request to mailing unsolicited sample issues.[5]

Publishers should please note that although librarians do take seriously requests from faculty, their requests do not translate into automatic purchases, particularly as monies become increasingly scarce. Also sample copies are important for selection decisions–but only when we request copies. Unless the title is requested and sent to the requesting individual it costs the library staff time to identify the title and then route it (MAYBE) to the proper selector. More often than not, the unsolicited issue is tossed.

Two other selection tools need perspective: book reviews and A & I services. Book reviews are considered an important selection tool; however, their importance varies. Some librarians depend on reviews for purchase, because their monies must only be spent on materials "approved" by the professional community. Other librarians use reviews only for the grey and ephemeral literature. For them reviews for trade materials appear for "too few" books, "too late." There is an increasing sense that by the time the review is published the book is already "op." If we don't choose the material through our approval plans, we may not get it.

When selecting a new journal title librarians consider it important that the title is included in an A & I service. I asked an informally gathered group of Stanford selectors how they evaluate serials for purchase. The science librarians tend to wait until a serial is established and covered in an A & I service before considering purchase. Social science and humanities librarians seem to depend less on this criteria and weigh content, editorial board, and publisher as the major criteria for purchase. The critical difference is the price. The Science librarians are making a major investment and seem more committed to "complete runs." The Social Science and Humanities selectors are able to take risks with the cheaper titles and consider it more important to get representative samples of scholarship into the library.

Once you have our attention and collection development staff have chosen to buy your book, the acquisition staff follow through with the purchase of the material. How can you make that task easier? Mary Chelton summarizes how publishers can make buying books an easier process for librarians–the points below are drawn from her article[6] and from responses to an ACQNET query on the same subject:[7]

1. give full author and title, including all subtitles and series
2. list the copyright date
3. list the full price (including shipping and handling)
4. give full information about the edition and the year
5. list the full ISBN–include the leading digits
6. cooperate with library vendors
7. use the terms "os" and "op" in a meaningful way

Publishers should not just count on the DO's and DON'T's stated above to make their marketing techniques more effective. It is important for publishers to remain aware of the environment in which collection decisions are made and monies are spent.

Libraries are in flux–organizational structures are being consolidated, resources are decreasing, automation and networking are increasingly important.

How Is Collection Development Changing?

Collection development has less staff to do the same amount of work and there are fewer dollars to build library collections. For bibliographers these truths translate into at least two trends: a greater reliance on approval plans and more time spent identifying serials for cancellations.

To give you an idea of the dollars spent on monographs and the impact of approval plans, in 1990-91 the ARL libraries spent between 32 percent and 80 percent of the total collection budget on serials, the median expenditure is 61 percent.[8] Of the remaining dollars, those spent on monographs purchased through approval plans varies widely. At Cornell about 25 percent of the monographs titles are procured through approval; at LSU this jumps to about 65 percent. Overall, Stanford acquires about 37 percent of its monographs through these plans. We try to monitor our subject profiles and vendor instructions so that fewer than 10 percent of the books supplied are returned.

Almost all libraries use approval plans–and the size of a library's approval plan may not be in proportion to the size of the library. Approval plans for American university presses are common in academic libraries; techniques for covering other types of publication vary greatly. Small press and other non-mainstream publications are not as easily supplied on approval plans as are trade press publications. Small press publishers have the most to gain by getting the collection development staff's attention.

Fewer dollars for collection development has influenced the nature of the collections being built. At Stanford, the sciences and social sciences are buying fewer current monographs and the humanities have substantially decreased purchase of retrospective materials. The 1987 survey reports "only 10% of all libraries cite availability at another library as a reason not to buy a book,"[9] but increasingly selectors are broadening their definition of "not building duplicate collections" from campus libraries to include regional peers.

Fewer standing orders are being placed for monographs and journals. This spring, selectors began to cancel selected numbered series and add these materials to the approval plan. The quality of monographs varies within some series and it is becoming more important to make sure every dollar is spent on high quality materials than to have all the volumes in a series.

Stanford used to order about 1200 new serial titles/year and we canceled about 200 to 400 titles/year. For the past several years we have ordered over 600 titles and have canceled almost as many titles as we've ordered. A nonscientific eye-balling of this year's serial cancellation and ordering data shows that many of the subject areas with new standing orders are also the areas with high cancellation rates (i.e., geology, engineering, education, art, and foreign areas studies). This pattern of canceling titles in order to purchase new titles is common.

At Stanford the criteria used to cancel science serial titles include: circulation; in house use; number of times cited by doctoral students; number of times cited by faculty; number of faculty articles published. The focus is on not only total price, and overall use, but on a ratio of price per use as a measure of quality.

The 1987 AAP/RTSD survey reports that only "8% of the largest academic libraries report price as a major decision factor."[10] In 1992 publishers are competing for a rapidly decreasing amount of money; material quality and pricing matter more than ever.

Static budgets and rising costs are forcing libraries to cancel and to not buy new journals. Many libraries are using or are considering experimenting with document delivery services to fill the possible intellectual gaps caused by these actions.

How Is Acquisitions Changing?

Libraries have fewer staff to perform the same work. Staff cuts have been at all levels. Cuts at the middle management layer are forcing consolidation of the functional responsibilities of monograph and serial librarians. We have fewer "experts." Within the last two years Stanford has cut staff by almost 20 percent. My Department has undergone two major reorganizations–four units have been consolidated into one. Line staff now concentrate on keeping up with incoming work and have less time to pursue acquisition of the esoteric materials. We have tried to carve out time to acquire the harder-to-locate materials (after all this is what a research library should collect!) by doing less complete pre-order searching for the majority of materials. We place orders using the information supplied in ads or catalogs. We do very little searching of print sources to verify bibliographic information. We primarily use online sources.

Smaller libraries and some state libraries have even fewer resources than Stanford. They have a harder time identifying smaller press materials and don't have much money for their purchases. Considering libraries' shrinking resources, publishers should not expect to expand their market share, but effective marketing may help to maintain current sales.

As monies become tighter, librarians are becoming more aware of accounting procedures. At Stanford we recently centralized and standardized invoice payments. This was important for control and audit regulations. However, there are disadvantages. In the past it was easy to sidestep the bureaucracy and pay the smaller publishers relatively quickly. Now it's harder to make exceptions. Educational institutions, in general, will find it increasingly difficult to make exceptions to standard procedures as money tightens and standardization is used to insure maximum efficiency.

What Marketing Strategies Do Librarians Like?

Continue to build relationships with librarians. Some techniques that have received good press on the librarian grapevine are:

> *Advisory Boards:* Bowker and Springer-Verlag are two companies with advisory boards. My experience on an Advisory Board has been very good—I gained some understanding of how difficult it is to choose what to publish, and the hardships of guessing what will sell. Publishers also had the opportunity to hear about the needs of librarians and library patrons, to solicit advice on the future of libraries and publishing, and to solicit reactions to products under consideration or development.
>
> *Focus Groups:* Focus groups provide a good forum for exchange of diverse opinions. These groups also allow in depth exploration and explanation of ideas. Jossy-Bass is sponsoring a breakfast at the annual 1992 ALA to follow up on a questionnaire mailed in the spring about its products.
>
> *Topical Programs:* Chadwick-Healy hosts a program at ALA on topics that are in some way related to a new product. At midwinter 1992, ALA librarians and faculty spoke on SGML and described how researchers use electronic texts. This program was planned in conjunction with the announce-

ment of a full text CD-ROM product Patrologia Latina (patristic and medieval texts).

Personal Contact: Make calls to gather information, not just to sell. I routinely spend time on the phone with vendors and publishers that I've met at SSP, NASIG or ALA. A well respected colleague wrote, "I appreciate the few publishers that take the time to call me on the phone and find out about our situation. And I am more apt to do business with them . . ."[11]

Continue to build relationships with book and serial vendors. While working on this paper I had occasion to talk to a variety of vendors, and I was surprised to learn that publishers and vendors do not collaborate more closely to analyze the library market. Some feeling persists that publishers have not fully accepted vendors as distributors; some even feel the vendors are competitors. Book vendors are in the best position to understand what librarians buy. Most of the trade and university press books that libraries buy are brokered by book vendors. All the vendors I spoke with work with publishers, all felt there could be closer relationships.

Publishers and vendors work together to market specific titles; they produce focus mailers and cooperate on advertising. I've read in several places that publishers say vendors won't give them marketing data. One vendor said that the publishers simply needed to describe what was needed and why. He said his company could offer book sales data stratified by type of library; for standing orders, specific sales data would be easier to compile. A second large book vendor sells a report on its international business, and also produces a report of the top 100 books sold on approval.[12]

The vendors can help publishers to identify the broad criteria librarians use to buy books and journals. I want the publishers to know what I'm buying. I want them to have adequate marketing information so print runs match demand. I want publishers to have sufficient profit so they can take intellectual risks. I want prices set at levels appropriate for the library market. I want to see a positive feedback loop to inform publishers about what I consider to be quality publications because what we buy is being held to increasingly strict standards of quality.

NOTES

1. Hendrik Edelman and Karen Muller, "A New Look at The Library Market," Publishers Weekly May 29, 1987:30-35.
2. Jane Treadwell and Lee Ketcham, "The Serials Marketplace," Library Journal 116, no.10 (1 June 1991): 83-84,86,88.
3. To see SERIALST discussions from April 1992, contact listowner Birdie MacLennan at e-mail address:
   BITNET: BMACLENN@UVMVM
   Internet:BMACLENN@UVMVM.UV M.EDU
4. Telemarketing was the least popular method in the 1990 ALECTS survey and was not well liked in the 1987 survey.
5. October Ivins, "Serials Prices: Column 14," Serials Review Winter 1991:70-71.
6. Mary K. Chelton, "Dear Publisher," Library Journal 117, no. 3(15 February 1992): 131-134.
7. To see ACQNET discussions from March 1992, contact listowner Christian M. Boissonnas at e-mail address:
   BITNET: CRI@CORNELLC
8. ARL Statistics 1990-91. Compiled by Sarah M. Pritchard and Eileen Finer. Association of Research Libraries, Washington, D.C. 1992. p. 34.
9. Edelman and Muller, "A New Look at the Library Marketplace."
10. Ibid.
11. Karen Schmidt, Acquisitions Librarian and Associate Professor, of Library Administration, University of Illinois, Urbana campus, e-mail message to the author, 19 March 1992.
12. From author's phone calls to vendors: Matt Nauman, Marketing Manager BNA, 8 June 1992; Bob Schatz, Sales Manager, Academic Book Center, 3 June 1992; Scott Smith, Regional sales Manager, Pacific Northwest BNA, 3 June 1992, John Secor, President, Yankee Book Pedler, 10 June 1992.

REFERENCES

Hoffert, Barbara, "Striking a New Balance of Power," *Library Journal* 117, no. 3 (15 February 1992): 124-128.

Melkin, Audrey. "Publishers, Vendors, Libraries: Troublesome Issues in the Triangle." In *Understanding the Business of Library Acquisitions* edited by Karen A. Schmidt. (Chicago: American Library Association, 1990).

Secor, John, "Friday the 13th/Saturday the 14th," *Dialog*, 1991, October-November: 1-7.

BREAKOUT SESSION H:
ARTICLE DELIVERY:
AN ALTERNATIVE TO OWNERSHIP?

Article Delivery: Shifting Paradigms

Anne McKee

Let me begin by stating how pleased I am to be able to speak to this diverse group on article delivery. We at ASU West believe a unique service is being offered to our constituents and we like to get the news out.

When considering the many forms document delivery has taken over the years, I am always reminded of an actual incident that occurred to a friend of mine who was a reference librarian in an academic library on the East Coast. At that time one of the original copies of the Magna Carta was touring the United States; a very dapper looking older gentleman (complete with a Derby hat, handlebar mustache and polished wooden cane) approached my friend at the reference desk. The gentleman inquired that he had heard of a "remarkable" service called "interlibrary loan." My friend nodded, explained a few basic facts of how the interlibrary loan

---

Anne McKee is Bibliographic Services Librarian, Fletcher Library, P.O. Box 37100, Arizona State University, West Campus, Phoenix, AZ 85069-7100.

system worked, and proceeded to ask if he could be of assistance. The gentleman replied "Yes, believe you can. I would like to request the Magna Carta by interlibrary loan." While the librarian sat there rather dumb-founded, the patron proceeded to assure my friend the manuscript would not be damaged–he simply wanted to study it.

Due to the first rate marketing efforts by libraries, many patrons are now convinced information does not need to be owned as long as it can be accessed–this was a user who took the library at its word and submitted what he believed was a perfectly reasonable request. While his expectations were a little unrealistic, still libraries must be ready to provide access to all information and items not readily accessible in-house. This can be accomplished by document delivery.

In this paper, I will be discussing ASU West's unique philosophy of access vs. ownership and how document delivery is handled at Fletcher Library. I will also discuss other innovative document delivery occurring within the United States. Finally, will address some aspects of vendor contract negotiations. To fully understand why document delivery is so prevalent ASU West, a brief explanation of the campus's history is necessary.

In 1972 a grass roots effort was launched by the "West Side Citizens Committee for Higher Education." This committee (comprised of citizens and legislators of western Maricopa County) began lobbying the legislature for higher education facilities. At that time, the "West Valley" was the largest metropolitan area in the country without an institution of higher learning beyond the community college level. In 1982 the state legislature responded, providing an exchange of 171.66 acres of general revenue lands for 300 acres of state trust land located in western Maricopa County. These 300 acres of state trust land now constitute the permanent campus of Arizona State University West, an upper level undergraduate and graduate institution.

The 95,000 square foot Fletcher Library, dedicated in March, 1988 was the first building constructed on the permanent campus. Besides housing the library, the building also served temporarily as space for faculty offices, classrooms, and offices for university administration until the core campus was completed in 1991.

Fletcher presently has a collection of 185,000+ volumes and

3000 serial subscriptions, but we also offer seamless access via document delivery/interlibrary loan to the excellent 2.6 million volume research collection at the Tempe campus (utilizing our online catalog CARL). We have a policy of "intentional reliance" upon the resources of the main campus, which has guided both our acquisitions policy and the development of document delivery services. A core collection is being developed at ASU West but fulfilling specialized research needs is left to the Tempe campus.

Our current "access budget" is 1.6 million dollars. Notice that we do not refer to it as an "acquisitions budget," a term that traditionally denotes purchasing monographs and serials for the collection. In our situation, it means so much more. We do purchase material for the library regardless of format. But we also pay all online database searching fees and meet costs associated with borrowing, delivery, photocopying, etc., detailed in our interlibrary loan contract with the Tempe campus. Like many institutions, ASU West has found that terms such as "document delivery" and "access over ownership" acquire new definitions, and require new ways of operating as paradigms continue to shift within the information-providing world at an ever increasing rate.

What is document delivery? Generally speaking, document delivery as defined in the Council on Library Resources 1983 Report is "the transfer of a document or a surrogate from a supplier, whether a library or a document service, to a requesting library."[1]

ASU views the process of requesting and receiving documents (either books, journal articles, or media) from one campus to the other as document delivery. Through our shared CARL catalog, the users can note exactly what each campus has to offer. If the material they need is at the other campus, they bring the CARL print-out to our reference desk, and the request is transmitted to the other campus via a "dove fax modem." (Through special software, our computer "speaks" to Tempe's fax machine.) This provides seamless access to the entire Arizona State University Libraries collection with an average turnaround of 48 hours.

This service is not just for faculty, staff and students, but is also available to anyone who holds a "community borrowers card." A community borrower is anyone who is an Arizona resident, over 21 years of age, and holds a driver's license or valid identification card from the state. For a fee of $25 a year, they have borrowing privileges from both campuses, can initiate document delivery and may request the copy service we provide to faculty and students for a nominal fee. Therefore, if a community borrower from Sun City, AZ comes into the library and requests material retained only on the Tempe campus, they are extended the same privileges as our own faculty and students.

Document delivery cannot be considered "seamless" unless there is immediate user satisfaction. Our constituents truly appreciate our service. The majority of our student body is composed of non-traditional students (people returning to college, midlife career changes and students who work full-time and attend classes part-time). Most classes meet every other day and it is far easier for our constituents to request a copy of a book or journal article through document delivery than it is to jump in the car, take off time from work, and drive 60 miles roundtrip to the Tempe campus. The users submit the request before class and two days later, when they are back on campus for another class, the material is waiting for them at the circulation desk.

When might it be cost-effective to actually purchase the monograph/videotape or subscribe to the journal rather than request document delivery? ASU West has grappled with that issue over the last few years and, while there is not currently a written policy, we do observe some general guidelines. Our Information Delivery Specialist produces a quarterly report, sorted by call number and type, of titles that have been requested either through document delivery or traditional interlibrary loan. The report tells how many times a title has been requested. To ensure patron confidentiality, patrons names are not kept, only the classification of faculty, graduate student, undergraduate student, or community borrower. These reports are then studied by the liaison librarians for collection development impact. If a publication has been requested frequently by either faculty or students, the title is considered for purchase. If a title has only been requested by community borrowers, the title would be considered for purchase if it fit the curricular needs of the campus.

When the University of Texas at Austin began a pilot study on commercial document delivery as a way to circumvent escalating journal prices, they soon experienced the same phenomenon as

ASU West. We both have come to view the document delivery process as an extension of the reference process rather than an unrelated, separate division of interlibrary loan.[2] Indeed at ASU West, is the reference staff that accept and verify the document delivery requests. Our constituent not care that the document delivery process is actually performed by three separate ASU West library units. All they want is the material within 48 hours of their request.

When interlibrary loan first started in the United States documents were requested by telephone, U. S. mail, or in some cases by teletype. Libraries set up reciprocal borrowing privileges, the request would be transmitted, and the document delivered either by courier, mail, a delivery service such as UPS, or even in person. While this service worked, and worked well, the "traditional" delivery routes were slow. How many times have patrons heard or librarians uttered those immortal words "Certainly, we can obtain that document for you but please don't expect it for three to four weeks." This slow turnaround time, combined with the fiscal implications of labor and delivery costs made it quickly apparent that more efficient, economic ways of delivery had to be developed.[3]

As stringent fiscal necessities have become a reality, private and public institutions are also employing innovative document delivery methods. Also vendors very quickly perceived a need in the library world for commercial document delivery and a market where libraries information needs could be fulfilled promptly. Let me briefly describe a few programs currently underway across the United States.

The "Electronic Reserve Room" pilot project at San Diego State University consists of an articles database set up by the faculty. The system provides for payment by student debit-cards on each article printed out. Usage records are kept by publisher name and a portion of each student fee is allocated for copyright royalties. Brett Butler from San Diego State, reported at the recent PSP conference in Washington, DC that the program will eventually enable students to access articles via their own personal computers locally and worldwide via Internet.[4]

At the same conference, CARL president Rebecca Lenzini, presented an update on Uncover2. More than 600,000 articles are being added annually. Articles are sent by fax, users pay the varying article costs by credit card, and the copyright fee is automatically built in. CARL has obtained rights to store materials by optical scan from 370 publishers.[5]

An excellent example of "electronic document delivery" is the exciting pilot program developed by the Copyright Clearance Center within the past year to examine storage and electronic distribution of copyrighted material. CCC (who is presently not releasing companies' names involved in the project) works in conjunction with user organizations, to obtain the rights to electronically convert, store, and distribute published works (such as journals, books, magazines and conference proceedings) via a personalized in-house database. The databases meet the highly specific information needs of the user organization in a more targeted fashion than do commercial databases.[6] For example, one company is using this service to support their nationwide quality improvement programs. They obtained permission to provide articles, book chapters, and various full-text materials electronically to their quality coordinators for use as a resource tool. This program has worked so well that the company is seeking to add other proprietary material to their large database. Pages are scanned and converted into ASCII format to provide maximum benefit.[7]

For the Copyright Clearance Center to consider an organization as a possible participant in the pilot program, the following conditions must be met:

1. The pilot location must include a significant number of workstations. Additionally, these must be for users who are likely to need the similar full-text information.
2. The workstations must be discrete–the material cannot be available to a wider network of users outside the pilot project.
3. The user organizations must define with some degree of precision what the primary information needs of the network are.
4. The body of material requested should be between 100-200 works.
5. User organizations must anticipate the hardware, software and network protocols needed.
6. The set of data output requirements with conditions of royalties must be discussed agreed upon by organization and the CCC.[8]

Recently ASU West's implementation of "document delivery" has been broadened to include commercial document delivery services. We have established accounts with CARL's Uncover2 and OCLC's FirstSearch. One agreeable feature of these services is the copyright fee is automatically built in. When neither campus can supply the requested material or if the timeline is too short to depend on traditional interlibrary loan, our Information Delivery Specialist will turn to these commercial sources for rapid turnaround time. The library currently pays all fees for our faculty. Our students and community borrowers also have the option to order their own documents from Uncover2 if they have a valid credit card and access to a fax machine. I have personally witnessed this service. A copy of an article was requested, charged against our deposit account and received within 15 minutes by telefacsimile. What user could resist that turnaround time?

How do publishers feel about document delivery? Some are wary, some interested, and others are taking a "wait and see" attitude. Publishers, states Karen Hunter, Vice-President at Elsevier Science Publishing Company "must do severe soul-searching and consider four alternatives in document delivery:

1. Actively support and encourage document supply services,
2. Ignore or tolerate them,
3. Vigorously oppose all delivery systems (an unrealistic attitude) or,
4. Do it yourself."[9]

It is imperative for both librarians and publishers alike to realize that the future is now. Malinconico states in a recent article that the same technology used to scan documents for facsimile transmission may be used to digitize them for electronic storage and dissemination.[10]

Libraries investigating document delivery services need to negotiate with a company to arrive at a mutually agreeable contract. When discussion turns to contracts, fees and legal implications–most librarians become visibly nervous and anxious; a fact that does not go unnoticed by the representative negotiating on the contractor's behalf. Michael Scott stated "the bottom line is the advantage will always be in favor of the vendor."[11] The literature however, can provide some assistance in how to handle negotiations:

A contract is a set of mutual promises between two or more persons—*not* a one-party document. While it is perfectly understandable that the vendor is in the business to produce a profit, it is also understandable the library has certain needs. Both parties expectations can be met, to the mutual benefit of all involved.

It is a common practice to place the lesser, unimportant items at the beginning of a contract. Therefore, if the vendor agrees to alter these elements, a better case can be made not to alter the more substantial items farther on in the contract.

Frank Bridge in a *Library Journal* article[12] states that the institution should attempt to identify why exactly a vendor wants to sell the product to you. Is it a new service? Are they trying to break into the region or market? If these reasons can be identified, the library may be able to negotiate for concessions. An institution can also negotiate financial penalties for poor system reliability. These penalties can either be daily fees or maintenance discounts. A common practice is to agree upon the percentage of time that the system or service is available. If the downtime exceeds these limits, financial compensation could be called for.[13]

Finally, even if not mandated by institutional policy, it is prudent that an attorney inspect the contract for any loopholes not readily noticeable to either the library or the contractor.

Document delivery paradigms will continue to shift and change due to emerging technology and the sobering fiscal realities. The "wonders" of today's technology will be the primitive machines of tomorrow. As budgets become tighter, funding continues to decrease and buying power is eaten up with increasing inflation; more and more institutions will discover that document delivery may no longer be an option, but rather a necessity.

We must all anticipate and embrace the future rather than fear it. I encourage you to examine your particular situation and incorporate the innovative programs currently being utilized or develop a pilot project that addresses your own particular needs. By providing document delivery, your institution can stretch its resources and still provide timely access to important information. The future is here!

NOTES

1. Richard W. Boss and Judy McQueen, "Document Delivery in the United States: A Report to the Council on Library Resources." ERIC Document #244-626 (Washington, D.C.: Council on Library Resources, Inc., 1982): p. 1.

2. Susan B. Ardis and Karen S. Croneis, "Document Delivery, Cost Containment and Serial Ownership," *C&RL News* 48, no. 10 (1987): p. 627.

3. Eugene Garfield, "Enter Credit Code... To Retrieve Data. Document Delivery Systems in the Information Age," *Phi Kappa Phi Journal* 63, no.3 (1983): p. 8.

4. Gayle Feldman, "Professional Publishing Goes Electronic," in "Professional Publishing," *Publishers Weekly* (May 11,1992): p. 32.

5. Ibid, p. 33.

6. Martin Wilson, "Copyright Clearance Center Pilots Electronic Access," *Information Today* 9, no.2 (1992): p. 18.

7. Ibid.

8. Ibid.

9. Feldman, p. 33.

10. S. Michael Malinconico, "Information's Brave New World," *Library Journal* 117, no.8 (1992): p. 39.

11. Michael D. Scott, "Commercial User-Vendor Litigation: The User's Point of View," *Computer/Law Journal* 5, no.2 (1985): p. 289.

12. Frank R. Bridge, "Negotiate Automation Contracts Yourself," in "Managing Technology," *Library Journal* 117, no.3 (1992): p. 143.

13. Ibid, pp. 142-143.

Document Delivery Vendors: Benefits and Choices

Martha Lewis

In the Library/Information Services department at Abbott Laboratories, we rely heavily on both commercial and non-commercial vendors to fill our document delivery needs. Although we also use vendors to provide copies of patents, this discussion will cover only copies of journal articles and book chapters. I will provide background to give you a feel for our operation, define types of vendors and the kinds of services they provide, and describe advantages of using vendors. I'll discuss how we manage the few disadvantages, our experiences in negotiating contracts, and how we evaluate vendor performance. I'll conclude with a few tips to help you get the best results in selecting and working with vendors. I am not able to mention individual vendor names or prices. However, in the May 1992 issue of *Online*, Georgia Finnigan presents a helpful review of document delivery technology and sources.[1]

ENVIRONMENT

Abbott Laboratories' motto, "Health Care Worldwide," describes our context. Abbott is a Fortune 500 company with diverse products in pharmaceutical, diagnostic, hospital, nutritional, chemical, and agricultural areas. The Library is located at our corporate headquarters and serves all employees worldwide. Our services support research, development, marketing, medical services to cus-

---

Martha Lewis is Head, Library Operations, Abbott Laboratories, Dept. 441, Bldg. AP6B, 1 Abbott Park Rd., Abbott Park, IL 60064-3500.

tomers, and management. From a journal collection of about 1300 titles, we are able to fill about 80 percent of the article requests we receive. We must also meet urgent deadlines: our patrons often need article copies within just a few hours in order to make critical business or medical decisions.

Of approximately 15,900 articles supplied by outside sources in 1991, about 1100 were received in one to two days; an additional 2400 were received in one to two weeks. Over 90 percent of the remaining 12,400 arrived within three weeks. Of these figures, roughly 90 percent represent articles supplied by commercial vendors.

We are a "net borrower," with a relatively small collection. We are unable to reciprocate with loans to match the wide variety and large number of items we need to obtain. Using vendors reduces the burden we would place on other libraries.

DEFINITIONS

Non-commercial vendors generally are based at major university libraries and fill requests from material in their own collections. They are not necessarily non-profit, but any profits they make usually support their library collection, building funds, or other educational purposes. They may offer special services as part of a membership program, charging for document delivery at cost but using membership donations to raise funds. They generally have more limited services than do commercial vendors.

Commercial vendors operate for a profit. They may have their own collections, which may be subject-specific. They usually supply photocopies; one major vendor supplies original pages, or "tear sheets." General commercial vendors, also called "general suppliers," rely on public or academic collections nearby (or sometimes not so nearby), using a network of "runners" to locate and copy articles in different cities or even different states. Some have offices or runners in other countries.

ADVANTAGES OF USING VENDORS

In the following discussion, I will not make specific distinctions between commercial and non-commercial vendors. Table 1 indicates which advantages are generally unique to commercial vendors.

Using document delivery vendors saves library staff time. Vendors accept our orders in a variety of formats, as we receive them from our patrons. Examples include handwritten citations on our own request forms, informal memos, references circled on a published bibliography, items marked on an online search printout, and formatted orders generated by electronic requesting systems we have created. Vendors do not require citation verification. Many of them do some checking on inaccurate citations as part of the base price of filling an order. Most offer to do online searches to solve citation problems for an added charge; a dollar limit can be set in advance. Consolidating orders also saves staff time. Orders are placed, received, and billed in batches.

Several general commercial vendors offer customized billing, with order details included on the invoice according to the customer's specifications, or subtotaled by department or patron, or with rush service and delivery charges either added to the cost of each item or totalled as a separate line item. Some vendors offer attractive savings for larger quantities of orders placed per month or per year. Some offer discounts for annual, semiannual, or monthly prepayment plans.

A few advantages of using vendors are especially important in our context. Vendors are highly sensitive to our rush needs and can work with deadlines in which rush can mean an hour rather than a day. Orders and article copies are frequently faxed or sent by express delivery services. Having vendors handle copyright payments for us relieves us of some of the record keeping related to copyright responsibilities. Vendors can track down obscure items for us, even contacting authors to obtain a copy. The confidentiality of our research and business interests is protected; when a vendor contacts an author or another company about a publication, the vendor is the buyer and we are anonymous.

We can place an order for a longer journal article, which may turn out to be a complete supplement issue, without too much concern about whether we will receive a photocopy or the original publication. Several general commercial vendors we have used are willing to obtain original journal issues or other complete documents when this is a better choice than photocopying. A dollar limit per item can be set in advance; then the vendor may order docu-

TABLE 1

Summary of Advantages

Labor savings: variety of formats

                    verification unnecessary

                    check inaccurate citations

                    * search online for problem citations

                    consolidation

*Customized billing

*Quantity discounts

Can routinely meet urgent deadlines

Handle copyright payments

*Locate obscure items; contact authors

Confidential

*Purchase documents

* Produce customized reports

Business relationship

Orders vs. Requests

Reduce "net borrower" burden

New services

* Indicates factors usually unique to commercial vendors

---

ments up to this price without needing to check with us for approval each time. The vendor handles prepayment if needed, saving us staff time and minimizing delays in obtaining the item.

Some commercial vendors offer customized reports detailing the history of transactions: how many orders filled per journal, per patron, etc. This data can be very helpful in analyzing document delivery activity and in suggesting future subscription orders, either for economic or copyright reasons.

Finally, the relationship between a commercial vendor and a customer is itself an advantage. It is a business relationship. The transaction between us and a vendor is an "order" rather than a "request." When we request material from other libraries, we are dependent on cooperation, goodwill, and the restrictions and pressures under which that library is operating at the moment. Of course our need is secondary to that library's mission to support its own institution. In contrast, commercial vendors are dependent on their customers. When we place an order with a vendor, successfully filling that order is very important to them. They need our business, and by using them we can reduce the burden a "net borrower" places on other libraries.

Commercial document delivery vendors visit our library just as subscription vendors do. A long term vendor recently visited to discuss at length what our needs are, in what additional ways they can serve us, as well as how they are performing for us. New services are continually developed.

MANAGING DISADVANTAGES

There aren't many disadvantages to using vendors. We pay a higher invoice cost per item, but labor reductions offset that. Vendors do not loan material, so Interlibrary Loan sources are still needed for sharing of books and other documents. Many vendors, particularly the collection based ones, specialize in specific subject areas, such as life sciences or business, requiring the use of multiple vendors to cover all the material we need. The general commercial vendor has a low failure rate when locating items; but the few items they can't locate we can usually get successfully from another vendor.

I don't consider it a disadvantage to use several commercial vendors. For one thing, their prices vary and orders can be assigned selectively based on subject strength and price structure. In addition, the reasons for using multiple document delivery vendors mirror the reasons for using multiple serials subscription vendors. In her presentation at the 1990 NASIG meeting, October Ivins listed six reasons to use multiple subscription vendors. I paraphrase her list with slight changes to fit the document delivery context:

1. The variety of published material is too great for any one vendor to handle.
2. Using multiple vendors avoids the risks involved in "putting all your eggs in one basket."
3. Fostering competition preserves choice.
4. We can identify vendors' differing strengths and weaknesses.
5. Our ability to compare performance and services is enhanced.
6. The potential for increased business keeps vendors "on their toes," resulting in better service.[2]

Using multiple vendors improves our ability to obtain any document. As one of our vendors says, if it exists we can find it.

NEGOTIATING CONTRACTS

Some vendors require contracts, but many do not. Even when a contract is not suggested by the vendor, the customer may want to have one to insure that copyright payments will be the vendor's responsibility. A vendor is more likely to require a contract if the customer will receive a price discount based on quantity of orders or based on a special prepayment plan. Vendors who do require them have standard contracts covering transmittal of orders, document delivery methods, copyright payments, prices per order, prices of added services such as rush handling, searching, fax or express delivery, and payment plans. The contract may also include statements about promised or expected fulfillment time and penalty charges if a minimum quantity of orders is not placed.

Contract discussions are quite informal, usually completed over the phone. My experience with vendors has been that they are often willing to modify the contract, the services included, and even prices, if asked. The key is asking. In selecting a vendor, even if these details are not included in the contract, it is wise to discuss customer service issues, such as reports on the status of orders in process. Pay attention to added costs. They may be more important than the base price. Charges for copyright payments, one or two levels of rush service, and fax or express delivery are usually "a la carte."

It is standard practice also to have legal review of the contract. Once I am satisfied with the terms of a vendor contract, it is forwarded for further review and approval within my company.

EVALUATING VENDOR PERFORMANCE

Some vendors offer customized reports summarizing order activity. These reports can be very useful. However, if several vendors are used, a library database including all orders from all sources may be preferable.

For each article or other item obtained, we enter one line of data identifying the patron, journal title and year, vendor used, number of sources or vendors tried, rush status, turnaround time, and other details. A one character code is sufficient for all except patron, journal, and year. We run a monthly analysis of vendor performance, looking at the percent of orders filled by each vendor, rush and routine turnarounds, and which items took longer than an acceptable time to fill. We use this information to initiate discussions with vendors regarding problems or desired changes in services and to adjust selection of vendors.

Accuracy in vendor selection is a major factor in evaluation of our own staff performance. Library technicians can easily be trained to make essentially all vendor selections. Routinely the first vendor selected is able to fill the order 93 percent of the time or better. A high quantity or proportion of rush orders indicates a heavier workload. The data analysis helps us recognize the work our own staff is doing, and give them feedback on performance.

Finally, we use the same data for collection development, identifying journals for future subscription orders. Some analysis is required to determine whether many orders for articles from the same journal represent an ongoing need for access to that journal or only a short term need, such as research on a project that may not be funded for future research.

SUGGESTIONS

In conclusion, I'd like to leave you with a few suggestions.

When selecting a new vendor, arrange for a trial period of at least three to four months before signing a contract or committing to a large quantity of orders.

Look carefully at hidden or "a la carte" costs. Analyze how your situation, especially your rush requirements, will affect the total average cost per item.

Ask for what you want. Don't hesitate to inquire about special arrangements to fit your needs. Most vendors want to know what you need, and will make adjustments, because they want your business.

NOTES

1. Georgia Finnigan, "Document Delivery Gets Personal," Online, 16(1992):106-108.
2. October Ivins, "We Need Department Store and Boutique Serials Vendors," Serials Librarian, 17(1990):99-106.

PRE-CONFERENCE WORKSHOP

Electronic Networking and Serials Resources: Quotidian Applications for the Curious and the Cynical

Birdie MacLennan
Workshop Leader

Robin B. Devin
Recorder

quotidian–1. Recurring daily. 2. Everyday; commonplace.

Birdie MacLennan began her workshop with the above definition. She explained that the purpose of the session was to inform people who have little or no experience with networking and/or electronic communications about the resources that are available to them, as well as to enlighten those already using networks about things that they may not be aware of. MacLennan is Serials Cataloger at the University of Vermont as well as Listowner and Moderator of SERIALST.

Robin Devin is Acquisitions Head, University of Rhode Island Library, Kingston, RI 02881.

© 1993 by The Haworth Press, Inc. All rights reserved.

MacLennan pointed out that electronic networking now includes more than 5000 computer networks in thirty-five countries which serve over a million people. She provided a brief historic overview of the various networks with particular emphasis on the BITNET and the Internet.

BITNET (Because It's Time Network) originated in 1981 when City University of New York and Yale University linked their IBM computers. It has since expanded to include ten cooperating networks worldwide. The majority of users are academic and use the network for electronic mail, file transfer, and interactive messages.

Internet is a network of networks connected through TCP/IP (Transmission Control Protocol/Internet Protocol). It developed out of a network called ARPANET which was designed by the Defense Department in 1969. In 1986 the NSFnet, administered by the National Science Foundation, became the backbone of the network. Current uses include electronic mail, ftp, and telnet. The Internet will form the basis of the future National Research and Education Network (NREN).

MacLennan then explained the importance that networks can have for serials work and handed out a list of electronic forums and discussion groups related to serials. These include SERIALST, Newsletter on Serials Pricing Issues, and SERCITES. A new addition to the list is NASIGNET, which was introduced this year to serve as the official electronic communications forum of the North American Serials Interest Group. Participation is limited to NASIG members.

At this point MacLennan introduced Shiela K. Osheroff, Serials Cataloger at Oregon State University, who discussed how to get connected to the networks. Many serials people have access to BITNET and/or the Internet through their institutions or places of employment. But for those who don't, Osheroff provided a directory of vendors who offer electronic services including e-mail and access to the Internet. She explained that to get connected you need a grounded electrical outlet, a computer, a telephone line with a modular jack, a modem, and communications software. For those who are selecting a commercial vendor, Osheroff advised asking the following questions:

1. Do the services match what you need?
2. How easy is the system to use?
3. Is the amount and type of support you need available?
4. Will you need a specific type of modem or software?
5. Is the mail system right for you?
6. Is the cost reasonable?

MacLennan continued her presentation with an explanation of basic network address concepts, practical tips on using e-mail, and information on e-mail ethics and etiquette.

The second half of the program was dedicated to network applications. MacLennan showed examples of e-mail messages using the IBM, VAX, and UNIX systems, demonstrated how to get a file list or index from listserv, and explained how to retrieve information from listserv archives. She showed examples of listserv retrieval using interactive searching with LDBASE and batch mode searching. The file transfer protocol (ftp) on Internet was also explained. MacLennan ended the session with a discussion of FREE-NETing using the "telnet" command.

Workshop participants received a packet of information which included handouts on NASIGNET, BITNET listserv command options, e-mail ethics and etiquette, networking resources, search and retrieval methods, a glossary of networking terms, and the directory of communications vendors, along with a workshop overview and synopsis.

WORKSHOP SESSION REPORTS

Cataloging Serial Computer Files

Colleen Thorburn
Rebecca Ringler

Workshop Leaders

Margaret Mering

Recorder

The purpose of this workshop was to examine problems specifically related to the cataloging of serial computer files and to discuss methods of providing catalog access to the newer types of computer files. Several examples of catalog records for various types of computer files were examined throughout the workshop. Colleen Thorburn, Assistant Librarian in the Cataloging Department at the University of Florida, began the workshop by giving an overview of the complexities of cataloging these "new tech serials." They can be cataloged using either the serials or computer files format. The environment of computer files is ever changing. Terminology is anything but set and can often be confusing. What to base the description on varies from file to file. Frequently, they lack a "title page." Sometimes, the cataloger does not have the physical item in

---

Margaret Mering is Principal Serials Cataloger, Serials Department, University of Nebraska-Lincoln Libraries, Lincoln, NE 68588-0410.

© 1993 by The Haworth Press, Inc. All rights reserved.

hand to base the description of the item on and is totally reliant on its documentation. Thorburn expressed concern that practices set locally and seen as important may conflict with standards set nationally and by other libraries, which in turn may effect bibliographic access to these serials.

Thorburn next compared the similarities and the differences between cataloging floppy disks using the serials or the computer files format. Regardless of format, the title, the beginning date of publication, and the subject headings can all be the same. However, some information is recorded in different MARC fields depending on which format is used. For example, system information is listed in the 538 field in the computer files format but in the 500 field in the serials format. Moreover, catalogers using the serials format may approach the same item differently than catalogers using the computers files format. Catalogers using the computer file format, for instance, are more likely to use a 520 field than a cataloger using the serials format. Thorburn showed one cataloging example where the same title had been given an added entry for the publisher when cataloged using the serials format but lacked this entry when using the computer files format.

Rebecca Ringler, Catalog Librarian at the University of California, San Diego, described the cataloging of magnetic tapes and the problems associated with them. Magnetic tapes are stored remotely on mainframes. The cataloger rarely has the actual item in hand. Gathering all the information required for a complete bibliographic description leaves the cataloger largely dependent on written documentation supplied by the publisher and other information supplied by the systems office and other sources. (In formation about the documentation is recorded in the 556 field in the computer file format.) Producers of computer reels tend to be noncommercial and are not usually good about giving a lot of bibliographic data.

Ringler talked then about the cataloging of CD-ROM disks. These make up one of the largest category of computer materials. They are usually issued by commercial publishers. Often printed counterparts of the disks exist. Linking notes between the two versions should be included on CD-ROM records. The contents of the two versions may not, however, be the same. The disks' version may not cover the entire run of the serial. Archival disks may be produced at future dates. Disks for the same title may have some overlap in their coverage.

One unresolved problem in cataloging CD-ROMs is how to handle product names which often appear in a prominent position on disks. They are frequently followed by trademark symbols. In reviewing OCLC records, Ringler discovered several solutions implemented by catalogers. Some have considered them to be part of the title proper. Others have recorded them as series statements or mentioned them in "At head of title" notes.

Next Thorburn spoke about the cataloging of single electronic journals available directly from the producer and full-text journals available in commercial databases. Bibliographic records for both types of journals will have notes explaining their universal modes of access and restrictions to their use. These notes will be retained in the master records. However, local public displays will also include in their bibliographic records local modes of access and specific holdings information. Journals from commercial databases will list contractual limitations to access. Because the amount of coverage of the same journal can vary between databases, a note in the bibliographic record addressing coverage is important.

The workshop concluded with an open discussion between the presenters and the audience. Everyone was in agreement that cataloging serial computer files calls for creativity on the part of the cataloger. Although the environment of computer files is still in flux and uncertain, it is an area of cataloging that catalogers should attempt to shape now rather than attempting to work with standards set up by others in the future.

Automating Binding Procedures: Using INNOVACQ vs. An In-House Database

Barbara Shaffer
Karen Aufdemberge
Lisa Macklin

Workshop Leaders

Paul Parisi

Recorder

Barbara Shaffer and Karen Aufdemberge, both Assistant Serials Librarians at the University of Toledo, began the workshop by discussing their experiences as the University of Toledo implemented the INNOVACQ binding preparation module. Prior to 1989 they had used a manual system for binding preparation. In 1989 they began using INNOVACQ to produce pull-slips and to display binding status in the OPAC. By April 1992 they were using the binding module in its entirety, including the printing of binding slips.

The main tasks required to get the INNOVACQ binding module up were the creation of the binding database and the design of an acceptable binding slip format that met both the library's and the binder's needs. Creation of the binding database was a labor-intensive effort that involved cooperation between the library and its binder. Records were organized, edited, and keyed into the database. Lists were printed out, proofed, and re-edited. Final lists were sent to the binder for final copy proofing and editing. Binding information keyed into the INNOVACQ check-in records included:

Paul A. Parisi is President, Acme Bookbinding Company, 100 Cambridge St., Charleston, MA 02129.

© 1993 by The Haworth Press, Inc. All rights reserved.

a. *Bind Information:* Binder's pattern number, color of print and buckram, and collating codes. This information prints in the binding instructions field.
b. *Bind Title:* The title to be printed on the spine of the volume.
c. *Bind Note:* This information prints on the pull-slip but not the binding slip. Bind notes are used to show variable information needed on the binding slip, as well as special instructions to library personnel concerning the binding of a title.

Once the system was implemented, the binding database is kept up to date by sending to the binder a paper copy of records to be added or changed before the INNOVACQ system is modified. This practice ensures that information needed by the binder is recorded correctly.

Shaffer and Aufdemberge displayed sample screens and forms for the participants' discussion. A binder asked if it would not be more efficient to have an automated interface between the library's automated system and the binder's binding module, so that machine-readable information could be exchanged, rather than paper binding slips that must be manually re-keyed by the library binder. Both Shaffer and Aufdemberge replied that use of the INNOVACQ binding module expedited binding preparation and improved public access to available holdings.

The second part of the workshop was presented by Lisa Macklin, Serials Records Librarian at the University of North Texas. Her institution had an in-house bindery until several years ago. When the administration decided to close the University's bindery and to use the services of a commercial binder, the library weighed its options to streamline binding preparation.

They first considered using HELPNET, the binding preparation software that their binder (Heckman Bindery) offered, but ruled this option out because necessary features were not available. They did not have the option of using an integrated binding module, so they decided to create an in-house system. They used several software packages during their development phases, including dBase and Paradox. Paradox offered network support and multi-user capability as well as a user-friendly programming routine.

Macklin explained the phases of their software implementation. First they defined the necessary data elements for a binding record which included: title, library workshop, color, collection, binding frequency, class code, rub/slot and notes. Information to create the database was garnered from plastic "credit" cards used to prepare periodical titles for their binder, from the kardex, and from the periodical acquisitions database. They keyed information into the database and printed and edited lists, creating four thousand (4,000) title records during a nine-month period. As with the INNOVACQ system, before they could update their database with new titles, title changes, or titles requiring a different lettering format (e.g., vertical), they had to send special paper forms to the binder and receive a master ticket with information that only the binder could supply.

The in-house system generates paper binding slips that the binder has to re-key at the bindery to meet the needs of their production process. Fortunately, the binder, Heckman, agreed to this arrangement. Macklin explained that they can communicate to the public sector what is at the bindery. They can print lists sorted alphabetically by collection for all volumes at the bindery. These reports include the date of the shipment and the library code which signifies one of the two library locations. They also can generate a purchase order report that calculates the binding cost of the shipment by library.

Several useful features of the system include: LOOK–an option that lets patrons inquire into the status or availability of periodical volumes; COUNT–an option that determines the number of binding tickets for each library per binding shipment; and ZAP–a deletion screen that allows a user to remove a title if the identification number and the first fourteen characters of the title match.

Macklin explained that they plan to put the LOOK function onto the local area network, to create a missing issue database and to generate cost projections by title. These "wish list" items are addressed by the hardware/software support staff that is essential to the development of an in-house module such as the one that the University of North Texas has developed.

At the end of the workshop a number of participants questioned the need for binding information to be part of an integrated system. An ALA committee (AVIAC) is currently in the process of writing standards for a generic interface between automated systems and binding modules used by library binders. Several systems vendors expressed interest in these developments.

The Footbone's Connected to the Anklebone, or, Enumeration, Checking-In and Labeling Instructions

Beverley Geer-Butler
Daphne Hsueh
Workshop Leaders

Lawrence R. Keating II
Recorder

The workshop focused on managing enumeration data in an on-line environment, and addressed the problems involved in reconciling various standards (bibliographic description, citation, holdings) and patterns (publication, binding), to provide users with consistent information. The presentation was predicated on the assumptions that a library has cataloged and classified its serials, has an automated environment, and has not adopted the USMARC Format for Holdings Data.

Beverley Geer-Butler, Head of the Copy Cataloging Section at The Ohio State University Libraries, began with an illustration of the maze of decision points for a user trying to retrieve cited information. Check-in and labeling are crucial functions, the first steps in serials control. Check-in can create more twists in the maze since it is an attempt to control inherently changeable materials. It is usually performed by first-level personnel who require extensive

---

Lawrence R. Keating II is Head, Serials Department, University of Houston Libraries, Houston, TX 77204-2091.

training in order to prevent the possible service failures caused by not recognizing title changes, numbering changes, etc. Check-in is not performed in isolation, but in relation to the enumeration/publication patterns which are integral parts of bibliographic description and binding.

Labeling (defined as marking the written representation of enumeration on the piece) is equally critical in user retrieval, yet the relative insignificance accorded to it in the serials control chain is indicated by the lack of either a local or national labeling standard. Standards exist for other aspects of serials control (e.g., MARC Serials Format, Library Binding Institute standards, USMARC Format for Holdings Data); some operate independently and do not present information in the same manner. Citation methods vary widely across disciplines, as illustrated with examples from library science, British medical, and humanities journals. The effort to achieve uniformity at OSU is based on the criteria that labeling information in the online catalog should agree with spine information, and should be uniform across all copies.

Daphne C. Hsueh, Chinese Studies Librarian at The Ohio State University Libraries, described how OSU achieves labeling uniformity in the absence of a standard. The OSU library system includes a main research library, an undergraduate library, 26 departmental libraries and some 40 other collections, all linked by the Library Control System (LCS). Acquisitions and Cataloging are centralized and part of Technical Services; Binding (also centralized), is part of Collection Maintenance (which includes labeling). Prior to automation, holdings were listed centrally as well as in departmental libraries; each location made its own decisions on the representation of enumeration levels, and customized binding decisions were made by the various locations. At present, OSU uses various systems for automated library functions (InnovAcq, LCS, Microvac), with a migration to OhioLink planned by the end of 1993.

In the mid 1970s, OSU converted serials holdings to the online system with a one-year project to transcribe information from the Central Serials Division check-in records. Completion of the project revealed variations in the representation of enumeration information among multiple copies held by different locations, and sometimes, even within the same copy. The need for standard identifiers for the physical pieces of a serial led to the formation of a committee and the issuance in 1983 of the OSU Labeling Policy and Procedures.

The committee's solution involved both policy and technical decisions. Policy decisions included: holdings descriptors for online display and bound volume spines of the same title should be the same for all copies; labeling patterns would be displayed online in the holdings file for all locations to follow; the Serials Cataloging Unit would be the sole authority for defining and changing any labeling pattern; and policy implementation would begin with 1984 with no attempt at retrospective updating. Technical decisions included: use of English descriptors, with English equivalents substituted for foreign terms; only selected commonly found descriptors would be used; and a labeling pattern could be given in as many levels as required for the serial's publication pattern. Detailed guidelines were worked out to deal with the format of the labeling instruction (levels of enumeration, as well as the order of levels), symbols to be used for communication, and the application of English equivalents of foreign terms.

Hsueh listed the advantages of the revised policy. A measure of uniformity has been achieved in marking pieces so that spine information agrees with the holdings file. Uniformity is carried over to all copies held by one or more locations. The work of the Bindery Unit has been eased with the elimination of customized practices. Disadvantages include the fact that while artificial substitution of English for foreign descriptors may have made it easier for users or library personnel, it strays from the goal of retaining the same consistent citation identifiers throughout the serials chain. Also, this type of practice could involve a possible conflict with cataloging standards, and inhibits the libraries' participation in any kind of union listing. The need for uniformity in identifying a serial item throughout the serials chain–from citation through description to shelf location–was re-emphasized.

Discussion following the presentations was lively and extended, and touched on such issues as staff training, input from Public Services staff on the decisions made, the difficulty of preparing a comprehensive manual, and the handling of various situations such as frequency changes.

Game Shows, Elevators, Full Plates, and Other Allegories: A Look at the Present State and Future Possibilities of LC Subject Headings

William E. Studwell
Workshop Leader

Sandy L. Folsom
Recorder

William Studwell, a Professor in the University Libraries at Northern Illinois University, began with an analogy, "Gorbachev and Me," comparing the breakup of European communism with the reform of subject access in libraries. The author recounted efforts made by himself and others throughout the 1980s to promote the idea of a subject heading code and revisions to LC subject headings. He also described the present, rather static, state of affairs in this area. The Library of Congress has announced no comprehensive plan for LC subject headings, and it is unclear whether the concept of standardization will be embraced.

To illustrate his ideas about LC subject headings, Studwell presented six allegories, three of which described the present state of LC subject headings. The first–"Will the real year of the subject code please stand up?"–was modeled on the old television show "To Tell the Truth." The author used this allegory to illustrate his point that in each year since 1988 there have been signs that a subject heading code was imminent but it has not yet come to fruition. The

---

Sandy Folsom is Serials Cataloger, Central Michigan University, 604 S. University, Mt. Pleasant, MI 48858.

second allegory, "least effort" and the implications of the least effort attitude has on subject access systems, suggested that systems become more logical, flexible and understandable in order to satisfy a body of patrons who are generally not patient or persistent. The final allegory describing the present situations was "consumerism," that is, the disinclination of patrons to be satisfied with services offered to them. The speaker found it likely that if dissatisfaction with LC subject headings continues, the LC monopoly on subject access and the LC subject system itself will be threatened by the rise of competing subject access systems.

The next three allegories suggested possible future directions for LC. The first of these was LC's "full plate." It described how LC has received a great deal of input on this issue from a variety of sources in recent years, to the point where a major decision should be forthcoming. The next allegory was called the "elevator dilemma." It illustrated how, like an elevator, LC has only three choices: up, down, or standing still. Since going down or standing still are essentially out of the question, the real issue is how far up to go. There is a great difference between going up only a few floors, the route of minor, reactionary modification, and going all the way to the top, which would result in substantial revision. The final allegory was the "three-pronged fork in the road," another question with three alternatives to be chosen by the library community. The signs over the three prongs read "LC Subject Access, Status Quo. Dead End. Soon to be Closed but Easy to Enter," "LC Subject Access, Revised, Upgraded and Codified. Much Improved Pathway. Must be Entered by Early in the Twenty-first Century," and "Subject Access by Other Means. Uncertain Roadway. Can be Entered at Any Time."

Mr. Studwell concluded his paper by stating that although the immediate course of LC subject headings may be unknown, without some kind of significant revision, the future of this subject access system appears bleak. Returning to the "Gorbachev and Me" analogy, he speculated how present efforts to reform LC subject headings will be viewed in future decades, and whether or not a Boris Yeltsin-type figure will emerge on the scene to complete the initiatives begun by others.

A wide-ranging discussion of related issues took place following the presentation. Mr. Studwell was asked what he thought a subject heading code should entail. He described it as being like an AACR2 for subject headings, consisting not only of rules but with guiding principles as well. *The LC Subject Manual,* 4th edition, was discussed. Mr. Studwell concluded that although it is helpful for everyday practice, it is entirely lacking in theoretical principles.

A question about ambiguous terminology in headings led to a discussion of possible multiple levels of codification, based on individual libraries' needs. Mr. Studwell emphasized the desirability for a "broader door" approach, whereby patrons with varying levels of sophistication would have enhanced access through the use of more subject headings and alternative approaches in searching. Along with this there was a discussion of the possibility of eliminating rigidity in the order of elements in specific strings, so that subject searching would have keyword-like flexibility.

Other topics of discussion included MESH and Precis and how they compare with LC subject headings, as well as how LC's "golden opportunity" for subject heading reform in the 1980s has become an imperative for survival in the 1990s. The session concluded with discussion about the present process of subject analysis at LC and the apparent inconsistencies in practice between subject areas. This inconsistency was attributed to the overall lack of guiding principles for LC subject headings.

The Changing Role of the Vendor: Developing New Products and Services

William Leazer
Marian Reijnen

Workshop Leaders

Lucy Bottomley

Recorder

This workshop discussed various research and development issues, including how new services are developed in response to library needs; how customers are consulted about new products; and the effects of new products on service charges.

Marian Reijnen, Area Manager North America, Martinus Nijhoff International, began by stating that user needs and requirements increase with technological advances. Today's vendor needs to focus on services to respond better to his clients' needs.

Reijnen provided a historical background on her company, a service-oriented organization, tracing the developments through the domestic, European and international services. Martin Nijhoff, a 19th century poet, established his own publishing and distribution house to facilitate the publishing of his own as well as his fellow-poets' and friends' works. After his death, the business was expanded to include international services, especially for European periodicals, which were extensively collected during the World War II years. Reijnen concluded the historical overview emphasizing that Nijhoff is investing in the future by developing new products and customizing its services.

Lucy Bottomley is Library Network Specialist, National Library of Canada, Ottawa, ON K1A ON4, Canada.

The traditional role of the vendor has been to act as an intermediary between the publisher and the client. The vendor is expected to supply the materials, to handle financial transactions, to express clients' concerns and needs to publishers, and to convey publishers' current direction and developments to clients. The vendor also realizes that services are different for each type of market segment—bookstores, libraries, individuals—as well as for each of the geographical segments, Europe, North America, Eastern Europe, and the Far and Middle East. Investment is made in qualified and specialized personnel who also are able to respond to client language needs. Nijhoff's policy reflects this, along with an ongoing co-operation and open communications between vendor, client and publisher.

Reijnen pointed out that Nijhoff's research and development not only respond to client requests but also anticipate them in some cases. Old services or products are refined or new ones provided. The feasibility of a new service or product is analyzed in terms of user type and size, application, cost (upfront, ongoing, hidden), results, and risks. Reijnen agreed that the competitive nature of the vendor market gives a greater impetus to the development of new services and products.

Reijnen next reflected on vendor expectations vis à vis the client. Nijhoff would like to see its clients play an active role in product development and in the follow-up activities. This implies that the client, as a consumer, has the responsibility to respond to vendor inquiries, questionnaires and surveys, all aimed at providing a better product or service. After all, Reijnen concluded, service is a shared responsibility because it depends on communications between the vendor and the client.

William Leazer, Vice President, Majors Scientific Subscriptions, began by providing a profile of his company. Majors serves medical libraries (95%) and some technical libraries (5%), and handles subscriptions and continuations for its clients.

Leazer elaborated on current service and usage. Clients have direct access to the database and are able to perform individual title searching, claiming and ordering. Future developments will include Electronic Data Interchange (EDI) with the application of X12 standards for ordering, claiming and invoicing. The draft subsets of the

X12 standards, specifically defined for the serial industry, are now available and some are ready for testing. Majors will be implementing the claim first, followed by the purchase order. Currently most operations are manual, and the information received is rekeyed. The manual aspect of the operation is useful in reconciling errors and in reviewing premature claims, especially for irregular publications. Automation has been applied to one message format, the Invoice, which is received as a combination of the X12 and MARC formats. Majors intends to comply with the X12 standard for all message formats.

Leazer stated that as new services are developed, the cost of implementing them is not always passed on to the client. If the new service saves time for the vendor, the cost is usually absorbed by the vendor. In developing new products vendors would like to see more cooperation from publishers. In conclusion, Leazer echoed Reijnen's statement that effective communications are crucial to customer satisfaction.

Check-In with the SISAC Symbol (Bar Code): Implementation and Uses for Libraries, Publishers and Automation Vendors

Tina Feick
M. Stephen Dane
George Wright, IV
Jim Young

Workshop Leaders

Marcella Lesher

Recorder

Tina Feick, Chair of SISAC and Serials Specialist for Blackwell Periodicals Division, Oxford, England, opened the session with a brief overview of the activities and purposes of the Serials Industry Systems Advisory Committee (SISAC). SISAC, formed in 1982, has worked to create a standardized identification code for serials. The standard is known as (SICI), the Serial Item and Contribution Identifier, and is encoded in a bar code (the SISAC symbol) which publishers can print on the cover of their journals.

SISAC activities have been concentrated in three areas: (1) standardization of formats to allow for computer-to-computer transmission of all business transactions for the serials industry (the ANSI XI 2 standard), (2) automation through a standardized machine-readable code to identify specific serial issues, and (3) standardiza-

---

Marcella Lesher is Periodicals Librarian, St. Mary's University, One Camino Santa Maria, San Antonio, TX 78228-8608.

© 1993 by The Haworth Press, Inc. All rights reserved.

tion of coding of contributions within serials. Feick then presented a list of publishers and automation vendors currently committed to implementing the SISAC bar code symbol.

George Wright IV, Vice-President, Product Identification and Processing Systems, Inc., discussed terminology surrounding the SISAC symbol and the SICI standard. He outlined the difference between the serial item identifier and the contribution identifier–the two elements comprising the SICI standard. The serial item data elements of the code (ISSN, chronology, enumeration) are currently being used by several publishers in conjunction with the SISAC symbol and for computer-to-computer communications. The contribution data elements (identification of individual articles) are not being commercially used at present. He also provided the audience with selected pages from the Z39.56-1991 American National Standard, "Serial Item and Contribution Identifier" booklet, and other pertinent material.

Stephen Dane, General Manager of Kluwer Academic Publishers, spoke about why publishers should be using the SISAC bar code. He pointed out that it is customer friendly–providing immediate access to the publication during the check-in process and has other potential applications such as inventory uses. He also used the "chicken vs. egg" analogy, pointing out that increased participation by publishers will encourage both systems vendors and libraries to utilize the technology.

He went on to explain the implementation process, indicating that bar codes could either be purchased externally or produced in-house using software. In Kluwer's situation bar codes are purchased by the production department and are ordered once the final repro copy is available from the typesetter. The bar codes are then inserted by the printer. Problems in using the bar codes have been minor, and include questions about the timing of purchase and location of the bar code on the journal.

Dane went on to outline other possible applications of the bar code, mentioning inventory, royalty computation and document delivery (when symbology is available for the contribution level identifier), and EDI (electronic data interchange) involving the provision of dispatch information and publisher-to-vendor invoicing.

Jim Young, President of Sirsi Corporation spoke about his company's experience as an automation systems vendor in developing bar code check-in software. He then used a CCD bar code scanner to check in a journal on the Sirsi system explaining that the scanner being demonstrated was comparable to a "grocery store's" laser scanner and could scan 25-30 times a second avoiding the problems of a light pen which sometimes requires several passes in order to pick up the code.

In the Sirsi system the bibliographic record and the control information (i.e., publication pattern) must be present to use the scanner. The scanner will read the ISSN and the volume and issue number. Information from the publication pattern will then complete the remaining chronology. Problems that Young addressed included dealing with multiple subscriptions to the same title, location of the bar code, and problems associated with a faulty scanner or bar code.

George Wright then returned to explain further how publishers could implement the SISAC bar code, noting that a worksheet to calculate the SICI was included in the documentation for the standard. Various software packages are available to create the bar code on an in-house basis. Use of film masters has been the traditional way to produce a bar code when the work has been done externally. Size, quality, color, and placement are extremely important variables in utilizing the bar code. For example, blue or black covers cannot be used with the bar code. As a final consideration, he noted that only recent model scanners are able to pick up Code 128 symbology which is the code selected by SISAC to display the SICI information. Special bar code scanners called "Verifie" are available to actually measure and verify bar code quality.

Publishing Opportunities: Getting into Print or Getting Involved

Cindy Hepfer
Julia Gammon
Workshop Leaders

Ellen Finnie Duranceau
Recorder

Cindy Hepfer, Head of the Serial Department at the State University of New York at Buffalo's Health Sciences Library and Editor of *Serials Review* since 1985, began the workshop by exploring traditional methods of getting published in the library literature, using a step-by-step overview of the publication process at *Serials Review* as an example.

In the first stage of preparing a paper for publication, Hepfer emphasized that a potential author should do a literature search to become familiar with what already has been written on the topic, where other articles on the topic have been published, and whether the topic has been exhausted. Noting which journals have published articles on the subject may help identify editors with an established interest who would be good targets for the proposed article. Subsequent stages include developing the concept and creating an abstract or brief outline; in the case of a research paper, the author should also develop the goals, objectives, and methodology for the study. Ideally, the author should then contact an editor to discuss submission guidelines and the publication process.

Once the paper is submitted to *Serials Review*, the editor and at

---

Ellen Finnie Duranceau is Associate Head, Serials and Acquisitions Services, MIT Libraries, Cambridge, MA 02139.

© 1993 by The Haworth Press, Inc. All rights reserved.

least two reviewers read the paper and prepare comments and suggestions. The editor may accept the paper as written (which is extremely rare); she may accept the paper with suggestions for brief or sometimes extensive revisions; or she may reject the paper outright, which is also rare. Typically, the author makes revisions, resubmits the paper, and then awaits a final letter of acceptance, while the publisher is sent a printed copy and a disk copy. The managing editor reviews and edits the paper, and the author, usually within a few weeks of submission, is sent a proof copy. The paper at this point enters a queue for publication, and is included in the next issue or rolled over for inclusion in the following issue, a decision which is based on layout and format rather than on editorial choice. The entire issue is then proofread and sent to the printer, who mails the issue out approximately one month later.

Hepfer followed her overview of the publication process by describing the results of a survey of the editors of thirteen publications that deal with serials or technical services, which consisted of nine questions about what material each journal publishes and what it expects of its writers.

In the final portion of her talk, Hepfer corrected the most common misconceptions that authors have about getting published. Despite potential authors' belief they have nothing to offer the library literature, Hepfer encouraged an author to trust that he or she has a unique viewpoint, and suggested that to find a good topic, authors can collaborate with a faculty member, develop a case study with wide applicability, do an interview, or leverage a personal interest into a bibliographic review piece. Hepfer noted that it is essential that this latter form be critical rather than merely descriptive.

A related misconception Hepfer also put to rest is the notion that "all of the good ideas have been taken." To find ideas, Hepfer suggested listening carefully at conferences such as NASIG, reading electronic bulletin boards such as SERIALST, and taking the time to do the necessary groundwork to sound out potential topics.

In Hepfer's experience, many writers mistakenly believe they are accomplished enough that they won't be asked to revise, but she reiterated that in fact it is extremely unusual for any article to be published without revision. Authors who believe it is acceptable to submit a manuscript to more than one journal at a time are also misled; the author has a right to ask the editor where the paper is in the review process and to follow up if no confirmation of receipt or editorial decision is forthcoming. (She later commented that six weeks is a fair interval to wait before calling an editor after submitting a manuscript.) Revisions can be negotiated with an editor, but the degree to which this is true varies dramatically from one editor to another.

Julia Gammon, Head of the Acquisitions Department at the University of Akron and a member of the University of Akron Press's Editorial Board, provided an overview of nontraditional methods of becoming involved in the publishing process, including focus groups, advisory boards, editorial boards, pre-publication reviews, surveys or questionnaires, journal monitoring task forces, and committees. Gammon gathered her information by calling publishers.

Gammon explained that publishers use focus groups for both old and new products, and will use librarians in these sessions to gain information that helps them market to libraries. Gammon has been in a focus group for CRC Press, and suggested that purchases and connections often lead to offers to participate. Advisory boards are more formal than focus groups, but also are used as marketing tools for publishers, since board members contribute views on whether a product should be offered and how it should be configured. Publisher's advisory boards vary in degree of structure; Gammon, who has participated on one, suggested that it is easier for the novice to become involved in the less structured boards.

Gammon's described own experience to demonstrate that a librarian who wants to be on a publisher's editorial board should make herself "indispensable." Gammon approached the Akron Press' board initially by volunteering her services, but it was only after she proved her value by contributing extensive and useful knowledge of the book market that she became fully accepted. Gammon has found participating on the board to be a two-way street: she offers them her knowledge, and in turn she finds that the experience has gained her credibility with publishers and vendors and has improved her interactions with them.

Some publishers, such as G.K. Hall and Oryx Press, use librarians to help them understand which of their potential products will be successful. Surveys and questionnaires sent by publishers are used for the same purpose, and Gammon stressed that a librarian's responses can actually mold a new product, which is a satisfying way to influence the marketplace.

Other publishers maintain journal monitoring task forces, which help them evaluate the overall health of a publication at routine intervals of about five to ten years. Gammon suggested that like committees, these task forces can be a direct means of shaping a publisher's offerings and of improving the quality of serial titles.

Gammon concluded with the thought that librarians have a valuable product to sell, and that getting involved in publishing, even without putting words on paper, benefits librarians as well as publishers. Her final words of advice to those who want to get involved were not to lose sight of the "four be's": be pushy, be seen, be heard, and be available.

Fine-Tuning the Claims Process

Dianne McCutcheon
Marjorie Mann
Stephen Giglio
Ted Barnes

Workshop Leaders

Martha Kellogg

Recorder

Can "fine-tuning the claims process" resolve the problem of claiming missing serial issues for the library and the serials vendor? What actually constitutes "fine tuning" of claims? In this workshop representatives of a large library with a significant serials collection–the National Library of Medicine (NLM)–and a major serials vendor–the Faxon Company–addressed an area of continuing concern to all members of the serials community.

With 85,000 serial records and 300,000–400,000 current receipts, the National Library of Medicine maintains a serials collection of mammoth proportions. Even with such a large scale operation, Marjorie Mann, Systems Librarian, and Dianne McCutcheon, Assistant Head of Serials Records at NLM, emphasized the application of human judgment at each step in the claiming process. Mann briefly described the library's Master Serials System and reviewed the library's claiming procedure. Most claims are entered at the time of check-in. Other sources of online claims include batch jobs for "overdues," "no check-in's," "on orders," and "nyp's." Each job is reviewed before claims are entered; records #1 can be reviewed serendipitously as well.

Martha Kellogg is Assistant Acquisitions Librarian, University of Rhode Island Library, Kingston, RI 02881.

© 1993 by The Haworth Press, Inc. All rights reserved.

NLM's serials operation presently does not have predictive check-in, but runs program cycles for overdues, all of which are subject to scrutiny. An "overdues review" job which produces online claims is run weekly. Overdues are reviewed for patterns of receipt, using data in other Master Serials System files before entering the online claim. Various parameters prioritize claiming or suppress claims as appropriate. A "proof cycle," also run weekly, pulls all claims entered in the past week and prints out claims and other relevant information (publication, payment data, etc.). Claims are reviewed against other information in the Master Serials System. If the claim is valid, another job finally prints the claims and mails them out by U.S. Postal Service.

NLM produces second and third claims by running a monthly "automatic claim reissue cycle" which identifies existing claims on which no action has occurred. The claims are re-reviewed at this step and updated to reflect any change, including reports received from vendors and publishers. After the third claim, missing items are cycled to the "Gaps File" (where claims go to die).

McCutcheon expanded on the timing of customizing and modifying the automated claiming system. NLM's database management program on a mainframe computer permits analysis of potential claims by utilizing appropriate data in the system. Professional library staff review all first time claims and a selective list of second and third claims. In a period of budgetary and staff constraints, claims can be prioritized, with #1 some claims suppressed if necessary.

Areas examined in a review of the claims process included: premature claims; percentage of receipts claimed; and return rate. In a study of 1992 claims, McCutcheon found that 7-12 percent of total receipts were claimed. Of issues claimed, about 40 percent came in as receipts; about 11 percent were never received (went to the Gaps File); about 25 percent were updated to "nyp"; and about 25 percent were still out in the second and third claim cycle. Claim failures were attributed primarily to NLM's increasing number of foreign titles (only 34 percent of the collection is published in the U.S.) and problems with bibliographic data such as cessations.

Future directions for NLM's serials program include: looking toward a MARC system to use with check-in, establishment of a predictive check-in, system, and implementation of electronic claiming with a goal to eliminate paper claims.

"Fine tuning," according to Stephen Giglio, Director, Medical Information Services Center, and Ted Barnes, Business Analyst of the Faxon Company, cannot solve the problem of serials claims; rather, "re-engineering" the whole claiming process is needed. For a large serials vendor which receives millions of claims each year, the time spent in claiming is viewed as a service failure of major proportions. With $30-50 million per year in library, publisher, and vendor costs, and 50-60 percent of Faxon customer service representative's time spent on claims, a Total Quality Management (TOM) effort was initiated at Faxon to deal with the claims problem.

Faxon analyzed the subscription lifecycle and identified the independent events that must occur in sequence for the library to receive issues efficiently. They looked for potential failure points in the process to try to track down the root cause of first claims. An analysis of 193 first claims from Faxon's computerized serials system (for academic and medical clients) found no single "root cause" of the claims. Eight problem areas were identified:

- Publisher order entry (about 5 percent)
- Dispatch and other data (32-38 percent)
- Defective issue (about 2 percent)
- Agent order entry (5-7 percent)
- Agent-library communication (1-5 percent)
- Invalid claim (12-20 percent)
- Distribution (about 5 percent)
- Undetermined (25-30 percent)

Publishers, agents, and libraries each have a role to play in re-engineering the process to insure effective delivery and prevent claims, Giglio asserted. Publishers can use EDI (Electronic Data Interchange) for dispatch data, to notify vendors and libraries of changes in publication, and to improve responsiveness to agent claims. Vendors can automate procedures with publishers and libraries for improved speed and accuracy. Vendors also can supply libraries with accurate publication data and use standard forms and procedures. Libraries can incorporate the publication data and vendor-supplied reports in their work flows. They can adopt standardized procedures and forms. All parties in the process can implement EDI to automate payment, dispatch, and receipt data for greater accuracy throughout the subscription life cycle.

Re-engineering the claims process by using automated data interchange, rather than fine tuning an outmoded system which has failed, was proposed by Giglio and Barnes. They also stressed the need for a national publication pattern database for predictive check-in. Combined with EDI, predictive check-in could eliminate human intervention in the claims process, a vision which moves beyond fine-tuning the claims process as most libraries know it today.

Following the presentations, workshop attendees commented on various aspects of the claims process, including problems with the postal service in non-delivery or delivery of mutilated issues; the time limit on claims required by publishers; and the potential for implementing EDI. Systems throughout the serials chain will have to adopt EDI standards to eliminate human intervention in the check-in/claims process. The Faxon representatives reported that use of EDI data for claims is presently in the testing stage.

Basic Training for Survival

Susan Davis
Louise Diodato
Cheryl A. Bernero
Workshop Leaders

Bonnie Naifeh Hill
Recorder

In this three part presentation, the foundations of serials work were discussed. "A Day in the Life of a Serials Manager," presented by Susan Davis, Head, Periodicals, SUNY Buffalo, gave an overview of serials work and the basic precepts behind it. Davis covered such topics as definitions of "serial" and publishing permutations such as title changes, splits, and renumbering. She discussed the need for and kinds of record-keeping, and stated it is important to evaluate the value of information kept vs. the cost of keeping it. The first step in record-keeping is to identify the name or title of a serial and keep track of the specific issues received, in order to ensure you are receiving what you paid for and to provide holdings information to patrons about what is owned by the library. Accurate record-keeping enables a library to know when to claim, to track costs, and to keep current with procedures for binding and routing.

Davis emphasized the business functions of serials as being important to a successful operation. Knowing your vendor's services and fees has been essential all along. New requirements for performing the business of serials include working with CD-ROM

Bonnie Naifeh Hill is Assistant Director to Collections and Technical Services, Tufts University, A & S Library, Medford, MA 02155.

© 1993 by The Haworth Press, Inc. All rights reserved.

licensing agreements and the new standards for EDI and X12. As always, good communication skills are important. The skills and talents that one should bring to a job in serials are the ability to prioritize and organize work, and the talent not to become too compulsive about it all. Problem-solving skills, attention to detail, and a good sense of humor are also needed.

In her presentation, "Educating the Future Serials Librarian," Louise Diodato, Adjunct Professor at University of Wisconsin-Milwaukee and Coordinator of Technical Services, Cardinal Strich College Library, gave an overview of a course in Serials Librarianship that she teaches at the University of Wisconsin-Milwaukee School of Library and Information Science. The class extends for eight weeks and requires as prerequisites courses in Acquisitions, Cataloging, Reference and Information Science. It begins with a series of definitions for "serial," including Philip Homes': "A serial is not a book." The initial part of the course covers the history of serials publishing, including the fact that the longest running serial to date began in China in 206 BC and continued until AD 1736.

The course introduces students to a variety of tools necessary for working with serials, such as printed guides to periodicals, vendor catalogs such as those produced by Ebsco and Faxon, union lists, local holdings, bibliographic utilities, local OPACs, and staff and colleagues. It then covers "nitty-gritty," theoretical and financial aspects; the "nitty-gritty" of serials work is check-in and claiming. Problems that arise in this area include knowing when to claim, working with title and frequency changes, and with titles published as parts of other serial titles. Diodato made an interesting point when she commented that new hires who recently have finished their education do not, as a rule, know how to read Roman numerals, and teaching this skill needs to be part of a training plan.

Selection policies, the difference between selection and acquisition, and gift and exchange as a means of acquisition, are examples of the theory discussed. Serial cancellations run the range, from how to design a project as a whole, to targeting specific titles within the framework of an overall design, to the public relations aspects of such projects. New topics which require attention are choosing a format (paper, micro or electronic), hardware requirements which play a role in some decisions, and whether or not to buy both the paper and fiche, or the paper and electronic versions of a title.

Budget management looks at budget formulas, ratios of monographs to serials, and the need to establish different ratios at different types of libraries in which a serials librarian may work. Serials automation is introduced by students developing a "wish list" and then discovering what actually is offered in the current market place. Demonstrations and site visits teach students about the features of various systems. Serials cataloging, which is not consistently part of a serials department, is also touched upon. The course next discusses where serials fit into the organization of a library, the difference between professional and support staff, and the advantages and disadvantages of working in serials. The final section teaches the skills needed to find a job, drafting a cover letter and resume, interviewing, and how to consider a job offer once made.

Cheryl A. Bernero, Account Services Manager, EBSCO Subscription Services, next discussed "What Your Vendor Can Do For You." Bernero began by defining and describing the purpose of a subscription agency, which is primarily to save a library a great deal of staff time by not having to deal with hundreds, if not thousands, of serials publishers directly. Their services are reflected in service fees, whose calculations should be explained by the vendor and understood by the client. A serials vendor is prepared to supply a library with background materials such as current-awareness newsletters, service brochures, handbooks, catalogs, and guides, and management reports customized to a client's account. EBSCO's Subscription Coordinator's Guide suggests formats for a variety of form letters to be used when communicating about serials acquisitions matters.

Vendors also conduct local, regional and national seminars on serials topics which are often focused on a type of library or a particular area of service; they exhibit their services at conferences and provide on-site training in such topics as effective claiming for their clients. Vendors possess a great deal of expertise on serials issues, such as how changes in the global market can affect your account.

The question period brought forth the suggestion that serials librarians could benefit from a better understanding of the publishing process for both serials and books. Other suggestions included having faculty editors of journals speak to classes about their role in the serials chain and share their perspectives as users of serials. Ms. Diodato concluded the session by saying "controlling serials is like nailing Jello to the wall."

Cataloging Computer Files That Are Also Serials

Colleen Thorburn
Rebecca Ringler
Workshop Leaders

Pamela Morgan
Recorder

Colleen Thorburn, Assistant Librarian, University of Florida, opened the workshop by stating that cataloging serial computer files is a combination of two "terribles" in the library world: serials and computer files. She then outlined several of the challenges facing catalogers.

MARC itself provides two separate formats, Computer Files and Serials. Thorburn provided an overview of the fields in each. Since MARC doesn't specify which format should be applied, a library must choose for itself, based on library needs and the utility or standard being used. When asked which format CONSER preferred, Thorburn replied that CONSER preferred the serials format.

Computer files are a new and constantly changing medium, with which AACR2 has not been able to keep pace. AACR2 does not provide interpretations for Chapter 9. Also computer technology is not set in concrete, but is constantly changing. Considerable discussion arose when participants were asked to define several concepts, such as OPAC and electronic journal, proving Thorburn's point that it is difficult to talk about something when it has no standard definition.

Pamela Morgan is Assistant Head, Technical Services Division, Health Sciences Library, Memorial University of Newfoundland, St. John's NF, Canada A1B 3V6.

© 1993 by The Haworth Press, Inc. All rights reserved.

Finally, the physical nature of the medium leads to the potential for different sources of information: labels, title screen, READ-ME files, documentation. While the preferred chief source of information is the title screen, most catalogers do not find this practical (since they don't usually have access to equipment to read the title screen) and so the majority use the documentation and item label.

In order to catalog a serial computer file, the librarian must first decide what information is needed locally for the OPAC, but must also consider what will be needed nationally if the record is going to be loaded into a large utility such as OCLC. USMARC formats provide examples, but they are not exhaustive. Since the rules are in a state of flux, the librarian must adapt them to best suit the library and its clientele. There are no easy answers for issues such as the new integrated format, multiple versions, and the changing role of the cataloger; each library must set its own policies. Thorburn then went through examples of cataloging floppy disk files in both the serials and computer file formats.

Rebecca Ringler, Catalog Librarian, University of California at San Diego, talked about the differences between cataloging floppy disks and other formats, specifically computer files on magnetic tape and CD-ROM.

Because files on magnetic tape are usually loaded onto a mainframe by the local computer center, they can generally be considered remote access. When creating records for remote access files the cataloger generally doesn't have the tape in hand, but is working with a codebook and whatever information the computer center has provided. Good relations with the person doing the mounting of tapes will make the cataloger's job much easier. Policy decisions have to be made regarding access and documentation. Will the computer file have a call number or a note directing the patron to the information desk? Will the documentation be cataloged with the computer file or separately?

Ringler then moved into a discussion of CD-ROM computer files, which can contain a variety of information (indexes, numerical/statistical, full-text, bibliographic) and tend to be cumulative. It is often difficult to ascertain the title main entry since each producer modifies the title somewhat to make it unique. Product names appear in a variety of places; the key is to create multiple 246 fields to track each variation. It is difficult to say whether one should use uniform titles since AACR2 rule 25.5B is contradictory, stating one thing for serials and another for computer files. The 362 field should include the dates of coverage, although they may be unusual since CD-ROM's compile wide ranges of data. The 260 and fixed fields should include the date of production. Records for print and computer file versions can be linked via the 580 and 787 fields. However, since the 787 is not usually indexed, it should be repeated in field 730. Because CD-ROM products tend to be licensed rather than purchased and must be returned to the producer, "limited retention" notes should be used and library holdings should reflect the dates of coverage accessible in the library.

In cases where a full-text CD-ROM contains more than one title and the library wishes to provide access to each of them, a Host/Component analytical relationship can be used. The host record would be a complete cataloging record for the database. The component record would be for each individual title available on the database, with a 773 field detailing its availability on the database. Host/Component records are identified by the bibliographic level in the fixed fields.

Ringler pointed out that when cataloging computer files, fields 256 and 538 must be used. Accompanying documentation should be included in 256$e if it is in print format, but in field 556 if it is machine-readable. Subject access is generally the same as for any type of material, however different subheadings apply: "software" for programs and "databases" for databases.

Thorburn finished up the session talking about electronic journals. Mode of access is important and the universal mode of access (i.e., the listserv address) is generally specified in either the 500 or 538 field. If the electronic journal has been downloaded to the library's OPAC, the local mode of access should be specified in local use field 590, which will not show in the records contributed to utilities. Remote access computer files usually need a separate location code.

Just as CD-ROM databases contain several other titles, an online service can offer access to a wide variety of titles. Again the library has the option of separately cataloging each title accessible through the database. However, the library has no control over whether the database elects to carry the title, drop it, or only partially carry a title, making it difficult for the library to keep records up to date. Also, two different subscriptions may provide access to the same titles. In this case, two records would have to be made since multiple versions require separate records.

Working Together for the Future: Librarian/Publisher/Subscription Agents

Keith Courtney
Margaret Radbourne
Brian Cox

Workshop Leaders

Lynne M. Hayman

Recorder

Stating that academics and publishers are "not pushing hard to get into new technologies," Keith Courtney, Sales and Marketing Director, Taylor and Francis, spoke about the decision-making process surrounding the launch of a new journal. First, research is undertaken to define the subject area and scope of the proposed journal, to assess the market, and to evaluate possible sources of articles. The potential quality of a journal's content is of crucial importance, as is the make-up of the editorial board. Avenues for publicizing the journal are explored, market research is conducted, and potential peer reviewers are identified.

Planning for a new journal includes identifying the "right person" as editor, defining the size, format, frequency and print runs, as well as setting revenue targets and subscription price.

It may take five years for a journal to become profitable (although publishers would prefer three) and eight to ten years to recoup the initial investment. If, by a certain year, the journal is not profitable, the publisher may need to increase the subscription rate or discontinue publication.

Lynne M. Hayman is Assistant Director, California Newspaper Project, Center for Bibliographic Studies, University of California, Riverside, CA 93521.

Actual launch of the journal means briefing editorial, production, marketing, sales and accounting staffs; issuing a "call for papers"; setting deadlines for publication; and compiling review and abstracting lists. An initial "dummy" issue may be produced to test the waters. Promotional materials are circulated to the academic community, librarians and subscription agents. The primary marketing targets for promotion are academics, rather than librarians.

More risk is entailed in the start-up of a journal, than in the publication of a book. The investment is greater; the publisher must commit to fixed ongoing expenses. On the plus side, there is a cash flow advantage, and, once a journal is established, increases and decreases in the number of subscriptions are somewhat predictable. Sources of revenue are subscriptions (which may compose 95% of revenue), special issues, supplements, back issues, offprints and permissions for republication.

Margaret Radbourne, Journals Administration Manager, John Wiley; spoke about journal fulfillment, the renewal process and customer service, and claims and queries. She stated that it is important to produce an agent's price list as early as possible for the new subscription year and to distribute in a time-sensitive manner, such as EDI (Electronic Data Interchange) or e-mail. Despite early announcement, renewals are often late and may be made at the previous year's rate, causing problems for publishers. Last year, Wiley experimented with full distribution of renewal notices directly to subscribers, and this had a positive impact. Librarians and subscription agents in the audience commented on the additional work this causes for librarians in reviewing renewal notices for publications managed by subscription agents. Subscription agents often advise that first renewal notices be ignored.

Brian Cox, Director of Journals Business, Pergamon, spoke about the activities of ICEDIS (the International Committee for EDI in Serials) and its pioneering of the use of EDI for the routine exchange of business forms, such as invoices and purchase orders, between publishers and subscription agents. The ICEDIS began in the United Kingdom as a working group of publishers. It is now a small independent international committee focused on defining standards for EDI for use by journal publishers and subscription agents. The membership consists of six international subscription agents and eight publishers of scholarly journals

The committee is presently addressing standards development for EDI transmission of claims and claims responses, journal subscription rates, and changes of address and publication dates. EDI has already been shown to be an effective means of communicating such information and facilitating the timely update of files and records. Existing standards which come into play are ANSI X12, EDIFACT (EDI for Administration, Commerce and Transport), TRADACOMS (the UK standard for tele-ordering of books) and SISAC.

Following these presentations, the claims process was discussed in more detail. Approximately 70 to 80 percent of claims to publishers are made too early. A major reason for this, one of the publishers speculated, may be generation of notices by automated library systems; however, a librarian in the audience noted that claim intervals are set in automated systems by users and are often set early due to publishers' requirements that claims be made within a brief time frame. Can EDI can be instrumental in addressing this problem? Ms. Radbourne noted that Wiley is now routinely ignoring first claims from automated systems and is not unique among publishers in doing so. Most legitimate claims, she noted, are the result of late ordering or late renewal by customers. A discussion ensued concerning the claims cycle and optimal time frames for submitting and fulfilling claims. The group questioned whether additional lenience on the part of publishers might be helpful in limiting the number of claims made too early.

Another standard noted and discussed was the SISAC barcode, which most major publishers are in the process of adopting and printing on publications. This new standard has already met with wide acceptance in the library and publishing communities.

The Role and Responsibilities of the Professional Serials Cataloger

Marilyn Geller
Eleanor Cook
Workshop Leaders

Jane Robillard
Recorder

When is a workshop not a workshop? When under the capable leadership of Marilyn Geller, Serials Cataloger, Massachusetts Institute of Technology Libraries and Eleanor Cook, Serials Librarian, Appalachian State University, it becomes a sharing of experiences by an audience composed mostly of serials catalogers. A tightly structured, seven-part outline kept the discussion moving in an orderly fashion and the participants needed very little encouragement to become actively involved.

1. AUTOMATION AND CHANGING JOB RESPONSIBILITIES

Topics covered under this heading included inputting, sources of copy, holding statements, and training needed for paraprofessionals to input holdings statements. Most catalogers did their inputting online from OCLC copy. Direct input allowed them to save time and to develop a better understanding of their systems. Few li-

---

Jane Robillard is Medical Librarian, VA Medical Center, Medical Library, Bldg. 11H, Perry Point, MD 21902.

braries are accessing other library catalogs through Internet or using the National Union Catalog or Union Lists. Holdings statements are sometimes input by Cataloging and sometimes by Acquisitions, generally using ANSI standards. Paraprofessionals play a large role in keeping the work flow moving smoothly since with minimal training they can input from edited copy. More one-on-one training is necessary for them to input holdings statements.

2. WHAT IS "PROFESSIONAL" WORK AND WHAT IS "PARAPROFESSIONAL" WORK?

There really is no cut-and-dried division of labor between these positions. A well trained paraprofessional with on-the-job experience can be as capable a cataloger as a professional. Most, however, do not know the theory and history of cataloging and may not be seeing the whole picture. One participant observed that we shouldn't expect a paraprofessional to do original cataloging when they are not being paid a professional salary. Finally, loading original cataloging into OCLC is considered to be very important but the upcoming OCLC searching charges are making people leery of inputting.

3. STAFFING ISSUES: QUALITIES OF A GOOD PROFESSIONAL CATALOGER AND A GOOD PARAPROFESSIONAL CATALOGER

Serials catalogers, whether professional or paraprofessional, are seen as people who tolerate ambiguity well; have an awareness of the impact of records on patrons and the rest of the library staff; understand that a catalog is a resource, not an object; are flexible about change; are detail-oriented; and love to do cross-word and/or jigsaw puzzles.

4. TRAINING ISSUES

This section divided into two areas: training technical services personnel and training public services personnel. Good training for technical services personnel is a necessity, whether training is one-on-one, through institutes and workshops, or by the sink-or-swim method. Also necessary is a knowledge of workflow. Without the whole picture firmly in mind a person will try to do everything instead of delegating. Support from fellow staff members, especially on the public service side is needed. Most people agreed that whenever possible public service people should be taught about MARC records, especially what field tags can do for them; an hour-long class with handouts was one suggestion. Another initiative has been used successfully. A reference librarian followed a serials cataloger around for a week watching what was involved in the cataloging of materials that ranged from "simple" to "difficult." Everyone involved thought the experience was helpful and the reference librarian began to understand just how difficult and time-consuming serials cataloging can be.

5. CATALOGING MODIFICATION

Streamlining records so as to input more of them rather then being able to input fewer full records is not looked upon favorably. People feel strongly that these kinds of cutbacks will only hurt the catalog in the long run. Serials catalogers have the obligation to do quality work and to expect their colleagues to do the same. "Do it right the first time or you'll redo it." The consensus here is that while catalogers understand the economics of modification and will do it, they do not have to like it.

6. INCORPORATING SPECIAL PROJECTS INTO THE STANDARD WORKFLOW

Establish priorities and document, document, document, so that the rest of the library can see what you are doing.

7. CAREER PATHS FOR CATALOGERS

Those that wish to go on to managerial positions have no trouble making the transition. Those who don't want to go into management can move to systems positions, bibliographic instruction, or work for vendors.

The presenters brought the workshop to a close with a series of questions designed to summarize the discussions. They discovered the following about the 96 participants:

- 83 people doing cataloging as part of their jobs
- 20 catalogers doing barcoding
- 49 catalogers doing holding statements
- 36 catalogers doing direct inputting
- 16 searching other OPACs on the Internet
- 62 catalogers editing of correcting in local systems
- 9 libraries were paraprofessionals do original cataloging
- 44 people trained in a one-to-one situation
- 19 people who received training at workshops
- 16 people who trained at institutes or preconferences
- 12 people who trained themselves
- 28 people discussing cataloging modification
- 38 people incorporating retrospective conversion into workflow
- 16 catalogers interested in managerial advancement
- 36 catalogers interested in technical advancement
- 3 catalogers wanting out

There was a common feeling among the participants that the work of serials librarians in general and serials catalogers in particular is misunderstood. Non-serials people do not seem to understand how time-consuming and tedious serials cataloging can be. The first workshop speaker concentrated more on sharing ideas on technical issues whereas the second brought up managerial issues. The most important issue seems to be the need for technical services administrators and public services librarians to understand the problems inherent in serials cataloging.

How to Plan and Deliver a Great Workshop

October Ivins
Tom Gearty

Workshop Leaders

Linda Meiseles

Recorder

October Ivins, Head, Serials Services, Louisiana State University Libraries, and Tom Gearty Operations Trainer, The FAXON Company conducted a workshop on how to plan and deliver great workshops.

Part 1: NASIG Workshops, led by October Ivins, a past presenter and Program Committee member, concentrated on workshop content and explained how the Program Committee operates. Her discussion was specifically designed to encourage members of the audience to develop and submit proposals for workshops at subsequent NASIG conferences. She began with a description of how the Committee evaluates and revises plenary session and workshop proposals. Plenary sessions are usually related to a theme, typically theoretical and comprehensive, treating many aspects of a particular topic. Often futuristic, many of the NASIG presenters have been non-librarians. Half or more of plenaries are invited papers. On the other hand workshops are much more specific, based on actual experience of the presenters. The goals of workshops are to provide guidance for someone wanting to do something similar, as well as to provide detailed information about a totally new area.

Linda Meiseles is Serials Librarian, Hofstra University, Hempstead, NY 11550.

© 1993 by The Haworth Press, Inc. All rights reserved.

Successful proposals incorporate both balance and quality. The Committee looks for proposals that will interest a diverse membership with different levels of expertise. They will include a wide range of activities for librarians, vendors, and publishers. Ivins emphasized that no two serials departments are identical. Some are highly automated while others are still operating manually. There is also a wide mix of positions and duties among serials librarians. To meet the needs of a diverse membership, workshops must offer varying levels of complexity. Some should provide some basic information, while others should be more advanced.

The Committee wants topics from across the entire spectrum of serials endeavors–pricing, vendor relations and evaluation, binding, automation, public service and access, retrospective conversion, handling new formats, and management and organization concerns. It is especially interested in workshops that can be combined, such as automation and binding, vendor performance and claiming, acquiring, cataloging and assisting patrons with electronic journals.

Ivins ended her session with a list of tips for successful proposals: examine proceedings from earlier conferences, follow electronic discussion groups, use your own direct experience, preview in your library or regional group, find a co-leader who balances you, ask a program committee or board member to react, submit multiple proposals, and if at first you don't succeed. . . .

While Ivins presentation was specific to NASIG, Gearty, experienced in training, focused on the techniques of effective presentations in general. He addressed several points: overcoming nervousness, the need for preparation, guidelines for successful presentations, and the purpose of overheads.

Gearty stated that giving workshops or making presentations can either be a trying experience or an exhilarating one. He spoke about how common nervousness is and offered several suggestions on how to overcome it. Converse with some of the audience beforehand. Focus on 3-4 people while making the presentation. Control the situation by recognizing your own style. For example, some people like to walk around, while some like to stand by the podium.

The key to an effective presentation is to prepare, but be adaptable by not being tied to your prepared remarks. One can over-prepare. Continually appraise your audience, and watch for cues. Flexibility allows for a change of directions if necessary. The guidelines for successful presentations are: write out the presentation and read it to yourself, a recorder, or an audience. After hearing it, edit it for the ear. Choose short words, not long ones. Quite often the audience gets caught up on erudite words and stops concentrating. Time the speech, and do not memorize. Note key points and use visual aids.

Overheads, he stressed, are an important part of the presentations. According to Gearty they accomplish several things. For one they keep the presenter and the audience on track. If either one loses concentration overheads serve as a prompt to get back to where the speaker is going. Overheads help pace the presentation and allow for an even flow of talk. They highlight keywords, which in turn stimulate memory. Without visual aids the audience remembers 10 percent of the information; with them the ability to remember increases to 80 percent or more.

Gearty then provided guidelines for the use of overheads. Do not have more than eight lines and use them just to support an idea. The location of the projector is important as well as the use of large typeface.

During the discussion period following the workshop some of the participants shared their past experiences in making presentations and offered suggestions for mitigating nervousness. One such suggestion was to practice in front of a mirror, another was to participate as a toast master at some function.

Ivins mentioned that to improve her skills in public speaking she went back to library school and took an oral communication course. Gearty ended the session by stating that a certain amount of nervousness is essential to a good presentation. It pumps up the adrenalin, while helping to keep the presenter from being monotonous.

Fewer Subscriptions = Increased Library Services: How ASU and ASU West Met the Challenge

Sheila Walters
Eleanor Mitchell

Workshop Leaders

Martin Gordon

Recorder

A case study on how access can be equal to ownership in providing quality service to users, this workshop detailed the symbiotic relationship between a major academic research library and its fledgling sister institution. In addition, it provided attendees with outlines of programs, policies and procedures that have been successful in employing dollars allocated for information in an optimum fashion through the careful balance of traditional modes of material purchase and more recent developments in document delivery.

Sheila Walters, Head, Inter-Library Loan and Document Delivery at Arizona State University (Tempe) began by introducing her audience to the main campus and the branch campus of ASU West (Phoenix) located twenty-five miles away. The Phoenix campus was not completed until 1991, although the library existed and housed other functions prior to that time.

Martin Gordon is Acquisitions Librarian, Franklin & Marshall College, P.O. Box 3003, Lancaster, PA. 17604.

Eleanor Mitchell, Information Delivery Specialist, Arizona State University (Phoenix) presented summary highlights of a collection development philosophy which considers access as important as acquisition in providing primary source material. As a consequence that policy from the outset has emphasized speed of delivery. The prevalence of upper division course requirements, non-traditional students, and both budget and physical plant restraints all contributed to this forward-looking "opening day" philosophy. She stressed that off-site realization of resources should be "seamless" and "virtually transparent" to the library's customers. In fact, a maximum period of forty-eight hours between request and material receipt is a formalized goal. Eighty percent of all needs are met within this time framework.

Mitchell developed a historical sketch tracing the evolution of document delivery, beginning in 1984 at the Tempe campus with the use of telephone and Teletype through the present day three department "partnership" using automated products such as the *Filemate Pro* database. The team effort of the staff at the information desk, journal department, and circulation desk is critical to the overall axiom of user primacy. Each step in the process is technologically efficient, including the use of electronic data bases by patrons in identifying citations that will support their research and curriculum needs.

At the end, Walters explained how incoming requests were tagged and put through a set of sophisticated verification filters. She stressed the scope and depth of these methods including an honest self-appraisal regarding the possible need to resume user notification of receipt. Management reports, some designed for collection development liaisons, were illustrated.

"Ask ASU" and "Library Express" programs for the faculty and students further assist the overall process of building user satisfaction. By establishing deposit accounts, faculty and students can have either ASU owned or borrowed books or journal article photocopies delivered.

Walters continued by describing ASU (Tempe)'s manner of on-site subscription reduction–moving down through layers of titles based upon frequency of use, duplication, price, and difficulty to administer (order, renew, claim).

A six month pilot program funded by $30,000 from the library's acquisition allocation provided free photocopy of articles for faculty. Between November 1 and December 31,1991, over 14,000 articles were received by fax (again underscoring a working commitment and not merely lip service to user satisfaction.)

Walters concluded this section of the presentation with the admonishment to other net lenders (her library is the highest volume net lender of all academic libraries on OCLC) that, without subsidy, even reciprocal agreements must be re-examined in light of today's budget climate. Use of commercial document delivery companies was investigated at ASU (Tempe) and results ranking the eleven listed on OCLC were made available to workshop participants.

In a conference permeated with anticipation regarding the use of technology as a means by which the tapestry of scholarly communication could be more economically woven, the experiences of ASU and ASU West were presented with the aim of illustrating more than just a few threads in such a fabric.

Managing Reference "Pseudoserials"

Christopher W. Nolan

Workshop Leader

Sharon Scott

Recorder

In response to the problem of "pseudoserials" in his Reference collection, Christopher Nolan, Reference Services Librarian at Trinity University, has devised a method of tracking those irregular and uncontrolled titles which seem to defy regular and systematic ordering. He began his presentation with his definition of a "pseudoserial," or "problematic" serial as he more commonly calls them. Those titles which are published as monographs, with new editions issued at irregular intervals, are the most familiar type of "pseudoserial." Many of these titles are published as frequently as true serials, but have not yet been designated as such. Nolan finds that keeping up with the latest edition of these publications is problematic, and in reviewing his reference collection, has found these are the most common items that "slip through the cracks" and are not reordered when necessary.

Nolan also defined those titles as "pseudoserials" for which the publisher does not accept standing orders even though they are true serials. Some local history publications, which are of great value, fall into this category. This material may not be published on a regular schedule so anticipating an order date is difficult, yet supplies may become exhausted soon after publication, so prompt ordering is important. Sometimes, even though a serial publication

---

Sharon Scott is Senior Serial Cataloger, University of Arizona, Serials Department, Tuscon, NV 85721.

© 1993 by The Haworth Press, Inc. All rights reserved.

can be acquired on standing order, the library may not want every new edition that comes out; this group, while not "pseudoserials," has many problems in common with them.

After examining the collection, Nolan decided to devise a method for tracking these "pseudoserials," so that issues and editions could be ordered or claimed in an efficient and timely manner. The Reference Department created a paper file, a method that was acceptable as long as the list of titles was not too long. However, the data in the list could not be manipulated. For instance, reports tailored to individual selectors were difficult to produce, and it was complicated to arrive at an estimate of funding needed to cover replacement of selected titles.

Nolan decided to create a small database file which would allow him to manipulate data in several ways. He selected dBase IV as his software in order to remain consistent with the rest of the library. A simple database structure was devised to provide the following information: title, publisher, call number, latest owned, price, purchase frequency, retention, last purchased, next purchased, and notes. Last purchased and next purchased areas provide data for predictive ordering. Paper forms were developed for the individual selectors to use when they discover a title to be added to the database. Nolan has several methods for identifying titles to be included. The first round of identification occurred during the reference weeding process; individual selectors were asked to fill out forms as they encountered a title which belonged in the "pseudoserial" database. Students often come to the reference desk looking for later editions of titles, which alerts the selector that the title is a candidate for the database. Approval forms are also used to select titles for inclusion. Budget cuts have forced the re-evaluation of certain reference tools, resulting in cancellations of some standing orders and the addition of these titles to the database.

dBase allows flexibility in generating reports and reports are easy to set up using this software. Information in the database can be manipulated to provide master reports of total renewals, total replacement costs, and other similar data. Smaller reports in specific subject areas can be provided for individual selectors. Nolan displayed a sample report designed to show the expected number of titles which should be purchased for the current year and the total purchase cost. dBase is more powerful and sophisticated than is really needed for this kind of database and may be difficult for some people to learn. Without additional programming it does not easily allow for calculating "next purchase" date based upon "frequency" and "last purchased" information. There are simpler softwares which may be easier to use; a good alternative is Microsoft Excel.

Nolan stressed the importance of written procedures when developing a new process. Some procedures in the Technical Services were modified, and close cooperation was required with the Acquisitions and Serials Departments.

Collection Development Assessment for Biomedical Serials Collections

Lynn M. Fortney
Judith Rieke
Workshop Leaders

Barbara A. Carlson
Recorder

Serving users who rely heavily on serial literature, health sciences libraries constantly face decisions about what to add and what to cut from their serials collections. Lynn M. Fortney, EBSCO Subscription Services, Biomedical Division Marketing Manager, and Judith Rieke, University of North Dakota, Special Projects Librarian, identified and discussed the key criteria that health sciences libraries traditionally consider when assessing their collections to make new purchase or cancellation decisions. Although, in general, these criteria are often the same for the two processes, the importance of each factor may vary significantly from library to library, depending on collection development policies and methods.

Fortney outlined the considerations libraries use when purchasing serial titles: faculty opinion, interlibrary loan requests, desired collection strength, quality, price, and accessibility. Without a doubt, faculty opinion is by far the most important factor considered when buying new subscriptions, with the cost of serials outpacing library budgets even a faculty request does not automatically trigger a purchase decision in most libraries. ILL requests, measurements of what is needed but lacking, are also good indicators of what to buy.

Bobbie Carlson is Head, Serials Management, Medical University of South Carolina, 171 Ashley Ave., Charleston, SC 29425.

© 1993 by The Haworth Press, Inc. All rights reserved.

Besides these user-generated requests, librarians build serials collections based on measurements of desired collection strength. Collection development policies often define prospective collection levels in specific subject areas by combining information on local programs with percentages measured against standard or ideal collection levels. The RLG Conspectus is used but is problematic for biomedical collection assessment, because it is based on the Library of Congress classification scheme.

Most workshop participants agreed that being indexed in *Index Medicus* assures a journal more consideration, because it goes through a very rigorous review process before being selected for indexing. Therefore, high journal quality has been deemed synonymous with being indexed in *Index Medicus*. It remains a positive standard for selection, although, it is by no means an automatic purchase guarantee. Additional factors are coverage by other primary indexing and abstracting services, the quality of the editorial board, publisher reputation, the country of origin, ISI impact factor, and peer-reviewed content. It almost goes without saying these days that price is usually a very important factor as well.

Accessibility, especially when a biomedical library is associated with a "main" academic library on campus, raises the issue of duplicate acquisitions. With resource sharing tools such as DOCLINE, health sciences libraries have the big advantage of using reliable and efficient ILL routing to compensate for material not owned.

Rieke reviewed the considerations from the opposite perspective–selecting titles for cancellation. Use, the number one criterion in most cases, can appear in the form of external circulations, in-house use, ILL requests, and photocopying. Use can be measured by automated or manual methods. Some discussion of the various techniques used to gather in-house use statistics revealed the extraordinary lengths librarians have gone to in order to collect such data.

When deciding to cancel a title (just as when deciding to subscribe to a title) price is looked at in conjunction with other variables. Fortney reminded the participants that price trends for titles can be supplied by subscription agencies. She suggested that the price trend of the dollar be factored in when non-U.S. titles are evaluated.

Availability in alternative formats, such as CD-ROM or full-text online, is the up-and-coming trend and will be an important factor in deciding what to cut. In relation to indexes and abstracts, it is especially important to decide whether to continue to buy print versions. The same decision has to be made for full-text periodicals online via such services as BRS Colleague and ADONISTM. There was much discussion by the participants concerning the pros and cons of ADONISTM, with many insightful comments on the current product and service.

During this part of the workshop, Fortney spoke of quality as a criterion in evaluating a journal for possible cancellation. She reiterated the significance of where a title is indexed and whether it is peer-reviewed, the lack of standard or core lists for biomedical literature beyond the Brandon-Hill lists, and the intended use and meaning of ISI impact factors. Many vendors can provide index source information. More difficult to determine is whether or not a journal has some editorial check on the quality of its content, and if so, to what degree. There was considerable discussion of why the ISI impact factor should not be used as an absolute measurement of quality and only as an indicator of what is being used and cited. Warnings to avoid comparing impact factors across different subject disciplines and the reality that research journals usually get cited more than clinical titles were helpful in putting this variable in proper perspective.

Speaking as a former serials librarian, Rieke offered manageability as a category to consider. Although subjective by nature and dependent on local library circumstances, the following problems are representative of how serials cost libraries money beyond their list prices: cataloging problems caused by frequent title changes, persistent claiming problems, binding problems such as narrow margins, and extensive shelf space for storage. Some positive signs to consider would be a journal's adherence to and use of standards, for instance, whether it accommodates the SISAC barcode or is printed on acid-free paper. Rieke urged librarians to talk with publishers about such matters.

Health sciences libraries have participated in regional cooperative collection development agreements, so they are in good positions to advance this concept. Rieke provided a list of steps librarians should plan for to put this idea to work: a proper communication system to access other libraries' holdings, a sense of the extent or quality of the other collections beyond the title level, an idea of the programmatic strengths of the other institutions, an efficient document delivery service, an informed administration and faculty that knows they may be dependent on other libraries' collections, negotiated or waived fees for document delivery, changed practices in ILL, and a willingness at each institution to look beyond its local concerns.[1]

When cutting titles, faculty opinion is given major consideration in medical libraries. Surveys are often conducted by sending faculty lists of titles to review. These methods will result in the inclusion of user biases, but are proof that health sciences libraries are responsive to the clientele they serve and know the value of good public relations. In conclusion, the assessment and development of biomedical collections is an evolutionary process that is dependent on weighing objective and subjective considerations from a broad base of information.

NOTE

1. Eva Martin Sartori, "Regional Collection Development of Serials," Collection Management 11, nos. 112(1989): 69-76.

Auditing the Automated Serials Control System

Carol Pitts Hawks
Sandra Weaver
Workshop Leaders

David Winchester
Recorder

Carol Pitts Hawks, Head, Acquisitions Department at the Ohio State University Libraries, and Sandra Weaver, Vice-President, Innovative Interfaces, Inc., collaborated on this workshop about the auditing of an automated serials control system.

By definition an audit is a methodical examination and review of a situation or condition, concluding with a detailed report of findings. An audit trail is a fundamental component of any audit. By way of background, Hawks explained that audit trails permit an auditor to identify each step in the acquisitions process from planning of the initial order through the receipt of the material. Audit trails may be traced "backwards" by following the material back through the acquisitions process to the original purchase order. Throughout the auditing process the auditor focuses on specific and primary concerns. Are appropriate controls built into the automated system, and are these controls being used properly? Hawks reported that one of the biggest issues is who did what, and by whose authority. An auditor may address these concerns by asking specific questions. Did the appropriate person sign the voucher for payment? Did the collection manager initial the request for purchase? Did the

---

David Winchester is Serials Librarian, Washburn University, Mabee Library, 1700 College, Topeka, KS 66621.

© 1993 by The Haworth Press, Inc. All rights reserved.

system verify the password of the person who signed on to the system to process the order? Were passwords made available to and used by inappropriate personnel?

Automated systems have built-in checks for identifying errors. In this process the key operative word is "prevent"–to prevent errors, fraud, or waste rather than to merely detect them. Hawks explained that there are two types of controls. General control mechanisms apply to all aspects of a system, while application controls are concerned with specific computer applications and the software used to perform the functions of the system. All controls must be balanced against cost effectiveness and carefully checked for redundancy.

General control mechanisms can be divided into those controls which separate computer data processing functions, and those that control access to equipment and data files. The segregation of staff is an example of the first type. In this example the staff, who maintain and service the physical system are segregated from those staff members who might perform specific serials tasks with the system. Limiting access to data files can be achieved by several methods. The primary and most obvious means of limiting access is through password controls. Actual physical access should be controlled by making the computers secure. The final method is by limiting the electronic access by external users of the system. This control becomes more significant as users increasingly use remote location access and as more vendors develop EDI capabilities.

In the discussion of application control mechanisms Hawks concentrated on activities and control by passwords. She presented three principal activities to be segregated: authorization, custody of assets, and accounting. These activities are translated in the acquisitions/serials system to mean purchase order preparation (authorization), receipt of material (custody), and invoice processing/payment (accounting). Passwords can be used to control many tasks in a system. They can block access completely, or can limit access to high-, medium-, or low-security files or data. Passwords can be very restrictive and allow extremely specific tasks. One password may only read data, while another may allow read and modify capabilities. Some systems may choose to separate, add, or delete data functions with unique passwords. While systems do allow for password flexibility, there are certain set conditions which govern password effectiveness. Passwords must be kept secret, not written down, and not shared with another user. The most secure passwords are those which are randomly generated. If passwords are not randomly selected, then they should be difficult to guess and be changed periodically.

A computer offers wonderful mechanisms to facilitate either the correct or incorrect recording of data and to assist in any auditing process. An audit may become a fact of life for most systems. Hawks concluded from experience that the auditing process raises important questions and accentuates areas that need attention. How long should you keep records and on what schedule should these be purged? A department head is vulnerable and it is wise to minimize the number of staff with so-called "super" passwords. Keep a watchful eye on the maintenance of paper/electronic trails in any purchase procedure. And perhaps most importantly, remember that a system cannot always detect human error.

Sandra Weaver concluded the workshop with observations from the viewpoint of an automated systems vendor. Innovative Interfaces has responded to the desires of both auditors and library staff to offer system enhancements. In discussions with auditors Weaver acknowledged that they are not always enemies. Auditors want to do things correctly; systems design should mirror this desire.

She has observed libraries which have gone through extensive audits, and she has found that auditors will listen to philosophical arguments. However, if a library has a minimal staff and an audit requires that a department have more layers of segregation of control than staff, does that library hire more staff? Everyone wants to do things correctly, but what is the price of control?

There are two different types of system audits. The first is an audit of the financial programs. This important, yet simple, audit checks that the dollars and cents add up. The basic goal is to add one and one to equal two. If a system cannot perform mathematical equations at this minimal level then it cannot hope to pass a financial audit at any basic level. Weaver acknowledged that from an auditing standpoint a system can have problems. One example can be observed in an acquisitions/serials system when a library attempts to delete funds from the system.

She complemented Hawks' discussion of access by raising and expanding on the issue of who has access to the system and to which parts of the system. As one might expect, libraries vary widely in their response to these questions. There are many different ways by which staff and non-staff alike can have access to any system. The constant element in any access question is that it gets more complex as the system gets larger. More options equal more complicated access. As a result, maintenance and back-ups become more complicated. With the element of access, system designers wrestle with control vs. flexibility.

Weaver raised questions specifically about the types of access. Where is the CPU located? What types of terminals are to be used and where? Is the system to offer dial-up ports? Does a single port support different types of services? How secure are technical services passwords when a system is confronted with Internet access? Can non-authorized persons get into operating systems levels? She argued that these are important yet basic questions which must be addressed.

A system needs a balance between control of access and cost effectiveness of providing that access. An audit may be a good check on procedures. Libraries are more frequently turning to the "one stop shopping" method of entering a record once and never having to touch it again; they are moving into EDI with less manual manipulation of data. Libraries seek to find systems which provide a combination of ease of use at greater speed with increased flexibility and the greatest savings in staff time. But who has control?

The Cost Effectiveness of Claiming

Marifran Bustion
Workshop Leader

Elizabeth Parang
Recorder

Marifran Bustion, George Washington University, reported on a study conducted while she was Head of the Serials Department at Texas A & M. The purpose of the study was to determine the cost, per title and issue, for claiming journal issues not received.

Bustion began with an overview of the reasons for claiming, identifying the two major reasons: skipped issues and lapsed subscriptions. Other reasons include incorrect number of copies received and defective or damaged issues received. She then discussed the relationships between librarians, agents, and publishers, identifying the roles of each: the librarian must correctly place orders, receive and claim orders, pay invoices, and organize and monitor tasks of the serials staff; the agent must centralize orders and payments, supply serials, and mediate between librarian and publisher; the publisher must handle orders and payments and supply publications requested.

Reasons for not claiming were examined next. These include bibliographic changes such as title changes, splits, mergers, cessations, and suspensions. Claims should not be sent if payment has not been sent, a postal strike is in progress, or war or other political turmoil is occurring in the country of origin.

Responsibilities of each of three parties in the claiming process

---

Elizabeth Parang is Head Serials Librarian, University of Nevada–Las Vegas, 4505 S. Maryland Parkway, Las Vegas, NV 89154-7007.

© 1993 by The Haworth Press, Inc. All rights reserved.

were outlined. The librarian is responsible for reviewing claims before submission. In addition to confirming that payment has been sent, the following should be examined: publication frequency, receipt pattern, publisher and vendor reports, beginning date of subscription, receipt recorded and enumeration and chronology. The agent must track payments and renewals, provide proof of payment, help determine action intervals, and provide status reports that include changes in publication schedules, bibliographic changes, and claims information, including responses. Publishers' responsibilities include printing enough copies for subscriptions and possible claims, responding promptly to claims, and providing status reports which include changes in publication schedules, frequency changes and bibliographic changes. Publishers should consider claims not just as claims. Prompt response to claims help libraries establish appropriate time intervals for claiming.

Bustion then remarked on the effect of automated systems on the quantity and quality of claims, noting the need to review the file completely at least four times per year. The increased frustration for publishers caused by automated claimed must be recognized; librarians need to know that publishers do not "toss" all first claims. Both the check-in and claims staff need to feel equally responsible for accuracy of information in the automated system; unfortunately these staff are often the lowest level with the least experience. Efforts to deal with claims need to be coordinated among librarians, agents, and publishers. Bustion mentioned Faxon's Claims Prevention Pilot Study as one such effort.

The claims study at Texas A & M attempted to determine the time spent by staff in identifying claims, determining the need to claim, and processing claim letters and responses from publishers and vendors. Also looked at were relationships between "problem" titles and use, between "problem" titles and subscription cost, and between "problem" titles and publisher. Between October 1991 and April 1992, the study followed the workflow through check-in, claiming, binding, and backfile (replacement) units. Forms were used which included some general information, such as NOTIS record number and price, and some information specific to each unit. The level of the person doing a task, as well as the time spent, was noted. Vendor reports were not reviewed as this was felt to be too time consuming. At the end of the study, only 1 percent of the titles included had been monitored by all four units; this constituted 25 titles. The study monitored 659 hours of work which averaged out to 16 minutes per issue with much of the time spent searching the shelves for the item. Approximately one third of the missing issues were found on a first cursory search. At an average pay of $5.50 per hour, the cost amounted to approximately $1.47 per issue. Both gift and high priced items caused problems. Each major scientific-technical publisher had problem titles.

Discussion after the presentation focused on fulfillment houses, the difficulty in matching titles from vendor reports to the titles entered on a library's system, damaged issues caused by poor packaging, and the definite need to claim.

Seventh Annual NASIG Conference Registrants, University of Illinois at Chicago, June 1992

Conference registrants

Adams, Agnes
Adams, Peter W.
Adrian, Philip
Aiello, Helen M.
Aitchison, Jada A.
Alexander, Adrian W.
Alward, Donna
Arcand, Janet
Arnold, Linda
Astle, Deana
Atkins, Patricia A.
Aufdemberge, Karen

Backus, Charles
Baia, Wendy
Baker, Carol M.
Baker, Mary Ellen
Baker, Sally
Barczyk, Ewa
Barnes, Ilse E.
Barnes, Jouliette
Barnes, Ted
Basch, Buzzy
Batten, Henry R.

Institutions

University of Nebraska
Moseley Associates
Rush University
Wesleyan University
University of Arkansas
The Faxon Company
Saginaw Valley State University
Iowa State University
OCLC Inc.
Clemson University
Upjohn
University of Toledo

Syracuse University Press
University of Colorado, Boulder
University of Calgary
California Polytechnic University
Indiana State University
University of Wisconsin–Milwaukee
University of West Florida
Association of University Presses
The Faxon Company
Basch Associates
Arthur Andersen & Co.

Battin, Patricia	Commission on Preservation and Access
Beatty, Deb	Dawson Subscription Service
Beckett, Chris	Blackwell's Periodicals
Bell, Carole R.	Northwestern University
Bennett, Kathryn	University of Toronto Press
Benson, Bill	Wright Laboratory Technical Library
Bentley, Ronald W.	Canadian Agriculture Library
Bergholz, Donna C.	Duke University
Berker-Nielsen, Tonnes	Aarhus University Press
Bernards, Dennis	Brigham Young University
Bernero, Cheryl	EBSCO Subscription Services
Berry, John	University of Illinois/Urbana-Champaign
Binks, Jon	Copyright Clearance Center
Blaes, Evelyn R.	American University
Blatchley, Jeremy	Bryn Mawr College
Blixrud, Julia C.	Council on Library Resource
Bloss, Alex	ALA/ALCTS
Boissy, Bob	The Faxon Company
Bonhomme, Mary	Chicago Public Library
Born, Kathleen	EBSCO Subscription Services
Borsman, Mary Linn	Massachusetts General Hospital
Bosse, Suzanne	University of Ottawa Press
Botero, Cecilia	University of Florida
Bottomley, Lucy	National Library of Canada
Bovenschulte, Robert	New England Journal of Medicine
Bowman, Mark	North Dakota State Library
Bowman, Mary	De Paul University
Breithaupt, John	Allen Press
Brenneman, Margaret T.	The Newberry Library
Broadwater, Deborah H.	Vanderbilt Medical Library
Broadway, Rita	Memphis State University
Brogan, Martha	Yale University
Brown, Gary J.	The Faxon Company
Buell, Vivian	Ballen Booksellers International
Bueter, Rita Van Assche	Blackwell North America
Burgett, Mary	Rice University

Burk, Martha	Babson College
Bustion, Marifran	George Washington University
Callaghan, Jean S.	Wheaton College
Cameron, Hamish	University of Toronto Press
Cameron, Linda D.	University of Calgary Press
Campbell, Cameron J.	University of Chicago
Canini, Tuula	University of Waterloo
Carlson, Barbara A.	Medical University of South Carolina
Cartwrite, Perry	Association of American University Presses
Case, Mary M.	Northwestern University
Chadwick, Leroy	Municipality Metro. Seattle
Champagne, Thomas	Ross & Hardies
Chan, Linda	The Newberry Library
Chang, Ling-Li	Loyola University
Christ, Ruth	University of Iowa
Christiansen, Christine	University of Miami
Chrzastowski, Tina	University of Illinois/Urbana-Champaign
Clack, Mary Elizabeth	Harvard College
Clay, Genevieve J.	Eastern Kentucky University
Clendenning, Lynda F.	University of Virginia
Coats, Jacqueline	University of Chicago
Cochenour, Donnice	Colorado State University
Cochran, Patti	University Microfilms International
Cohen, David	College of Charleston
Coleman, Shirley	Purdue University
Coles, Janet	Information Access
Collins, Dorothy	Readmore
Compton, Bruce	Louisiana State University
Conley, Laura	John Wiley & Sons
Conway, Cheryl L.	University of Arkansas
Cook, Eleanor	Appalachian State University
Cooley, Elizabeth A.	University of Virginia
Corbett, Gloria	CISTI
Corrigan, Anne-Marie	University of Toronto Press
Coulter, Cynthia M.	University of Northern Iowa

Courtney, Keith — Taylor and Francis
Cousineau, Marie — University of Ottowa
Cox, Brian — Pergamon Press, Oxford
Cox, John E. — Blackwell's Periodicals
Creesy, Charles — Princeton University Press
Crinion, Jacquelyn A. — University of Texas at San Antonio
Crump, Michele — University of Florida Library
Cunliffe, Christina — CAB International
Curasi, Suzanne C. — University of Wisconsin–Milwaukee
Curtis, Jerry — Springer-Verlag
Czech, Isabel — Institute for Scientific Information

Dabkey, Lee — EBSCO Subscription Services
Dabkowski, Charles — Niagara University
Dane, Stephen — Kluwer Academic Publishers
Darling, Karen — University of Oregon
Davidge, Lyn — University of Michigan
Davidson, Leanne B. — Ball State University
Davis, Allan W. — University of Wisconsin, Whitewater
Davis, Carroll Nelson — Columbia University
Davis, Renette — University of Chicago
Davis, Sheryl — University of California–Riverside
Davis, Susan — State University of New York/Buffalo
Dawes, Joan A. — Houston Academy of Medicine
Dawson, Julie Eng — Princeton Theological Seminary
Day, Nancy — Linda Hall Library
Debacher, Richard D. — Southern Illinois University Press
DeBuse, Judy — Washington State University
Degener, Christie T. — University of North Carolina at Chapel Hill

Delgadillo, Jose L. — Information Access
Derr, Louise — Dynix
Deurell, Anne — Phillips Research Library, Hanscomnb Air Force Base

Devin, Robin — University of Rhode Island
Devlin, Mary — The Faxon Company
Diodato, Louise — Cardinal Stritch College

Divereaux, Dorothy	Association of American University Presses
Douglass, Janet	Texas Christian University
Doyle, Colleen	Blackwell's Periodicals
Dudley, Lenore	Appalachian State University
Dungey, Phyllis	Upjohn
Duranceau, Ellen Finnie	Massachusetts Institute of Technology
Eaglesfield, Jean	Michigan State University
Echt, Rita	Michigan State University
Edelman, Marla	University of North Carolina at Greensboro
Edwards, Keith R.	Collets Subscription Service
Elliott, Maxine	Clemson University
Entwistle, Stephen	Blackwell's Periodicals
Ercelawn, Ann	Vanderbilt University
Erickson, Annmarie	Student
Eslami, Eva	Princeton University
Evans, John R.	University of Missouri–Columbia
Evans, Tom	Canisius College
Evilsizer, Martha	University Microfilms International
Feick, Tina	Blackwell's Periodicals
Feliciano, Olga Edleen	Chicago Public Library
Ferley, Margaret	Concordia University
Fetch, Deborah	Pennsylvania State University
Field, Kenneth C.	Trent University
Fisher, Fran	North Dakota State University
Fisher, Heidi A.	Princeton University
Fisher, Janet S.	East Tennessee State University
Fitchett, Christine	Vassar College
Folsom, Sandy L.	Central Michigan University
Forney, Marlene G.	Minitex
Fortney, Lynn M.	EBSCO Subscription Services
Foster, Constance L.	Western Kentucky University
Frade, Patricia	Brigham Young University
Franq, Carole S.	Indiana University Medical Library
Fritsch, David R.	The Faxon Company

Fugle, Mary — Elsevier Science Publishers
Fullerton, Janet — Ferris State University

Gaisford, Janet — Metro Toronto Reference Library
Gammon, Julia — University of Akron
Gans, Alfred J. — ISA Australia
Gartrell, Joyce — Columbia University
Gasser, Sharon S. — James Madison University
Gbala, Helen — NOTIS Systems
Gearty, Tom — The Faxon Company
Geer-Butler, Beverly — Ohio State University
Gelenter, Win — National Agricultural Library
Geller, Marilyn — Massachusetts Institute of Technology
Gentz, William — Carnegie Mellon University
Gifford, Caroline — New York Public Library, Research
Giglio, Stephen J. — The Faxon Company
Gillespie, E. Gaele — University of Kansas
Gimmi, Robert D. — Shippensburg University of Pennsylvania

Glasgow, Kay — State University of New York at Binghamton

Goforth, Kathleen — Academic Book Center
Gordon, Christine M. — Information Access
Gordon, Martin — Franklin and Marshall College
Gordon-Gilmore, Anita — Fort Hays State University
Gormley, Alice — Marquette University
Grande, Dolores — John Jay College
Greene, Philip E.N., III — EBSCO Subscription Services
Guay, Gisele — Canadian Centre for Architecture
Gurshman, Sandra J. — Readmore

Hahn, Barbara G. — University of Kentucky
Hale, Kimberly A. — Columbia College Library
Hall, Kyle — EBSCO Subscription Services
Hamilton, Fred — Louisiana Tech University
Harnum, William — University of Toronto Press
Harri, Wilbert — Moorhead State University
Harris, Jay — University of Alabama at Birmingham

Hasiuk, Anne Z.	University of Chicago
Hawks, Carol Pitts	Ohio State University
Hayman, Lynne	University of California
Heinemann, Peg	University of New Mexico
Hendrickson, Kent	University of Nebraska
Hepfer, Cindy	State University of New York/ Buffalo; and, *Serials Review*
Hill, Bonnie	Tufts University
Hill, Martha	Institute of Paper Science and Technology
Hill, Thomas W.	Self Memorial Hospital
Hinders, Thomas	Oberlin College
Hinds, Isabella	Copy Clearance Center
Hinger, Joseph P.	Case Western Reserve University
Holland, Jeffrey	University of Nevada, Reno
Holley, Sandra H.	University of Texas Health Science Center at Tyler
Holloway, Carson	EBSCO Subscription Services
Holzenberg, Phyllis	University of Colorado, Boulder
Hor, Annie Y.	Williams College
Howard, Martha	Association of American University Presses
Hsieh, Cynthia	Columbia College
Hsueh, Daphne C.	Ohio State University
Hudes, Nan	R.R. Bowker
Hudson, Christopher	J. Paul Getty Museum
Hurst, Brenda	CISTI
Hutto, Dena	Pennsylvania State University
Hyman, Barbara T.	United States Postal Service Library
Iljin, Kristina	University of Alabama
Impellittiere, Agnes J.	Pergamon Press
Irvin, Judy	Louisiana Tech University
Ivins, October	Louisiana State University
Jaeger, Don	Alfred Jaeger, Inc.
Jaeger, Glenn	Serialsquest
Jakubowski, Kathi L.	University of Wisconsin–Milwaukee

James, Darryl Dean	HAM-TMC Library
James, David Willis	Johns Hopkins University
Janes, Jodith	Cleveland Clinic Foundation
Jayes, Linda D.	University of Chicago
Jen, Ping-Chih Esther	Lake Forest College
Jensen, Deborah	The Faxon Company
Johnston, Judith A.	University of North Texas
Jones, Ann L.	Art Institute of Chicago
Jones, Daniel H.	University of Texas Health Sciences Center at San Antonio
Jones, Florence	University of Colorado
Kanter, Dorothy A.	CHS Health Sciences Library
Kasper, Carol	Association of American University Presses
Kavanaugh, Karalyn	EBSCO Subscription Services
Kean, Gene	Allen Press
Keating, Lawrence R.	University of Houston
Kellogg, Martha	University of Rhode Island
Kellum, Cathy	Tec-Masters
Kennedy, Kit	Readmore Academic Services
Kercher, Marilyn L.	Ohio State University
Kerr, Linda	University of Alberta
Kersey, Harriet F.	Georgia Institute of Technology
Ketterman, Kathleen	Indiana University Press
Khan, Mumtaz A.	Wright State University
Kietzke, Naomi K.	University of North Carolina
Kimberlin, Robert H.	Elsevier Science Publishers
Kirkland, Kenneth L.	De Paul University
Kisilinsky, Stuart	Association of American University Presses
Knapp, Leslie C.	EBSCO Subscription Services
Knotts, Barbara	St. Louis Public Library
Kostecki, Janine	Student
Kramer, Nina	American Society of Civil Engineers
Kropf, Blythe A.	New York Public Library
Kwan, Cecilia	University of California, Davis

Ladjen, Nadia	New York Public Library
Lamborn, Joan	University of Northern Colorado
Landesman, Betty	George Washington University
Lange, Janice	Sam Houston State University
Lawrence, Jane	Harcourt, Brace, and Jovanovich
Lawton, Wesley	CRC Press
Leatham, Cecilia A.	University of Miami
Leazer, William V.	Majors Scientific Subscriptions
Lebron, Maria	*Current Clinical Trials*
Lecian, Jane E.	University of Akron
Lee, Maureen	University of Toronto
Lehman, Charlene	University of Iowa
Lehmann, Terry	Lehmann Bookbinding
Lesher, Marcella	St. Mary's University
Lewis, Martha	Abbott Laboratories
Lewis, Susan	Penn State Press
Lin, Selina	University of Iowa
Lindquist, Janice	University of Missouri–Kansas City
Llewllyn, Tony	Butterworth-Heinemann
Loafman, Kathryn	University of North Texas
Loranz, Claire T.	Wellesley College
Loslo, Joan	University of Northern Iowa
Lowry, Anita	Columbia University
Lucas, John	Medical College of Ohio
Luther, Judy	The Faxon Company
Lutz, Linda	University of Western Ontario
Lynch, Clifford	University of California
MacAdam, Carol	Princeton University
MacArthur, Marit	Auraria Library
Macklin, Lisa A.	University of North Texas
MacLennan, Birdie	University of Vermont
Madarash-Hill, Cherie	University of Akron
Maddox, Jane	Harrassowitz
Magee, Elizabeth	University of Regina Library
Magenau, Carol	Dartmouth College
Malawski, Susan	John Wiley & Sons

Malinowski, Teresa	California State University, Fullerton
Malone, Debbie	Ursinus College
Mann, Marjorie F.	National Library of Medicine
Mapes, Frank	EBSCO Subscription Services
Markley, Susan	Villanova University
Marks, Betty	The Faxon Company
Markwith, Michael	The Faxon Company
Marsh, Corrie	NOTIS Systems
Marshall, Karen	University of Western Ontario
Martin, Sylvia	Vanderbilt University
May, Charles	SOLINET
McCafferty, Patrick	Case Western Reserve University
McCalla, Anna	Trent University
McCann, Kris K.	Dawson Subscription Service
McCarty, Willard	University of Toronto
McClary, Maryon L.	University of Alberta-Edmonton
McCollough, Amy F.	Southwestern University
McCutcheon, Dianne	National Library of Medicine
McGrath, Kathleen	University of British Columbia
McKay, Beatrice	Trinity University
McKay, Peter	Harcourt, Brace, and Jovanovich, London
McKee, Anne E.	Arizona State University
McMahon, Suzanne	Stanford University
McQuiston, Karhleen	Philadelphia College of Pharmacy and Science
Meiseles, Linda	Hofstra University
Meneely, Kathleen	Cleveland Health Sciences Library
Mering, Margaret	University of Nebraska
Merrill, Claire	The Faxon Company
Merrill-Oldham, Jan	University of Connecticut
Mesner, Lillian	University of Kentucky
Metcalf, Walda	University of Florida Press
Meyers, Barbara	Meyers Consulting Service
Michael, James D.	University of South Florida
Miller, Daphne	Write State University
Mitchell, Eleanor	Arizona State University–West
Moe, Gary	Dynix

Moore, Patricia L.	Michigan Tech University
Moran, Sheila	Massachusetts General Hospital
Morey, Laura	Gauthier-Villars North America
Morgan, Pamela	Memorial University of Newfoundland
Mouw, James	University of Chicago
Murden, Steven H.	Virginia Commonwealth University
Murphy, Lynne F.	McGill University
Narang, Sat P.	Eastern Illinois University
Neal, James G.	Indiana University
Ney, Michael V.	Indiana University Department of Surgery
Nicholas, Patty	Fort Hays State University
Nichols, Catherine	The Faxon Company
Nigoghosian, Alice	Wayne State University Press
Nolan, Christopher	Trinity University
Nordman, Alan	Dawson Subscription Service
O'Connor, Michael	Harvard University
O'Donnell, James J.	University of Pennsylvania
Oberfranc, Gretchen	Princeton University Press
Oberg, Steven	University of Illinois/Urbana-Champaign
Okerson, Ann	ARL
Olson, Dianne	Loyola University Medical Library
O'Malley, Terrence	Cleveland State University
Osheroff, Sheila Keil	Oregon State University
Osmus, Lori	Iowa State University
Ostrander, Gloria	Boise State University
Pabbruwe, Herman	Kluwer Academic Publishers
Pangallo, Karen	University of San Diego
Paradis, Olga	*The Citadel*
Parang, Elizabeth	University of Nevada, Las Vegas
Paredes, Providence F.	United States Postal Service Library
Parisi, Paul A.	Acme Bookbinding

Patterson, Susan L. — Butterworth-Heinemann
Peterson, Joseph G. — Association of American University Presses

Plotkin, Wendy — University of Illinois/Chicago
Preisser, Julie — Sinclair Community College
Preston, Cecilia — University of California–Berkeley
Prior, Albert — UK Serials Group
Proctor, David — Texas Tech University
Putney, Patricia — Brown University

Radbourne, Margaret — John Wiley & Sons
Raines, M. Diane — Dynix
Ralston, M. Joan — Villanova University
Randall, Kevin M. — Northwestern University
Rast, Elaine K. — Northern Illinois University
Rauch, Theodore G. — Columbia University
Ravinder, Sarita — Princeton Theological Seminary
Raymond, Lorraine M. — University of Washington
Reed, Joy — University Microfilms International
Reed, Virginia R. — Northeastern Illinois University
Reich, Vicky — Stanford University
Reijnen, Marian — Martinus Nijhoff International
Revas, Robert — University of Utah
Reynolds, Regina R. — Library of Congress
Riding, Ed — Dynix
Rieke, Judith L. — University of North Dakota
Riley, Cheryl — Central Missouri State University
Riley, Teri A. — Information Access
Ringler, Rebecca — University of California–San Diego
Rioux, Margaret A. — Woods Hole Oceanographic Institution

Risop, Ingrid — IR Publications
River, Sandra — Texas Tech University
Roberts, Sally — Information Access
Robillard, Jane A. — Veteran's Administration
Robischon, Rose — U.S Military Academy
Rogers, Marilyn L. — University of Arkansas–Fayetteville
Rossignol, Lucien R. — Smithsonian Institution

Rowlison, Lisa	University of California, Berkeley
Rowson, Richard C.	W. Wilson Center Press
Rumph, Virginia A.	Butler University
Salk, Judy	R.R. Bowker
Salony, Mary	Clarion University
Sanders, Susan	NIST
Sarazin, Georges	Faxon Canada
Saxe, Minna C.	City University of New York Graduate School
Sayler, Terry	University of Maryland
Scarry, Patricia	University of Chicago Press
Schaafsma, Carol A.	University of Hawaii
Schmidt, Karen A.	University of Illinois/Urbana-Champaign
Schmidt, Kathy Wodrich	University of Wisconsin–La Crosse
Schmidt, Vincent	EBSCO Subscription Services
Schwartz, Marla	American University
Scott, Jo Anne	University of Chicago
Scott, Sharon K.	University of Nevada, Reno
Sederstrom, Gene	University of South Dakota
Settle, Huguette M.T.	University of Alberta
Shaffer, Barbara A.	University of Toledo
Shaw, Deborah L.	Oklahoma State University
Sheridan, Bill	Hertzberg–New Method
Shipp John	University of Wollongong
Shropshire, Sandra	Idaho State University
Sisak, Kathleen A.	City University of New York Graduate School
Slawik, Nora B.	University of Alabama Press
Sleep, Esther L.	Brock University
Smets, Kristine	Center for Research
Smiley, Julie	Heckman Bindery
Smith, Sue	B.H. Blackwell
Sommer, Susan	State University of New York at Albany
Sonn, Lark Lee	Ferris State University
Sowa, Kathryn A.	New Mexico State University

Sozansky, Bill	University of Minnesota
Stamison, Christine	University of Chicago
Stanley, Nancy M.	Pennsylvania State University
Steele, Heather	B.H. Blackwell
Steer, Carol	University of Manitoba
Stickman, Jim	University of Washington
Stimac, Susan C.	Michigan Technological University
Striedieck, Suzanne	North Carolina State University
Studwell, William	Northern Illinois University
Sturge, Peggy H.	Memorial University of Newfoundland
Su, Julie	Indiana University/Purdue University at Indianapolis
Sutherland, Laurie	University of Washington
Tagler, John	Elsevier Science Publishers
Tang, Lorna Y.	University of Chicago
Taylor, Kay E.	University of Minnesota
Teague, Eliane E.	Burroughs Wellcome Company
Teaster-Woods, Gale	Winthrop College
Teel, Katherine	Columbia University
Ten Hare, Elizabeth D.	Michigan State University
Tenney, Joyce	University of Maryland at Baltimore
Terry, Nancy	Grand Valley State University
Thatcher, Sanford G.	Penn State Press
Thompson, Margery	Georgetown
Thompson, Steve	Brown University
Thomson, Mary Beth	University of Houston
Thomson, Sarah	University of Massachusetts–Amherst
Thorburn, Colleen	University of Florida
Thornberry, Pat	University of South Florida
Thornton, Christopher P.	Case Western Reserve University
Thornton, Glenda	Auraria Library
Tong, Dieu Van	University of Alabama at Birmingham
Tonkery, Dan	Readmore
Topfer, Sue A.	Wilkes University
Tucker, Ruth	Boston College
Turitz, Mitch	San Francisco State University

Tusa, Sarah D.	Lamar University
Tuttle, Marcia	University of North Carolina
Unver, Amira	George Washington University
Valino, Nenita M.	Anne Arundel Community College
Van Andel, Ken	Aurora University
Van Auken, Gayle J.	Linda Hall Library
Van Cura, Mary Ann	Hamline University Law Library
Van Eysinga, Frans	Kluwer Academic Publishers
Van Goethem, Jeri	Duke University
Van Lerssel, Harry	University of Toronto Press
Van Velzen, Antoon	SWETS Subscription Service
Velazquez, Arturo	Universidad Nacional Autonomo de Mexico
Vent, Marilyn	University of Nevada, Las Vegas
Vertrees, Linda S.	Chicago Public Library
Vidor, Ann B.	Emory University
Vogt, Norman	Northern Illinois University
Von Wahlde, Barbara	State University of New York at Buffalo
Wachel, Kathy	University of Iowa
Walford, Leo	Chapman & Hall
Wall, Colleen	3M Technical Library
Wallace, Patricia M.	University of Colorado
Walters, Mitchel	University of Texas at Dallas, Southwestern Medical Center
Walters, Sheila	Arizona State University
Ward, Jeannette	University of Central Florida
Ward, Sharon	Arizona State University
Waring, Jonathan	Collets Subscription Service
Warren, Karen T.	University of South Carolina
Weaver, Sandra	Innovative Interfaces
Weaver, Terry	Marion Merrell Dow
Weir, Barbara	Swarthmore College
Weisser, Teresa A.	Lafayette College
Wen, Sheila	North Central College

Weng, Cathy	Temple University
Weyhrich, Larry	Illinois State Library
Whiting, Peter	Student
Wiles-Young, Sharon	Lehigh University
Wilhelme, Judy	University of Michigan
Wilhite, Marjorie	University of Iowa
Wilke, Mary	Student
Wilkerson, Judy	University of Oklahoma
Williams, Geraldine	Northern Kentucky University
Williams, Sheryl	University of Nebraska Medical Center
Williams, Sue	University of Colorado, Boulder
Williamson, Josephine	University of Delaware
Wilson, Sally	University of Pittsburgh
Winchester, David	Washburn University
Wirtz, Theresa M.	Yankee Book Peddler
Witsenhausen, Helen	John Wiley & Sons
Wood, Don E.	Southern Illinois University
Woolfrey, S.	Wilfrid Laurier University Press
Wright, George	Publication Identification
Yegerlehner, Shirley	Indiana University/Purdue University at Indianapolis
Young, Jim	Sirsi Corporation
Zake, Semei	Columbia College Library
Zappen, Susan H.	Rensselaer Polytechnic Institute
Zhang, Yvonne W.	Northwestern University
Ziegler, Roy	Southeast Missouri State University
Zook, Ruth Ann	United States Bureau of Reclamation Library
Zuidema, Karen	Student
Zuriff, Susan Rom	University of Minnesota

Index

Abstracting and indexing services 179,184,200-201
Access versus ownership 159,161,173,176,208,281
ACQNET 201
Acquisition on demand 10-11
ADONISTM 291
Advertising to libraries 189
Advisory boards, Publishers' 183-185,204,255
Alexandria library 22,37
American Chemical Society 127
American Association for the Advancement of Science 125
American Geophysical Union 128
American Mathematical Society 127,134
American Mineralogical Society 127
American Physical Society 127
ANSI X12 standard. *See* X12
ANSI/NISO Z39.2 standard. *See* Z39.2
Any Text Scholar's Package 66
Approval plans 201-202
Archie 54
Areopagitica 79,85
ARIEL 115,169
Arizona State University West 207-214,281-283
ARPANET 226
ARTFL: American and French Research on the Treasury of the French Language 65,69-70,89
Artificial intelligence 33-34,158
ASCII 51
Association of Research Libraries 115,130,176

statistics 164,167-169
Atkinson, Ross 100
Audit trail 293-294
Aufdemberge, Karen 233-234
Augustine, Saint 24,38
Authorship in electronic media 35

Barcode. *See* SISAC barcode
Barker, Joseph 102
Barnes, Ted 259-260
Bernero, Cheryl A. 263-264
Berners-Lee, Tim 50
Bible 24
Bibliographic description of Internet resources 50
Bibliographic Information Interchange. *See* Z39.2
Binding preparation, Automated 233-235
BITNET 226
Book as physical format 22,79
Book reviews 200
Books for College Libraries 151
Bovenschulte, Robert 123-125
Bowker, R. R. 183-196,204
Brain Research 131
BRS Colleague 291
Bryn Mawr Classical Review 84-85,95-96
Bustion, Marifran 297-299
Butler, Brett 211

C. Elegans 9
California State College System 162
CARL 209
   UnCover2 115,211-213

© 1993 by The Haworth Press, Inc. All rights reserved.   *317*

Cassiodorus 24-27,38-39
Cataloging modification 275
Cataloging standards 50
  for computer files 230,265
Catalogs, Cooperative 170-171
Catalogs, Publishers' 195
CCITT X.400 53
CD-ROMs 75,77
  cataloging 230-231,266-267
  licensing 64
  Bowker products 186-191,193
Center for Electronic Texts in the
    Humanities 69-70
Chadwick-Healy 204
Check-in, Serial 237-238
  predictive 258-260
  scanning software 251
Christians, Early 23,38
CIC. *See* Committee on Institutional
    Cooperation
Circulation 149
City University of New York 226
Claims 257-260,271
  causes 259,297
  cost effectiveness 297-299
Clemson University 131
Coalition for Networked Information
    20,50,111,145
Collection Development and
    Evaluation Section (RASD)
    198
Codex 23-25,38
Collaboration
  between libraries 164
  in marketing 205
  in networked environment 9,115
  in scholarly communication 83-84
Collection development functions
    198-199,201
Colson, Barbara 200
Columbia University 64,143
Commercial information in
    networked environment 17
Committee on Institutional
    Cooperation 162

Communication system standards
    53-54
Concordances 28
Consensus building 85-86
CONSER 265
Contribution identifier 250
Control mechanisms in serials
    control systems 294-295
Cook, Eleanor 273-276
Cooperation between libraries 164
Copyright 119,124,143,173,179
  Act of 1976 62-64,145
  ownership 14-15,146
  law 13
Copyright Clearance Center
    11,154,179,212
Cornell University 152-153
Corporate sponsorship of
    information access 12
Cost-per-use studies 133-134
Council on Library Resources
    44-45,169,209
Courtney, Keith 269-270
Cox, Brian 270-271
CRC Press 255
Customer services, Publishers'
    193-194

Damaged issues 299
Dane, Stephen 250
Dartmouth College 69
Dartmouth Dante Project Database
    69-70,89
Data, Standards for 45-52
Databases, Network access to 144
Davis, Susan 261-262
dBase 234,286-287
DIALOG Information Services, Inc.
    70
Diodato, Louise 262-263
Direct mail marketing
    187-188,192,198-200
DOCLINE 290
Doctrine of fair use 62-64
Doctrine of first sale 62-63

Document delivery 115,124,169,
  208-213,282-283
 commercial
  13-14,173-174,176,211,283
 contracts 213-214,222-223
 fulfillment rates 218
 instead of journal subscriptions
  131,203,210-211
 vendors 218-222
Docutek printer 118,151-153
Doing more with less 118-119
Dougherty, Richard M.

EBSCO Subscription Services
  115,137-142,263
EDI 51,246-247,250,259-260,
  270-271
 in serials control systems 294,296
Editorial boards 255
Editorial process 253-255
Electronic bulletin boards 106
Electronic discussion groups
  80,86-88
 related to serials work 226
Electronic editions 80,88-92
Electronic information 76-77. See
  also Networked information
 copyright of 65,143
 monographic 65,144
 networking of 174-175
 pricing 145,174
 reproduction 64,66
 restrictions on use
  13-14,61-71,144-145
 serial 66,144.
Electronic journals
  41,75-77,146-147,174
 cataloging of 231,266-267
 publication of 125-126
 ISSN for 56
Electronic mail
  34,86,120-121,226-227
Electronic media 33-35,81-82,85
 effect on scholarship 80,82,93-95
 use for concensus-building 85-86
Electronic publications
 models for access 144-145
 value in tenure and promotion
  process 84
Electronic Reserve Room pilot
  project 211
Electronic seminars. *See* Electronic
  discussion groups
Electronic Text Service 64-68,143
Elsevier Scientific Publishers
  8,20,111,131
Enumeration data 237-239
Eusebian canon tables 27-28,39-40
Expert systems 53

Facsimiles, On-demand reproduction
  of 152-155
Faculty
 involvement in serials
  cancellations 292
 ownership of copyright 14-15
Faxon Company 115,259-260,298
Fayen, Emily 174
Feick, Tine 249-250
File transfer protocol 226-227
Fire upon the Deep, A 20
Fleming, Janice 128
Flexner, Abraham 101
Florida higher education 74,76
Florida Center for Library
  Automation 171
Florida Library Automation Project
  162
Focus groups 204,255
Franklin and Marshall College 151
FTP. *See* File transfer protocol
Fulfillment houses 299

Gammon, Julia 255-256
Gearty, Tom 278-279
Geer-Butler, Beverly 237-238
Geller, Marilyn 273-276
Glossa Ordinaria 35,41

German, Paul 175
Giglio, Stephen 259-260
Golden Fleece awards 75-77
Gopher 54
Gorman, Michael 106
Government's role in scholarly
    communication 124
Graphical user interfaces 52
Gutenberg 119

Hall, G. K. 255
Harris, Pat 47
Hawks, Carol Pitts 171,293-295
Health science journal prices
    137-142
Health science libraries 289-292
Hepfer, Cindy 253-255
Higher education 74-78,130
Holistic librarianship 101
Hsueh, Daphne C. 238-239
Humanist Discussion Group 86-87
Humanities, Computing in the
    86-87,145
Humanities databases 69-71
Hypertext 8,41,54,120
HYTELNET 54

IBID project 153-155
ICEDIS. *See* International
    Committee for EDI in Serials
Idea of the University 81
Image scanning of documents
    151-155
Indexes 28
Index Medicus 290
   price study of journals indexed
       137-142
Indiana library networks 157-159
Information access
   cost 11-12
   in electronic media 33-34
Information chain 112,116,117 (ill.)
Information infrastructure
    44-46,112,119
Information interchange Format 57
Information management, Library
    model of 18-19
Information soup 102-103
Information technology
   effect on scholarly communication
       6-7
   role in librarianship 102-106
Information transfer in networked
    environment 116
INNOVACQ binding preparation
    module 233-234
Innovative Interfaces 295-296
Intellectual property rights 15,19
Interdisciplinary scholarship and
    electronic media 83-84,
    86,89
Interlibrary loan 130,207-209,211
   automatic 170
   cooperative 171,173-174
   costs 14,175
   effect of resource sharing on
       171-173
   limitations for networked
       information 13
International Committee for EDI in
    Serials 270-271
International Union of
    Crystallography 127-128
Internet 43,111,158-159,162,226-227
   cataloging on the 50
   access to articles 211
   text delivery 120
Invisible college 83-84,101,106
Invoice stuffers 195-196
ISDS 51
ISSN 179-180
   use for electronic journals 56
Ivins, October 200,277-278

Josey-Bass 204
Journal articles, Acquisition on
    demand of 10-11
Journal fulfillment 270

Journal monitoring task forces 256
Journals 29-32. *See also* Serials
   launching new 269-270
   price increases 138-141,175
   price studies 127-128
   selection 200-202,289-290
Journals, Print 29-31
   competition with electronic journals 146-147
Just in time acquisitions 13-14,130,173

Keller, Michael 175
Kinko's Copy Centers 63,67
Knowledge, Organization of 28-29
Knowledge management matrix 112,116;113 (ill.)
Knowledge management methodology 9
Kuhn, Thomas 109-110

Labeling, Serial 238-239
Leases for electronic information 64-69
Leazer, William 246-247
Lebron, Maria L. 123,125-126
Lenzini, Rebecca 211
LEXIS 68
Librarians' relationships with publishers 178
Librarianship as a profession 101-104
Libraries. *See also* Research libraries
   automation 104-105
   budgets 75-76,129-131
   circulation 149
   collection-based versus access-oriented 14,76-77,114-115
   competition with publishers 124
   control of electronic information 61-71
   development of networked information systems 17-20
   financial support of publishing 18
   impact of networking on 115,157-159
   medieval 24-25,38-39
   mission 9-10
   nonprint communication and 18-19
   resource sharing 161-176
   role in scholarly communication 7,9-10,20,114,116
   service to remote users 173
Library of Congress Subject Headings 241-243
Library schools 262-263,196
Library users, Self-sufficient 176
Licensing agreements for electronic information 13-14,64-69, 144,146,174-175
Linguist's Software, Inc. 66
List of Journals Indexed in Index Medicus 138-139
LISTSERV discussion groups 32,41
Longitudinal studies 132-133,135
Lowry, Anita 143-145
Lucier, Richard 9
Lyman, Peter 8
Lynch, Clifford 50,111

Macklin, Lisa 234-235
MacLennan, Birdie 225-227
Major Scientific Subscriptions 246-247
Mann, Marjorie 257-259
Manuscripts, Medieval 26-29,39-40
Manuscripts, Submitting 254-255
MARC format 51,247
   for cataloging serials computer files 229-230,265
   use in serials check-in systems 238,258
Market research, Library 183-205
Martinus Nijhoff International 245-246
Matheson, Nina 9

McComb, Gillian 100
McCutcheon, Dianne 257-259
McGill University 54
McLuhan, Marshall 25,33,121
Medical Subject Headings
    139-141,243
Medium, Influence on content
    25-26,33
Metamorphoses 79,91
Meyers, Barbara 127-128
Milton, John 79,85,92
MITT Media Lab 18
Mitchell, Eleanor 282
Modern Language Association 70
Modern Language Association
    International Bibliography
    database 70
Modernization
    of scholarly communication 8
    effect on publishing costs 10,12
Moline, Sandra 134-135
Monographs, Obsolescence of 30-31
Multimedia databases 8-9

NASIGNET 226
National College Bookstore
    Organization 176
National Information Standards
    Organization 178,180
National Library of Medicine
    139-140
    serials operations 257-259
National Science Foundation 226
Neal, Jim 157-159
Net lending libraries 283
Network access to electronic
    databases 144
Networks, Electronic 226-227
New Oxford English Dictionary, 2nd
    ed., on CD-ROM 68-69
New technology, Cost of 130
Networked information. *See also*
    Electronic information
    as part of scholarly
        communication system 6-7

costs 20,111,118,120
distribution options 11-12
evaluation 9,16-17
intellectual property rights 15
need for information-organizing
    technologies for 18-19
peer review 17
publishers and 19
role of libraries in 9-10,17-20
shift from print to 110-121
technical standards 43-44,46-59
Networking, Cooperative library
    158,161-162
Newsletter on Serials Pricing Issues
    226
Newsletters 194
NISO. *See* National Information
    Standards Organization
Nolan, Christopher 285-287
Nonlinear access to information
    25-29;39-40
Nonprint communication, Libraries
    and 18-19
NOTIS 170
NREN 226
NSFnet 162,226
NYSERNET 162

OCLC 115,125,162,283
    networked information 19,50
    FirstSearch 213
Ohio Link Project 162,171
Ohio State University 238-289
Okerson, Ann 145
Oliver, Valerie 174
On Mendelian Inheritance In Man
    (OMIN) 9
Online Journal of Current Clinical
    Trials 123,125-126
Online public access catalog
    29,33,40
Operating system standards 52
Optical Society of America 127-128
Orynx Press 255
Osheroff, Sheila K. 226-227

OSI/LSP 53
Out of print material 150-151
Ovid 79,91

Packard Humanities Institute (PHI)
    CD-ROM 65,67
PACLink project 170-174,176
Paperless society 105
Paradigm shifts 109-110
Paradox software 234
Passwords in serials control systems
    294-295,296
Patrologia Latina CD-ROM 205
Peer review 17,32,114,126
Pelikan, Jaroslav 81
Penniman, W. David 44,59
Pergamon Press 20
Permanent paper 181
Perseus project 9,65
Personal digital interactive
    appliances 52
Peters, Paul 8
Political correctness 74
Polly, Jean Armour 53,59
Precis 243
Predictive check-in 258-260
Preorder information 201
Preservation of library collections
    150-152
Presentations, Delivering 278-279
Preservation
    of networked information 55
    of scholarly communication
        13-14,18
Price studies 127-135,137-142
Pricing models 176
Princeton University 70
Print
    cost 124
    fixity of 35
    introduction of 21,36-37,119
Product information cards
    194-19
Product reviews 190-191

Professional associations as
    publishers 147
Programs, publishers' 204-205
Proxmire, William 75
Psalter, Commentary on 26-27,39
PSYCOLOQUY 41
Publication in electronic formats
    75-77
Publication pattern database 260
Publish or perish 83,85
    effect on library budgets 10
Publishers
    and networked information 19
    cost-cutting strategies 125
    customer service 270
    exhibits 191-192
    relations between librarians and
        124,178
    response to claims 298
    restrictions on use of electronic
        information 66-71
    role in information chain
        112,114,116
Publishing 6
    by librarians 253-256
    by professional associations 147
    costs 75-76,83
    financial support from libraries 18
    modernization 8,10
    pricing structure 146
    role in scholarly communication 7
    serials librarians' understanding of
        263-264

Quality as criterion for journal
    deselection 291
Quality control in electronic media
    35
Quinn, Judy 176

Radbourne, Margaret 270
Ranganathan 103-104
READI program 145

Reciprocal borrowing agreements
    211,283
Reference collections, Serials in
    285-287
Regional cooperation between
    libraries 291-292
Reijnen, Marian 245-246
Remote access computer files,
    Cataloging 230-231,266-268
Renewal process 270
Research. *See* Scholarship
Research and development by
    vendors 246-247
Research libraries. *See also* Libraries
    as brokers to access-oriented
        libraries 14
    collection budgets
        6,15-16,19-20,202
    preservation of scholarly
        communication 13-14,18
    role of 5-6,175
Research Libraries Group 162
Reserve reading room material,
    Networking of 176
Resource sharing, regional
    161,164-176
*Responsa Project/Global Jewish
    Database* 69
Retention of records in serials
    control systems 295
Retrospective conversion 158
Reynolds, Regina 178-180
Rights for Electronic Access to the
    Delivery of Information.
    See READI program
Ringler, Rebecca 230-231,266-267
RLG Conspectus 138-139,141,290
Royalties for reproduction of journal
    articles 11,13,63
Rogers, Michael 176
Running headers 28
Rutgers University 70

Saffo, Paul 119
Sales teams, Publishers' 192-193

Sample issues 200
Saxe, Minna 181
Saxenian, AnnaLee 121
Scanning technologies 118
Schatz, Bruce 9
Scholarly communication
    82-86,93-94,110
    effect of information technology
        on 6-9,19-20,124,157-159
    role of government in 124
    role of libraries in 5-7
Scholarly publishing
    crisis 79-80,84-85,94,124
    future of 123-126
    role of libraries 5-7
    role of publishers in 7
Scholarship
    effect of electronic media on
        80,82,93-95
    public's willingness to support
        75-78
Scroll 22,37-38,120
SERCITES 226
Serial Item and Contribution
    Identifier 181,249-251
Serial item identifier 250
Serials. *See also* Journals
    cancellation 170-171,174,202
    criteria 203,290-292
    collection development 142
    control of irregular 285-287
    review process 131-135
    selection criteria 289-290
Serials catalogers 173-176
Serials computer files, Cataloging of
    229-231,265-268
Serials control systems 293-298
Serials Industry Systems Advisory
    Committee 249-250
Serials Review 119,253-255
Serials work 261-264
SERIALST 226
SERLINE database 140
Shaffer, Barbara 233-234
Shera, Jesse H. 101-102

SICI. *See* Serial Item and
    Contribution Identifier
SilverPlatter 67
Sirsi Corporation 250-251
SISAC barcode
    180-181,245-251,271
Small press marketing to libraries
    202
Social-context cues in networked
    information 87
Springer-Verlag 204
Staff cuts 203
Staffing of serials cataloging 274
Standard identifiers 50-51,249-251
Standards. *See* Technical standards
Stanford University 197-204
State University of New York
    Centers 161-176
Stewart, Mary R. 48,59
*Structure of Scientific Revolutions,
    The* 109-110
Studwell, William E. 241-243
Subject access systems 241-243
Subject heading lists in collection
    analysis 139-141
Subscription agencies 263
SULAN 157-159
SUNY Intercampus Data Network
    (ill.) 163
SUNYNET 162
Syracuse University 46
System audits 295-296

TCP/IP 53,226
Technical services librarianship
    100-101,104-106
Technical standards 47-49
    development of 57-58
    for format and arrangement of
        serials 178-181
    for interfaces between library and
        binder systems 235
    in networked information
        43-44,46-59

Technology, Assimilation of
    80-81,119
Telemarketing 189-190,199
Telesophy system 9
Telnet 226-227
Tenure and promotion process
    9,31,84
Texas A & M University 298-299
Thatcher, Sanford 145-147
Thinking Machines 54
Thesaurus Linguae Graecae
    CD-ROM 65,67,89
Thornburn, Colleen
    229-231,265-268
Title changes, Serial 180-181
Total Quality Management 259
Transformation of scholarly
    communication 8-9
Tresor de la Langue Francaise. See
    ARTFL
Trinity University 286-287
TULIP project 8,20,111

UMI 115
UnCover2. *See* CARL UnCover2
Unit cost of journals 131-132
Universal Document Identifier
    proposal 50
University of California system 162
University of Chicago 69
University of Minnesota 54
University of North Texas 234-235
University of Texas at Austin
    210-211
University of Toledo 233-234
University of Wisconsin-Milwaukee
    262-263
University presses 146-147
University System of Florida 74,76
Usenet Newsgroups 20
Utah State University 132-133

Vendors 245-246
    marketing 205
    performance evaluation 223-224

Vinge, Vernor 20
Virtual library 105,111-112,159
Virtual reality environments,
    Shared 9

Walters, Sheila 281-283
Wax tablets 23,37
Weaver, Sandra 295-296
Wide Area Information Servers 54
Wilson, H. W., Company 67
Wilsondisc CD-ROMs 67
Workshops, NASIG 277-279
WorldWide Web 54

Wright, George IV 250,251
Writing, Introduction of
    21,36-37,26,39

X.500 53
X12 51,246-247,249
Xerox Corporation 118,151-153

Yale University 226
Young, Jim 250-251

Z39.1 178-181
Z39.2 51
Z39.50 53

For Product Safety Concerns and Information please contact our EU
representative GPSR@taylorandfrancis.com
Taylor & Francis Verlag GmbH, Kaufingerstraße 24, 80331 München, Germany

www.ingramcontent.com/pod-product-compliance
Lightning Source LLC
Chambersburg PA
CBHW071800300426
44116CB00009B/1153